WORK, IDENTITY, AND
LEGAL STATUS AT ROME

Oklahoma Series in Classical Culture

WORK, IDENTITY, AND LEGAL STATUS AT ROME

A Study of the Occupational Inscriptions

Sandra R. Joshel

University of Oklahoma Press : Norman and London

Library of Congress Cataloging-in-Publication Data

Joshel, Sandra R. (Sandra Rae), 1947–
    Work, identity, and legal status at Rome : a study of the
occupational inscriptions / by Sandra R. Joshel.
        p.   cm. — (Oklahoma series in classical culture ; v. 11)
    Includes bibliographical references and index.
    ISBN 0-8061-2413-X (cloth)
    ISBN 0-8061-2444-X (paperback)
    1. Labor—Rome.   2. Working class—Rome.   3. Slaves—
Rome.   4. Occupations—Rome.   5. Inscriptions, Latin.
I. Title.   II. Series.
HD4844.J67   1992
305.5'62'0937—dc20   91-34749
                                                                        CIP

Text and jacket design by Bill Cason

Work, Identity, and Legal Status at Rome: A Study of the Occupational Inscriptions is Volume 11 of the Oklahoma Series in Classical Culture.

The paper in this book meets the guidelines for permanence and durability of the Committee on Production Guidelines for Book Longevity of the Council on Library Resources, Inc. ∞

To Robert and Frances Joshel

CONTENTS

TABLES

PREFACE

When I think of antiquity, the detail that frightens me is that
those hundreds of millions of slaves on whose backs civilization rested generation after generation have left behind them
no record whatever. We do not even know their names. In the
whole of Greek and Roman history, how many slaves' names
are known to you? I can think of two, or possibly three. One is
Spartacus and the other is Epictetus. Also, in the Roman room
at the British Museum there is a glass jar with the maker's
name inscribed on the bottom, "Felix fecit" [Felix made this].
I have a mental picture of poor Felix (a Gaul with red hair and
a metal collar around his neck), but in fact he may not have
been a slave; so there are only two slaves whose names I defi-
nitely know, and probably a few people can remember more.
The rest have gone down into utter silence.

(George Orwell, Looking Back on the Spanish War)

PSAMATE · FURIAE
ORNATRIX · V · A · XIIX
MITHRODATES · PISTOR
FLACCI · THORI · FECIT

Psamate, slave of Furia, hairdresser, lived eighteen years. Mithrodates, baker of Thorius Flaccus, made (this).[1]

(CIL 6.9732)

ORWELL WAS MISTAKEN about records but correct about silence. Classical literature gave him the names of a gladiator and a Stoic philosopher. Spartacus, leader of one of the few large-scale slave revolts in Roman history, threatened the imperial society that had enslaved him; the doctrines of Epictetus appealed to senators, who faced their own brand of master in the emperor. Archaeology provided (possibly) the name of an artisan whose life made no such claim on the attention of freeborn authors. Orwell was unaware of the hundreds of slaves named in Roman inscriptions like the epitaph of Psamate, the hairdresser, written by the baker Mithrodates. But, like this epitaph, they rarely tell stories or express sentiments. The words carved in stone effect a particular silence: they offer no direct answers to questions about relationships, feelings, and work, yet their very inscription assumes them.

At the beginning of my research, inspired by recent work, especially feminist, on the unrepresented, I had hoped to give voice to silent Romans. This project became more modest. Beyond the problems of speaking for the "other," I found it difficult to elaborate the verbal sparseness of epitaphs like Psamate's without more information on similar inscriptions. So I began with descriptions of what this book calls the occupational inscriptions—the epitaphs and dedications from the city of Rome in which at least one person names his or her work. In the end, I have examined 1,470 individuals who lived and worked in Rome during the first two centuries A.D. My focus became questions of identity: (1) how did slaves, freed slaves, and freeborn Romans represent themselves? and (2) how did work figure in the framing of an identity?

The book pursues two strategies. First, I attend to the ways of thinking about muted groups discussed by feminist scholars and critical ethnographers. This involves calling into question ancient Roman accounts of work and workers in order to reorient our ways of looking at Roman workers. Second, I use descriptive statistics to represent various patterns in the inscriptions. The elements that compose Psamate's identity and the social relations reflected in her epitaph can be compared not only with those of other hairdressers and service workers but also with those of individuals in different employments. These strategies produce the book's structure. It moves between general methodological questions, on the one hand, and textual and statistical analyses, on the other. Of necessity, the latter are quite technical, but they lay the ground for the last chapter's case studies of artisans and domestic servants, which open out the question of identity in Roman society.

SANDRA R. JOSHEL

Boston, Massachusetts

ACKNOWLEDGMENTS

THE HELP OF many people was essential to the completion of this book. I am especially indebted to Peter Weiler, Kathleen Weiler, and Amy Richlin. Kathleen and Peter Weiler took time from their own work to read mine and offer invaluable comments and criticisms. Their friendship and support have sustained me throughout the entire project, and I thank them for their patience and generosity. Amy Richlin gave the book a good critical reading, and her own work has helped me to think about Roman society. I have long relied on her conversation and good humor.

Other colleagues and friends offered their advice on various chapters or on the entire book. Alan Bowman, Eleanor Huzar, Donald Engels, and John Lenaghan read the earliest drafts of different chapters and listened attentively to my thoughts on Roman epitaphs. Michele Salzman, David Konstan, and Paul Breines made valued observations on later versions of the whole book. James Ruebel offered useful suggestions on many matters, great and small, and I am especially grateful for his careful and considered criticisms. Debra Riley helped me to sort out what I wanted to say. Andrew Herman commented extensively on chapters 1 and 2 and on statistical problems at many points; in addition I have benefited both from his kindness and from his knowl-

xv

edge of the sociology of class and work. Sandra Zagarell, whose friendship was important to my work in its final stages, provided an important perspective on the issues of representation in chapter 1.

Stephen Pfohl, Irit Rogoff, Andrew Haase, Teresa Podlesney, Jenny Sharpe, and Helen Tandler provided support of various kinds. Avery Gordon contributed to the writing of this book in ways difficult to calculate; my work has been enriched by her insights, sociological and otherwise. I regret that my former colleague Janet James died before she could read my words of gratitude for her help. The collegiality of members of the Women's Classical Caucus was a constant source of encouragement; in this context, I owe a special debt to Judith Hallett.

The staffs at the Boston College Library and the Library of the American Academy in Rome provided much valued assistance. I relied on the Boston College Computer Center during the project and especially wish to thank Larry Zaborski and Alex Wirth-Cauchon. Grants from the National Endowment for the Humanities and from the American Philosophical Society have supported my research and enabled me to make two trips to Rome.

WORK, IDENTITY, AND
LEGAL STATUS AT ROME

ABBREVIATIONS

ABBREVIATIONS FOR ancient authors can be found in the *Oxford Classical Dictionary* (Oxford, 1970). In two cases, I do not follow the forms listed there: Gaius (for Gaius, *Institutes*) and Pet. (for Petronius, *Satyricon*). Abbreviations for journal titles are those of *L'Année Philologique*. The following merit special notation:

AJAH   *American Journal of Ancient History*

ANRW *Aufstieg und Niedergang der römischen Welt*, ed. H. Temporini (Berlin, 1972–)

CIL   *Corpus Inscriptionum Latinarum* (Berlin, 1863–)

DE   *Dizionario epigrafico di Antichità romane*, ed. E. de Ruggiero (Rome, 1895–)

FIRA   *Fontes Iuris Romani Anteiustiniani*, ed. S. Riccobono, et al. (Florence, 1940–43)

ILLRP   *Inscriptiones Latinae Liberae Rei Publicae*, ed. A. Degrassi (Florence, 1957–65)

ILS   *Inscriptiones Latinae Selectae*, ed. H. Dessau (Berlin, 1892–1916)

OLD   *Oxford Latin Dictionary*, ed. P. G. W. Glare (Oxford, 1982)

PIR   *Prosopographia Imperii Romani*, ed. E. Klebs, H. Dessau, E. Groag, and A. Stein (Berlin, 1897–98; 2d, 1933)

RE   *Real-Encyclopädie der klassischen Altertumswissenschaft*, ed. A. Pauly, G. Wissowa, and W. Kroll (Stuttgart, 1893–)

· I ·

LISTENING TO SILENCE

Problems in the

Epistemology of

Muted Groups

Say, what do you make of that guy?
You name it—that's the man he has imported for us.
Grammarian, rhetorician, geometer, painter, trainer,
Seer, tight-rope walker, doctor, magician
The hungry little Greek can do it all.
Tell him to fly, he is in the sky.

(Juvenal, Satire 3.74–78)

The point at which people live, not borrow, their class destiny
is when what is given is re-formed, strengthened and applied
to new purposes. Labour power is an important pivot of all this
because it is the main mode of active connection with the
world: the way par excellence *of articulating the innermost*
self with external reality. It is in fact the dialectic of the self to
the self through the concrete world.

(Paul Willis, Learning to Labour)

THE PROBLEM OF EXCLUSION: LITERATURE AND INSCRIPTION

JUVENAL, a Roman satirist, and Willis, a British sociologist, comment on the significance and function of work
for "little Greeks" (a term Juvenal seemingly applies to
slaves, ex-slaves, and foreigners) and "people" (Willis examines working-class boys). For Juvenal, work reveals the outsider's attempt to please; it is not something in which the

3

"little Greek" really invests himself, nor does it constitute his true identity. For Willis, work is a place of real engagement—a way of expressing the self in the material world, not a duplicitous strategy with some other purpose.

What Juvenal and Willis say about the place of work in their subjects' self-conceptions has much to with the perspective from which each looks. Here, although both speak *about* the perspective of the people they observe, the satirist is making up a story about his subject's point of view, whereas the sociologist makes this his ethnographic problem. While Juvenal's pose seeks to reveal what the "little Greek" is really doing, he does not share the point of view of the slave, ex-slave, or foreigner; his discourse, in fact, is not really about little Greeks at all, but about the corruption of Roman society and his fears for his own economic position. The little Greek, who may have had some actual counterpart in Roman society, becomes a literary vehicle: the stereotypical foreigner or successful "outsider," whether freed slave or free noncitizen, he succeeds not by hard work but by sycophancy, a practice permitted by decayed social values. Juvenal employs his creature to criticize society, and, through him, the poet can denigrate "outsiders" and assert his own position as an "insider." In other words, although Juvenal's fiction presents the other, it excludes him. In contrast, Willis attempts to see or think through the point of view of his subjects—the others whom he observes. His text is an analysis of how work may function for them, a narrative that puts the excluded into the story. Whether that story is the truth or simply a different kind of account, and itself a fiction, is another question.[1]

The point is not to rebuke the satirist and applaud the sociologist or to complain that Juvenal should have been more accurate, scientific, or sociological. Questions about representation and fictions must be posed for Willis no less than for Juvenal. Writing also engages the sociologist in the practices of creating. He, too, constructs his subjects' lives, attitudes, and thought processes. His account does not simply replicate his subjects' actions and words. He chooses which actions compose the narrative, and the subjects' words are re-presented, interpreted in light of the sociologist's own observations and understandings, and infused with meanings assigned by him. And sociologist, as well as satirist, aims to comment on his society. What we must attend to in either author's work is the relation between what is asserted about social meanings and the point of view of the observer— poet, sociologist, or historian.

This relation underlies my discussion, which looks at groups of people who named themselves as servants, tradesmen, and professionals in Rome in the early empire and asks about the significance work had for them in contrast to the attitudes toward it articulated by those who for the most part did not work. My study follows Willis in his attempt to look from the place of its subjects, and I find his general observation about "labour power" useful. In what follows, work is seen as a means of active connection with the world for these Roman workers; as a way of re-forming and reapplying, in Willis's phrase, "what is given." For Willis, class shapes the material circumstances, cultural context, and structured possibilities in which his subjects live and frame their identities. Without denying the significance of wealth and privilege, I assign this formative role in the slave society of imperial Rome to legal status, the individual's relation to freedom. Here, "what was given" refers to the conditions set for the freeborn citizen, the slave, and the freedman.[2]

Law and literature describe the conditions of what was given. Law defines the legitimacy of freeborn citizen, slave, and freedman; it sets out the family and property rights that belonged to the free and the disabilities suffered by the slave. In various ways, law articulates the honor of individuals with respect to others and the state, drawing clear connections between honor and power. The conditions outlined in law are complemented by information and attitudes drawn from the literary sources. Poetry, satire, letters, moral tracts, history, and biography rarely focus on legal status itself, but because such texts distinguish sharply between those of servile origin and freeborn citizens, they reveal much about the denigration of the former and the social respect claimed by the latter.

While law and literature allow us to write a history of Roman society in the early empire, this is a narrative based on exclusion. For however much legal and literary texts describe social reality, they do not truly represent the nonprivileged groups who lived and worked in the city of Rome because, quite simply, these texts were not written by those they describe. Law outlines the boundaries within which action took place and the roles determined by rights and privileges, but it does not delineate the living actors. The figures in literature serve the descriptive, moral, or humorous purposes of their creators. They inscribe the values and attitudes of freeborn author and audience. Even where Roman writers speak directly about slaves and ex-slaves, they do so from the perspective of those who did not work—of masters, usually members of the upper ranks of the "legitimate social order."[3] Although in certain ways they may account for those they dominated, they occlude the slaves' and ex-slaves' experience.

Literary stereotypes, which may seem to represent slaves more directly than they are represented anywhere else, in fact obscure them as powerfully as any other mode of expression. The classicists Lloyd Thompson and Keith Bradley note how Roman stereotypes rationalize behavior toward out-groups and slaves, and they emphasize the importance of belief and perception in their functioning. Both assume that stereotypes contain a core of untransformed truth. For Thompson, negative stereotypes "often reflect a reality of group conflict or haunting memories of past tension and conflict." Commenting on the crafty slave of Plautus's comedies, Bradley observes that "the trickery essential to [the slave's] schemes," if not the schemes themselves, "makes sense only if it were developed from a popular conception that slaves, in reality, were deceitful and conniving, and such a conception can have only derived from the observed behaviour of slaves in everyday life."[4] Hazel Carby notes the difficulties with analyses similar to these in her discussion of black female sexuality in the antebellum United States: they regard "literary stereotypes as a directly related expression of social processes in terms of resemblance, homology, or analogy."[5] Such analyses also underestimate the formative quality of the in-group's or master's perspective. The social realities represented cannot be divorced from the viewpoint that conditions them. Stereotypes construct not only particular realities but also particular truths. As Carby argues, "the objective of stereotypes is not to reflect or represent a reality but to function as a disguise, or mystification, of objective social relations."[6]

The "lazy slave" is a case in point. Bradley sees the frequent references to servile idleness "as a firm indication of its prevalence." With Bradley, we might see such slaves to be acting out a resistance to their servitude, or, with Eugene Genovese, observe that they take their labor into their own hands by working according to their own rather than their master's schedule.[7] Yet even the interpretation that tries to divine the slave's reality passes over the masking function of the stereotype: "lazy slave" inscribes as legitimate—even natural—the master's claim to his slave's labor and eclipses the power relations that uphold it.

Inscriptions from the city of Rome provide a different kind of account, recording the actions of those whose experience is excluded from law and literature. Dedications to gods, emperor, officials, private individuals, and occupational or religious associations document benefactions, gratitude for benefits bestowed, or the hopes of future favors. In epitaphs the living remember the dead. Within the limits of a conventional vocabulary, we find slaves, freedmen, and freeborn citizens alike representing themselves. In inscriptions in which men and women named their work, we can see what they did with what was given by the conditions of legal status.[8] The question, however, is not simply how work connected with legal status but how work, from the workers' point of view, articulated an identity and re-formed one's legally determined status. In light of the conditions set by law, how did individuals and groups, through their work, present themselves?

Although epitaphs, which constitute most of the inscriptions considered here, record the world of the dead, they bespeak a lived social reality. In Rome, death was followed by prescribed rituals that purified the living, gave forms for their grief, and commemorated the deceased. Stone epitaphs with the name of the deceased and often the commemorator were part of the material process of commemoration: as Hopkins notes, like tombs and funerary portraits, they are "the long-surviving residues of [the] social rituals and personal experience" of death at Rome. The wealthy, especially senators and aristocrats, had elaborate funerals; costly tombs and often lengthy epitaphs recorded their existence. The least fortunate residents of the city received unmarked burial in mass graves. Funerals and burial for everyone else fell between these two poles: tombs range from small ash urns to large elaborate structures; epitaphs from plaques with only the deceased's name to elaborate accounts of the deceased's life or the commemorator's grief. But even the simplest plaque in a *columbarium* (chamber tomb) recorded an individual's existence. The epitaph also made the dead present for the living during the public festivals and private ceremonies that took place at the tomb. The audience were primarily those connected with the deceased—family, friends, and associates—although epitaphs that call upon the passerby to stop and learn about the deceased self-consciously address those outside an intimate circle. In a way foreign to most modern funerary practices, ceremony and epitaph "attempt[ed] to secure the social survival of the dead in the world of the living."[9]

Because commemoration depended on social relations as well as on financial resources, an epitaph often reflects the social experience of commemorator and deceased. For those with little or no resources, nonfamilial connections would have been critical. The deceased's family had the primary responsibility for commemoration, but often aid came from those outside this group—friends, colleagues, and peers, including fellow slaves and ex-slaves.[10] Wealthy families with large domestic staffs established *columbaria* with rows of niches for ash urns labeled with small plaques that identified the deceased; a burial society of slaves and freedmen saw to the burial of their fellow household members. Such popular societies (*collegia*) were composed of the slaves and freedmen of one family, of those with the same occupation, or of men and women whose shared interest was named burial. The contributions of members and donations of wealthy patrons ensured named burial for those undistinguished by social rank.[11] The practice of inscribing the name of the epitaph's commemorator as well as the deceased memorialized the dead, the living, and their relationship. Thus, men and women without a voice in the literary sources were presented to the living, inscribed in history as it were, by themselves and those who shared their lives (see Tables 2.5 and 3.3).

Epitaphs do not offer perfect images of life. They speak primarily of a world of loss and the dead; the information about commemorator and the deceased is limited, often consisting only of a name, legal status, and occupation. The social relations evidenced in the circumstances of burial can often only be surmised, guessed at by noting who commemorated whom, who was to be included in the tomb, and who was associated in the dedication of an epitaph. Nevertheless, this information often provides our most direct access to the experience and perspective of an individual; we must rely on the evidence of death as a mirror of life that reflects how men and women saw themselves.

Even when we accept this premise, we still face a problem of interpretation, one posed essentially by a particular condition of silence. In epitaphs, we can observe what the deceased and the commemorators did. We have pieces of information given at death, representations of the epitaph's authors and subjects. To understand how they conceptualized themselves, however, we must move from these representations to what they thought of themselves. Such a move involves acts of reading. How do we understand the facts given in epitaphs, the circumstances of lives captured in the discrete minutiae of names, statuses, occupational titles, indicated relations? Compared to the *Digest* and Gaius's *Institutes* or to a Pliny, Seneca, Martial, Juvenal, or Petronius, the inscriptions are inarticulate. The problem is likely to lie with our ears and eyes, for I suspect that these stones spoke clearly to their primary audiences, for whom their visual, ceremonial, and written languages were easily accessible.

STRATEGIES OF LISTENING:
WOMEN'S HISTORY AND ETHNOGRAPHY

Women's historians and ethnographers offer a strategic approach to interpreting the lives of the unprivileged men and women in Latin inscriptions. Feminist writers have long struggled with the problem of writing about those excluded from the dominant historical narrative: for some, the problem can be conceptualized as a question of truths and fictions. Ethnographers who are critical of the standard practice of ethnography deal directly with this question and provide a perspective on writing about those defined as "other."

Speaking eloquently of the shifting names for "woman's causality," Catherine Clément associates exclusion with an imaginary place that for her must become the focus of a project of retelling. "Somewhere every culture has an imaginary zone for what it excludes, and it is that zone we must try to remember *today*." Remembering requires the writing of history (or vice versa) and different readings from different points of view. Clément goes on to elaborate the essentially fictive nature of this history and its particular truth.

> It will be a history read differently, at once the same in the Real and an other in the Imaginary. These narratives, . . . these fragments of evidence, these tail ends of history do not compose a *true* history. To be that, it would have to pass through all the registers of the social structure, through its economic evolution, through analysis of the contradictions that have made and are making its history. This is not my object. Instead, it is a history, taken from what is lost within us of oral tradition, of legends and myths—a history arranged the way tale-telling women tell it.[12]

From the perspective of what Dominick LaCapra calls the "'documentary' model of knowledge," Clément's history lacks "hard" facts and proper scientific method: by the "objective canons of historiography," it remains a myth or a fiction.[13] Feminist retellings of the past, of course, responded to the demands of an extensive women's movement: as Linda Gordon explains, a "new wave of women's historians . . . had first to render the invisible visible, the silent noisy, the motionless active." Living between a social movement and the academic discipline of history, women's historians "were soon dissatisfied with myth-making," but they could not relinquish the project of including the excluded. According to Gordon, "two poles of philosophical assumption and self-consciousness" directed the writing of women's history. Seemingly, the assessment of truth or fiction depended on whether one accepted the "objective canons of historiography" or rejected such canons as historical and political phenomena, equally fictive in their claims to an objective truth.[14]

Well aware of the political issues involved, Gordon seeks a "method in-between," a "liminal method" in which the tension between these two poles cannot and should not be avoided.

> It is wrong to conclude, as some have, that because there may be no objective truth possible, there are not objective lies. There may be no objective canons of historiography, but there are degrees of accuracy; there are better and worse pieces of

history. The challenge is precisely to maintain this tension between accuracy and mythic power.[15]

The question of a feminist methodology and epistemology draws Gordon to the histories of others excluded from the dominant historical narrative. After all, she notes, "historians once considered black people outside of history, too." Following "in paths already opened," women's historians redefine "what counts as evidence," namely, "material once thought of as outside history—gossip, menstruation, latrines."[16] A focus on gender attunes the historian to evidence that may differ from that where race or class is the central concern, yet the pattern persists. In order to remain within the discipline of history, women's historians, like their predecessors who listened to African-American or working-class voices, cope with the problem of using the master's tools to rescript a master narrative.

The implication, of course, is that the dominant historical narrative is conditioned by structures of power. The very existence of particular documents is not accidental, and they determine the narrative that can be constructed by historiographical canons. Further, who becomes the subject of history, what actions compose its narrative, and how meanings are assessed as significant are influenced by the identification of the historian with a particular social class, race, ethnic group, and gender. As Clément argues, history "transmits itself making changes in accordance with historical and cultural evolution. It varies, it changes feathers, but it only dies with the people who express it and whose contradictions it serves to resolve."[17] The dominant narrative itself, no less than new histories of women, blacks, or the working classes, is a political response, though it is not always recognized as such by its practitioners.

Writing about the other has also been the concern of ethnography, a discipline whose methods have recently become attractive to historians.[18] Ethnographers' self-critique in particular seems relevant to the question of "fictions" and the poles of "fact" and "myth." Vincent Crapanzano compares the ethnographer with Hermes:

> . . . a messenger who, given methodologies for uncovering the masked, the latent, the unconscious may even obtain his message through stealth. He presents languages, cultures, and socie-

ties in all their opacity, their foreignness, their meaningless-
ness; then like the magician, the hermeneut, Hermes himself,
he clarifies the opaque, renders the foreign familiar, and gives
meaning to the meaningless. He decodes the message. He
interprets.[19]

The analogy is especially apt for ancient historians, because
their "dialogue with the dead" seeks the reconstruction of
the long absent. The self/other dichotomy that informs ethnographers' relations with their subjects characterizes historians' relations with the past: for ancient historians, there
is a great distance across which the foreign culture has to
be rendered familiar. When they study people who did not
author the sources from which history is written and who
are represented only by those who were their masters and
social superiors, the dichotomy is doubled and the distance
extended.[20]

In light of this distance, Crapanzano's attention to the
relation between interpretation and presentation is especially important. According to Crapanzano, although ethnographers conventionally acknowledge the provisional nature of their interpretations, they tend to assume final and
definitive readings. In effect, they build "definitive presentations" on "provisional interpretations," obscuring the con-
ditional basis of the former.[21] When James Clifford calls such
writing "fictions," he does not mean invention as opposed
to fact or lie as opposed to truth, but rather something made
and made up. Facts and their means of communication cannot be disentangled: interpretative and literary processes
inform ethnographic and historical work from note-taking
to book writing. It is not simply a matter of "all truths are
constructed"—historical no less than mythical; historical
methodology, checks against self-contradiction, and attention to the limits of the evidence, however much they separate history and myth, do not insulate the historian from the
politics of representation. Construction involves "systematic, and contestable, exclusions." Moreover, such exclusions are already present in the evidence: "what appears as
'real' in history, the social sciences, the arts, even in common sense, is always analyzable as a restrictive and expres-
sive set of social codes and conventions."[22]

The point, to return to Gordon's poles of fact and myth,

is less what is fiction (i.e., untrue) and what fact (i.e., true), but what sort of "fictions," in Clifford's sense, do we write? He urges more than a passing acknowledgment of the incomplete quality of ethnographic accounts: "a rigorous sense of partiality" ought to be incorporated into both the production and writing of those texts.[23]

Ancient historians, well aware of the haphazard and incomplete nature of their sources, have recognized the partial nature of their interpretations. Such an acknowledgment needs emphasis for the subjects of this study. The absence of the experience of slave and ex-slave, tradesman and servant, produces a history based on exclusion. The hegemony of certain groups in Roman society is inscribed in its law and literature. However "true," historical accounts based on these sources must be viewed as fictions and as partial. Yet, if we attempt to fill the gap by reading the epitaphs of Roman workers and tradesmen with assumptions drawn from legal and literary texts, we simply reinscribe hegemony and exclusion, for we are led, conceptually, by the viewpoint of the master.

Certainly, law and literature have much to tell us. The expectations embedded in texts written by men who in most cases were slaveholders figured in the lives of the people in this study, the majority of whom were slaves and ex-slaves. For example, Roman authors' assumptions that slaves should please and could (and should) be corporally punished for a task poorly done suggest certain terms: the master's centrality and his power over those who served him. But the slave occupied a different position in a relationship with the master and in the larger society and could, therefore, be expected to read these same terms differently. The question must be, how did the slave read them? How were they altered from his or her point of view? The testimonies of masters and slaves in the American South, for instance, demonstrate not only that master and slave had different readings of the same terms but also that slaves had other concerns, feelings, and understandings of their masters and themselves than appear in masters' comments on their slaves.

Further, an analysis that reflects on the arrangements of power suggests that we reevaluate the assumptions that seem transparent and immediate in the master's discourse. In chapter 5, for example, I argue that a consideration of what is said in a text in light of its author's social position shifts our understanding of the master's terms. The assumption that the slave should please speaks of an upper-class master's need for a sense of his own self-importance. And assumptions about the master's power also involve his pleasure in a visceral experience of command in a period when the emperor restricted the political and military authority of the senatorial class.[24]

The very articulateness of the dominant narrative and the unexamined reinscription of its terms, which persist into our own time, make it difficult to write about the slave's reading of the master's terms or to assess his or her own terms. The frame of the dominant narrative is so embedded as to seem natural, self-evident, or unworthy of reflection. And when epitaph and dedication are the texts to which we look for the other's subjectivity, the absence of a language that says "I think" or "I feel" increases the difficulty.

This study sees epitaphs and dedications as a language, with a readable vocabulary, grammar, and syntax. It assesses the inscribed representation of men and women, and from representation moves to rewriting in order to consider other meanings. In this process, it seems neither possible nor desirable to erase the language of law and literature. In fact, to find other meanings, the claims and terms of the latter must be examined critically. Taken apart, they can be seen as meanings themselves, as ways of thinking about the world from circumscribed points of view. We need to remember that, as Clifford argues, "every version of an 'other,' wherever found, is also the construction of a 'self.'" The image of the sycophantic little Greek constructs the Roman satirist or his poetic persona; the image of cook or hairdresser being flogged depicts the master's centrality and power. Only by assuming this analytic position will it be possible to break historians' implicit identification with the point of view of their more articulate evidence and, as Clifford points out, "to dislodge the ground from which persons and groups securely represent others."[25] Then, we can at least consider the meanings of those who did not write.

In what follows, literature, law, and inscription will be read in terms of their genre and the social power of their authors. Carroll Smith-Rosenberg's proposal for women's history also fits the project undertaken here:

> By applying the critical techniques of close reading to deduce the relations not only of words to words within a literary text but of words of one genre and one social group to the words of quite different genres and social groups—and, lastly and most fundamentally, of words to specific social relations within the ebb and flow of a particular culture—we will begin to re-form history and to hear women's stories with fresh clarity.[26]

This approach opens important possibilities for reading the epigraphical evidence. Inscriptions often refer to a particular social context; the legal status of individuals in these inscriptions names positions within the Roman structures of power. If we consider the discrete information given for individuals in an inscription itself in light of the social relations within Roman culture, our ability to speak about the lived experience that informs the particular vocabulary and syntax of individual inscriptions is widened. The slave baker Mithrodates, author of the epitaph quoted in the preface, for instance, was probably the slave of Thorius Flaccus, proconsul of Bithynia under Augustus. The identity of the master suggests the social context for the slave's use of occupational title—the upper-class domestic household, which often included a host of servants. "Baker" lived and worked among "cook," "waiter," "provisioner," "steward," "secretary," "musician," and "maid." Work in the service of Flaccus associated them; job in particular distinguished each, as Mithrodates distinguished himself as "baker" and Psamate as "hairdresser," although she was not a slave in the same household (unless her mistress Furia was Flaccus's wife). Further, Mithrodates names a trade that was not unimportant to his master's social position, since the proper domestic staff was supposed to have its own baker.[27] Of course, such readings must be understood as partial and as sets of possibilities. In the following chapters, I focus on possible readings of the representation of experience and speculate about how men and women with occupational titles conceptualized themselves.

THE OCCUPATIONAL INSCRIPTIONS: SAMPLING AND ANALYSIS

I began the collection of epitaphs and dedications in which individuals left occupational title with the appropriate section of the *Corpus Inscriptionum Latinarum*, volume 6 (*CIL* 6), the major collection of Roman inscriptions, "Tituli Officialium et Artificum" (pt. 7), the supplements to the original publication, and the editors' cross-references to inscriptions in other sections. Using the *index vocabulorum* created by E. J. Jory and D. G. Moore (*CIL* 6.vii), I found other inscriptions omitted in the editors' cross-references. I then reviewed inscriptions published in *Notizie degli Scavi di Antichità* since the last supplement to the *Corpus* and those not included in *CIL* 6.

The bearers of occupational title considered here, 1,262 men and 208 women, generally worked for private individuals or in the marketplace.[28] Men who noted public posts, *apparitores* (assistants to the magistrates), senatorial magistrates, equestrian officials, and more generally members of the senatorial and equestrian orders are omitted, as they, in fact, did not name an occupation per se. The slaves and freedmen of the emperor and his family, too, are not considered, except for comparative purposes. These individuals, especially members of the imperial bureaucracy, require and have already received detailed treatment in the works of Weaver, Chantraine, and Boulvert.[29] For similar reasons, those who worked in the theater, circus or arena, soldiers, and the military support staff are not included. Since they, too, need special attention, their inclusion would expand the scope of this study to unmanageable dimensions.

Generally, the inscriptions here date from the late first century B.C. to the late second century A.D.; most fall in the period between the reign of Augustus and the death of Commodus. Dating by means of paleography, type of stone, and archaeological setting is impracticable for many inscriptions published in *CIL* 6 because the information is often insufficient or inaccurate.[30] Locating every extant stone used in this study, an overwhelming task in itself, seemed unproductive: archaeological settings in most cases are unknown, and the paleographic criteria are problematic. For the most part, dating here relies on internal evidence: the names of consuls, titles of emperors, identity of upper-class masters, and certain usages and formulas. My primary concern has been to eliminate inscriptions of a later date: in practice, this excludes Christian inscriptions, those that name an individual who lived later than the second century, and a few where external evidence points to the later empire. The attempt to establish an internal chronology is limited to a few inscriptions dated to a particular year or period by an identifiable master or patron.

Whether these men and women with occupational title represent the Roman work force is a difficult question. They are a small group of individuals in terms of the entire body of inscriptional evidence. In antiquity, they were neither a class nor an order;[31] in fact, they exist as a group only in one source of Roman history, and there only on the basis of their titles. They are not a homogeneous group, and the various social and economic conditions depicted in their epitaphs and dedications also characterized the lives of others who did not name their work.[32] In other words, by other criteria of classification, individuals with occupational titles belonged to the same social groups as those without title (e.g., slaves in a large elite household or propertied members of the nonprivileged classes).

However, such considerations make these individuals a unique group for the study of identity. As those who labeled themselves workers and tradesmen, they constitute a self-selected group: their use of occupational title in situations where it was more commonly omitted suggests a certain self-consciousness about the role of work in their existence. The social contexts in which occupational title was used placed these men and women in positions to experience keenly certain dynamics of work and legal condition in Roman society. Slave attendants and maids of upper-class masters, for instance, living in close proximity to those they served and among many other slave workers, had an intimate encounter with slavery as a form of involuntary labor.

The information on individuals with occupational title and the circumstances of their appearance were classified and coded for statistical analyses.[33] This process involved an initial translation of information into distinct categories of three types: the characteristics of the individual with occupational title, the description of his or her family (family of origin as well as family of creation), and the data on the inscription itself. With the elements in each category, I could explore what constituted the elements of identity. The individual's characteristics include name, gender, age at death, legal status, information on master or patron, occupation, affiliation with domestic, religious, or occupational *collegia*, role in inscription. The description of families covers the family as a whole (e.g., number of children and name pattern) and considers individual family members separately. I recorded the legal status, factors determining status, age at death, and, where relevant, gender for parents, siblings, spouses, and children. In addition, I noted the names of spouses, the identity and social standing of the spouse's master or patron (if the spouse was a slave or an ex-slave), and the extrafamilial relation of spouses. The data on epitaphs include the size of the burial plot, the location of the epitaph, the number of named deceased, the formulas that indicated who was included in a tomb, the commemorator, the deceased and their relationship; the data on dedications cover the identity of the person, deity, or institution to whom the dedication was made, the reason for the dedication, and the substance of what was dedicated. The recurrence of this information is far from uniform. For example, of the 1,051 deceased (who bore occupational titles), only 17.5% ($N = 184$) recorded an age at death.

For the discussions that follow, another sort of translation has been necessary: the evidence of death has become the evidence of lived conditions. The analyses of social relations and the use of epitaphs as assessments of material resources best exemplify this translation. An individual with an occupational title has a particular role in an epitaph, usually as the commemorator or the deceased, and the other men and women who appear have a relation to him or her in these terms. If the epitaph is considered as a whole, it delineates a nexus of social relations. In some cases, the outline of relations is partial; an epitaph cannot record the totality of a man's or a woman's social connections, although presumably it records significant ones. It may also capture only one moment in time: the future of a commemorator and the past of the deceased may have been different. Yet, for that moment and at least in part, we have in death and commemoration an articulation of the circle in which an individual lived and worked.

Epitaphs and tombs measure an individual's or family's wealth, specifically the ability to expend resources. More elaborate epitaphs and larger tombs required more extensive material resources. "Even cheap [epitaphs] may have cost roughly the equivalent of three months' wages of unskilled labor."[34] The physical dimensions of the tomb or burial space are infrequently noted: 3.9% (N = 47) of the epitaphs in this study note the size of the plot. However, the number of deceased named and formulas like *suis* (for children or, more generally, family) and *libertis libertabusque posterisque eorum* (for freedmen and freedwomen and their descendants) allow us to estimate the number of persons intended for inclusion in the tomb. The epitaph itself, therefore, offers some indication of the expense of the tomb and the resources of the commemorator. With certain exceptions, I have used the number included in the tomb as a barometer of these resources.[35]

This is perhaps the appropriate point to comment on the class bias of the epitaph material. It is usually assumed that the cost of inscribed epitaphs means that they generally represent "the *respectable classes*—a suitably vague term . . . which . . . convey[s] something like small shopkeepers and above."[36] Certainly, epitaphs better represent those with financial resources. The poorest and those without connections ended up in the city's potter's fields, or their ashes were placed in unmarked amphorae like those found between the tombs and at the edge of the cemetery at Isola Sacra. And some burials were probably recorded on wood or stucco, which have not survived.[37]

However, the general assumption that the humblest are excluded from the epitaph material involves some exaggeration, because individual and family incomes were not the sole determinants of commemoration. Burial clubs, domestic organizations, occupational associations or their officers provided burial to those who otherwise would have lacked the means for commemoration. The slaves and freedmen of upper-class families who were given space in a *columbarium* appear in Roman inscriptions by virtue of their connection with a household, not because of their wealth. In addition, this generalization does not consider the pooling of funds, aid from friends, fellow slaves, and fellow freedmen, or a desire for commemoration that may have strained the means of those with very little, even if it resulted only in a simple plaque with the deceased's name.[38]

The information on epitaphs and dedications is presented here in a series of tables. I analyze the patterns represented in these tables against the background of the conditions determined by freedom or slavery and the attitudes toward work expressed in literature. I emphasize "patterns"—the distribution of individuals in different categories—rather than statistical significance and inference. The latter is less important than the picture that we can construct from observing the characteristics of certain individuals and groups. I give percentages in nearly all the following tables; used descriptively, they are a more convenient mode of exposition and in most cases a more meaningful reflection of particular situations.[39]

THE OCCUPATIONAL INSCRIPTIONS
AND ROMAN SOCIAL HISTORY

The study of inscriptions in Roman social history is not new. A primary source for the study of the population as a whole, and especially of the lower classes, inscriptions have been used to describe aspects of Roman society and the economy: age, status, and family structures; marriage and manumission patterns; patterns of wealth and expenditure; the organization of the imperial bureaucracy and imperial household; and the functioning of specific institutions like the *familia*. Work on status indication and nomenclature has enlarged our ability to discuss legal condition, even if recent studies have made historians more cautious in claiming freed or servile status for certain individuals in inscriptions.[40] Most immediately relevant here are those studies that use the occupational inscriptions—general studies and those focused on the trades of particular groups. Although some describe specific employments or discuss economic organization and work environment, as a whole they have been especially concerned with the legal status of those with occupational title and often engaged in attempts to ascertain the actual status structure of the Roman work force.[41]

The older and more comprehensive studies, like those of Kühn and Gummerus, are seriously flawed. Susan Treggiari has pointed out that their figures are outdated.[42] They also lack clear articulation of their methods of classification, can be faulted for their assumptions about nomenclature, and often are biased by obvious ethnocentric or racist assumptions. Some years ago, F. G. Maier criticized their use of statistics and raised important questions concerning any conclusions about status, ethnic, and economic structures drawn from inscriptions. The problem of representation and the omission of certain groups from the epitaph material cannot be ignored in moving from descriptions of the epigraphical material to observations about Roman society.[43]

Although the entire body of work on the occupational inscriptions and the studies of nomenclature and status indication make possible the study undertaken here, the articles of Susan Treggiari and Pertti Huttunen's *Social Strata in the Imperial City of Rome* require special comment because of their importance in the following chapters. At points I rely on their findings, which describe general patterns as well as specific social and occupational groups. At other points I am in dialogue with them as well as with other scholars in this field.

Treggiari's articles carefully examine the work and often the legal status of major groups found in the occupational inscriptions: women in trade, artisanry, and domestic service; aristocratic households in the late first century B.C. and early first century A.D.; Livia's urban staff; and urban labor in Rome (*mercennarii, opifices, tabernarii*).[44] She discusses the structure, organization, and conditions of work for these groups and raises some important questions about the reasons informing the use of occupational title. The experience of working closely with many epitaphs seems to underline her observation in "Jobs for Women" that "with all their conventionalities, odd spellings, and varying choice of material, the inscriptions allow us to grasp something of the personalities and lives of the slaves and freedwomen to whom they were set up."[45]

Huttunen seeks to fill an important methodological gap: no study that uses a group of published inscriptions assesses its relation with the entire collection of published inscriptions. Using a sample of every fifth epitaph in *CIL* 6, Huttunen constructs a broad quantitative and qualitative perspective on the epitaph material. And it is primarily as a framework for comparison that Huttunen's work is important in chapter 2, "Slavery, Freedom, and the Construction of Identity."[46]

In what he calls the "quantitative part" of his study, Huttunen tries to estimate the correspondence between the deceased mentioned in epitaphs and the actual population of Rome. He discusses the occupations named in epitaphs and tries to assess "to what extent and in what way the representation of the different occupational groups corresponds to the probable occupational and social structure of Roman society." He also attempts to show which groups are absent from the epitaph material. In the "qualitative part" of his study, Huttunen is primarily concerned with how patterns of thought, burial practices, and funerary etiquette affected the notation of occupation and legal status in Roman epitaphs.[47]

The work undertaken here differs from that of Huttunen and Treggiari in scope. Where Treggiari studies specific groups among those with occupational title, I examine the general patterns for all the men and women with occupational title within the limits noted earlier and then look closely at domestic servants and artisans against the background of these patterns. Huttunen is concerned with the entire body of epitaphs in *CIL* 6. His sample includes 657 deceased and 287 dedicators with occupational indication, although his figures include 140 senators and equestrians (101 deceased and 39 dedicators), those who in Roman terms would not be considered to have a trade.[48] Huttunen's sample cannot provide a thorough study of the occupational inscriptions themselves, nor does he claim that it does.

My focus also differs from that of Treggiari and Huttunen. The major reference point in their work is ultimately Roman social and economic realities; both try to map the actual structures of these realities. Although I analyze the extant epigraphical material that features occupational title, providing a current and thorough description of the inscriptions, I assess neither the actual occupational structure nor the status structure of the work force. My questions turn on different issues: What claims did people make with their occupational identification? Did these claims address Roman

society as a whole or a subculture? Did the identities constructed by domestic servant and artisan differ? Did those
constructed by slave and free? What aspects of work figure
especially in the epitaphs of slaves and ex-slaves?

The issue, as noted above, is what we can say of the lives
of Roman workers and tradesmen, how we move from their
representation to our reading of it, and what frames our interpretation. My concern with this sort of analysis sharply
distinguishes this study from Huttunen's and Treggiari's
work. Huttunen's conclusions about patterns of thought, although important, tend to be general or not fully explored.[49]
At points, his assumptions about the attitudes of workers
and tradesmen omit factors that have received detailed consideration here: the specific nature of their work, differences
in occupation, and the environment of work—household or
marketplace.[50] Although Treggiari especially makes careful
and knowledgeable use of literature and law, neither her
work nor Huttunen's examines the terms of law and literature specifically with a view toward a critical understanding
of how assumptions drawn explicitly or implicitly from
them inform our reading of the epitaphs and dedications of
the nonprivileged.[51]

WORK, IDENTITY, AND LEGAL STATUS AT ROME

The following chapters explore the varied conditions of life
in Rome and the factors that affected identity; as a whole,
the book speaks to the question of who used occupational
title in Roman inscriptions. Chapter 2 focuses on the legal
status of those with occupational title: what these men and
women named in this regard, and what we can know about
their legal condition from circumstances other than status
indication. The factors that suggest legal status where it is
not formally stated provide a picture of the names, associations, and families of individuals with title and make it
possible to estimate the actual number of slaves, freedmen,
and freeborn citizens in this population.

Most of those who claimed their work (more than 60%)
were slaves and freed slaves. Because this representation is
unusual (it does not characterize the epitaph material as a
whole), an initial consideration of the special significance of
work for slave and freed slave seems necessary. This specu-
lative and theoretical interpretation attends primarily to

what was given and, in fact, denied by legal condition. I examine particular claims and identities in later chapters, but they fall within the general perspective I outline here.

I suggest that the slave's claim to work may originate in social poverty and what Orlando Patterson calls natal alienation—the denial of rights, socially acknowledged kin, a past and a future, and membership in the legitimate social order. Work is one mode of identity not refused by the master, however much he devalued and denigrated specific jobs and livelihoods and would not or could not acknowledge work's social value. It is precisely this value that these slaves may have grasped. Certainly, though implicitly, the claim to work was a claim to physicality and an active interaction with the world by those denied physical integrity and defined as socially dead persons.[52] A servile past would not be erased by manumission, although the ex-slave could claim kin, citizen rights, and membership in society. Whereas that membership was a second-class one, and the ex-slave's position had aspects of marginality, the claim to work may nevertheless shift the terms of identity from birth to productive activities, from what one is to what one does. In this shift, the socially marginal freedman appears on the inside.

Chapter 3 addresses the naming and claiming of work. I set the claims to labor made by men and women in Roman inscriptions against the definitions of jobs and attitudes toward trade voiced in literature. In chapter 4, the most technical part of the book, I look at the social contexts in which occupations were named. These are divided into two broad categories, public and private. The analyses in chapter 4 break down and cut across the categories of legal status and occupation and point to the social diversity indicated by the occupational inscriptions.

Chapters 2, 3, and 4 examine more general patterns; chapter 5 focuses on two groups chosen because of their typicality: freed artisans in the marketplace and slave domestic servants in large households. Detailed consideration of these two groups returns directly to the larger perspective set out in chapter 2.

· II ·

SLAVERY, FREEDOM, AND THE CONSTRUCTION OF IDENTITY

"Who are you?" said the Caterpillar. This was not an encouraging opening for a conversation. Alice replied, rather shyly, "I—I hardly know, sir, just at present—at least I know who I was when I got up this morning, but I must have been changed several times since then."
(Lewis Carroll, Alice in Wonderland)

The primary distinction in the law of persons is this, that all men are either free or slaves. Next, free men are either ingenui *(freeborn) or* libertini *(freedmen). Ingenui are those born free,* libertini *those manumitted from lawful slavery.*
(Gaius, Institutes 1.9–11, trans. De Zulueta)

"Losing one's virtue is a crime in the freeborn, a necessity in a slave, a duty [officium] for the freedman." The idea became a handle for jokes, like "you aren't doing your duty by me" and "he gets in a lot of duty for him."
(Seneca, Controversiae 4.praef.10, trans. Loeb)

ALICE CANNOT ANSWER the caterpillar's question because she has difficulty with what for her are the components of identity: "I can't remember things as I used—and I don't keep the same size for ten minutes together."[1] For Gaius, the jurist, the distinction between slavery and freedom functioned like Alice's memory and size, determining the answer to "who are you?" at Rome. By moving from one to the other, the freedman, like Alice, changed identities over time. The juridical designations slave, freeborn, and freedman (*servus, ingenuus,* and *libertinus*) expressed Roman identity in terms of rights, obligations, and powers that defined fundamental social realities and attitudes, as the orator's bon mot makes clear.

Roman inscriptions often lack the clarity of law and literature. On his epitaph, the doctor C. Hostius C. l. Pamphilus (9583: *medicus*) identifies himself as a freed slave; the name of the carpenter Q. Haterius Evagogus (9408: *dec. coll. fabrum tignuariorum*) tells us only that he was free. Omitting status indication, it does not record how he came by his freedom. Formal nomenclature and status indication, as in Pamphilus's case, directly convey legal condition. Other circumstances of commemoration frequently suggest actual legal status where it was not specifically noted: in Evagogus's case, the names of his wife and child point to his status as a freedman (see below).

In this chapter I take the question, Who are you? in two directions. First, who of those who named their occupations were freeborn citizens, slaves, or freedmen? By paying special attention to the use of formal status indication, I look at the degree to which these Romans stated their identity in terms of legal condition as well as work. Second, in what terms should we consider the identity constructed by work for those who used occupational title most frequently— slaves and freed slaves? I begin with a short review of legal status for those unfamiliar with Roman society. Like the "class destiny" of Willis's working-class boys, Roman legal status marked out what was given for the freeborn citizen, the slave, and the freed slave. Since work involved physical interactions with the world, I stress other material conditions—family and physical integrity. My discussion attends to what Keith Bradley calls the "negative side of the slave-master relationship." I do not deny the privileges accorded some slaves, the comparative liberality of Roman manumission, or the possibility of intimacy between individual masters and slaves. But I want to focus on the "Roman slavery system as a whole" and the practices that followed from making a woman or man a commodity.[2]

LEGAL STATUS: THE COMPONENTS OF WHAT WAS GIVEN

Freeborn Citizens (Ingenui)

The freeborn Roman citizen (*ingenuus/a*) was a legitimate member of the social order, and the legal rights of citizenship reflected that legitimacy in terms of family relations. Paternal power (*patria potestas*) characterized proper family order; it was peculiar to Roman citizens and, as pointed out below, undisturbed for *ingenui* in a way that it was not for freedmen. The *ingenuus/a* was free, but not from the authority of another who held the power of life and death (*ius vitae necisque*) over his children as well as his slaves. Indeed, the liabilities of the son or daughter in paternal power were similar to the slave's, although they were not as drastic and had different repercussions. The child's position was considered an honorable one, because obedience was owed to a father, not a master. Moreover, he or she succeeded to the father's position and property, at least by the lines of intestate succession. For males, this succession had a particular significance. Not only could male, like female, *ingenui* contract a proper Roman marriage and have children who were legitimate members of society, they also gained paternal power over their own children.[3] From his family of origin, the *ingenuus* received a legitimate place in the society; in his family of creation, he passed that heritage on to his own children. The lines of paternal power traced a past, a present, and a future in the social order.

The freeborn citizen released from paternal power (*ingenuus sui iuris*) had claims that gave him control of his property, made him responsible for his actions, and granted him legal recourse in the courts. The action for injury or outrage (*iniuria*) that in principle enabled him to defend his person, honor, and that of his family outlines a scale by which his respectability can be measured against that of the slave and freedman. Inflicted on an individual's body or his standing (*dignitas*), injury resulted when one person asserted his power in relation to another: striking a person with a stick, fist, or sword; flogging him; forcibly entering his home; preventing him from fishing in the sea, catching birds, bathing publicly, taking a seat in the theater, or associating with others in public; behaving in a lewd manner toward a proper Roman woman; raising a public outcry; or advertising someone's property for sale as if he were a debtor.[4] That most of the offenses listed in the legal sources were physical in nature suggests that honor and physical integrity were inextricably intertwined. The assertion of power offended the victim because he was treated, contrary to his status as freeborn citizen, as if he were a slave, a being without power and physical integrity. Failure to recognize that an individual had power denied him membership and position in the legitimate social order. Thus, the offense was most serious if committed in public, even when the physical damage was negligible, for the offended person was shamed before his peers and others of lesser rank.[5]

Divided by income and social status, *ingenui* formed neither a class nor an estate. Access to standing was limited by birth and property, and since the distribution of wealth in Roman society was extremely unequal, so too was the distribution of prestige.[6] Thus, while in principle the law favored free over slave, citizen over free alien, *ingenuus* over *libertinus*, by the late first century A.D., in fact, inequalities of wealth and rank produced further inequalities in legal privilege. Men of lower rank (*humiliores*) were tried in different courts and received harsher punishments than the socially prominent. The latter had greater access to the right of appeal and the material means to use the legal system effectively. The class bias of judges and magistrates, too, gave them an advantage.[7] Nonetheless, any *ingenuus* could identify himself as a member of a family and of the legitimate social order. Even if he lacked privilege and power in relation to his social betters, there was another whose position was at least defined as lower—the slave.

Slaves (Servi)

The slave's lack of rights and claims, label of alien, and subjection to another person defined him or her as powerless, not a legitimate member of society. The slave was property, actually or potentially in another's ownership. Although his or her humanity was acknowledged in fact and in law, the slave, like other property, could be sold, lent, mortgaged, given away, and willed.[8]

Legal actions in which a plaintiff asserted his rights of

ownership against another party (*actiones in rem*) associate the slave as property with the Roman notion that the slave was an outsider, regardless of the mode of enslavement—conquest, capture, birth, or penal condemnation—and despite the Romans' own distinction between homeborn slaves (*vernae*) and others.[9] The plaintiff touched the "thing" claimed with a rod that represented a spear, the symbol of lawful ownership (*iustum dominium*), according to Gaius (4.16), because the Romans thought that things that they had seized from the enemy were lawfully theirs. The person enslaved in war was not simply something captured from the enemy; he or she had been the enemy. Thus, in court, this ritual replaced the act of violent seizure. The practice relegated the slave to the status of the foreigner whose powerlessness had been manifest in capture.[10]

If brought from outside Rome, the slave lost an ethnic or national heritage; if born within Rome, he or she had none from birth. The slave, in Finley's words, was "a deracinated outsider."[11] The Romans did not ignore the origin of the slave; it had to be stated for every slave put up for sale, because the slave's personal qualities were in part judged by *natio*. However, ethnicity became an individual idiosyncrasy that buyers assessed for slaves' potential utility and acquiescence to subjection, or a set of personal characteristics that satirists used to discredit successful foreigners.[12]

The slave's status as an outsider was furthered by his or her lack of socially acknowledged kin. Roman society did not recognize slave spouses as husband and wife (*contubernales*), and their union itself existed as a privilege "that could be granted unilaterally by a slaveowner, and withdrawn unilaterally." Law took into account slave motherhood, because slave children belonged to their mother's owner. But in social and legal terms no male slave could be a father, and no slave, male or female, had a father. The master could dispose of his property as he wished, so, in principle, the slave family had no stability as a social unit; in fact, husbands and wives, parents and children were often separated.[13]

M. I. Finley and Orlando Patterson emphasize the slave's kinlessness and loss of ethnicity as critical factors in the slave's existence. Patterson describes these interconnected losses as "natal alienation," a term that

> goes directly to the heart of what is critical in the slave's forced alienation, the loss of ties of birth in both ascending and descending generations. It also has the important nuance of a loss of native status, of deracination. It was this alienation of the slave from all formal, legally enforceable ties of "blood," and from any attachment to groups or localities other than those chosen for him by the master, that gave the relation of slavery its peculiar value to the master.[14]

Ownership expressed the only socially and legally acknowledged relationship a slave had, the relationship with his or her master. The master's legal power of life and death and claim to the slave's productivity summarize his control of the slave's physical existence.[15]

This control was manifested in part through the slave's lack of physical integrity. In scenarios of corporal punishment found throughout the literary sources, authors raise the question of abuse but do not deny the master's right to use physical punishment. Indeed, the topos of Roman humor that plays on flogging slaves assumes the practice.[16] Finley has characterized the slave's sexual vulnerability as a "manifestation of the answerability of slaves with their bodies." References to the master's "boy," slaveholders' advances on their male and female domestic servants, the purchase of slaves for sexual relations, and the alteration of a slave's physical appearance (long hair) and body (castration) for sexual purposes are fairly commonplace in satire and moral tract.[17]

Petronius's freed characters deny the disgrace of fulfilling the sexual needs of masters and mistresses (75.11, 45.7–9): the master orders; the slave is forced to comply. Yet, as Petronius well knew, in the wider social order the physical vulnerability and lack of power so directly expressed in the slave's sexual relations with the master were a source of dishonor.[18] For Seneca the Elder, the slave's necessity is the freeborn male's misdeed. In Quintilian's imaginary case of a raped *ingenuus* (*Inst.* 4.2.69), the male victim hangs himself, presumably out of shame. As Amy Richlin has shown, in Roman literature threats of oral or anal penetration humiliate the victim.[19] The pathic role makes a man the object of another's assertion of power—a position to be endured by woman or slave, but not freeborn male.

Imperial legislation limited the corporal treatment and sexual abuse of slaves: freedom for abandoned sick slaves; regulations against prostitution, castration, and condemnation to the arena; rulings against excessive cruelty and murder. None of this denied the master's physical domination of his slave or the slave's vulnerability, nor did it interfere with the master's sexual relations with his own slaves.[20] Further, slaves had difficulties in bringing complaints to the attention of the authorities. They could not prosecute on their own or anyone else's behalf and had recourse only to refuge at a temple or a statue of the emperor, or to an extralegal appeal to a magistrate. Magistrates, however, were themselves slaveholders, and their class bias favored the wealthy, who were the largest slaveowners.[21]

Ultimately, slaves' physical integrity and honor were not issues; in law, they had none. Unlike the freeborn, slaves could not personally suffer *iniuria*; in cases involving a slave, it was the honor of the master that was affronted by what amounted to an assault on some extension of himself. Wounding or killing a slave was damage to property; it was the master who sued under the Lex Aquilia for the recovery of a loss to property.[22] The state, too, treated the slave as physically vulnerable. Slave testimony was taken under torture—a treatment that, at least until the second century A.D., was used exclusively for slaves, as originally were punishments like crucifixion, burying alive, and the fork. When applied to the free of lower standing, they marked a denigration of their status since one of the primary distinctions between slave and free was erased.[23]

This cruelty notwithstanding, slaves figured in ways within the legal system that indicate their economic prospects when engaged in various businesses. They made contracts that were legally binding, participated in all sorts of transactions involving property, and paid for actions that caused offense, damage, or loss to others. Like sons in paternal power, some slaves had de facto control of property, called a *peculium*. Ultimately, however, the master was responsible for the slave's actions, and *de iure* the *peculium* belonged to the master, who could take it away at will. In general, whether the action lay against the master for acts committed by the slave or with the master for acts committed on the slave, the slave, unlike the son, appears in law as an extension of the master's will or person, or simply as his property.[24]

Freedmen (Libertini or Liberti)

Manumission brought an end to the slave's status as a property object and membership in the legitimate social order with its attendant rights: the slave of a Roman citizen manumitted according to the regulations in the Lex Aelia Sentia (A.D. 4) became a Roman citizen. Freedmen could contract a proper Roman marriage and have legitimate children. They could make contracts binding in their own name, sell or transfer property, write a will, and sue and be sued in their own right. However, legally and socially, freed slaves suffered disabilities that freeborn citizens did not share. Especially important in this respect were the stigma of a servile past and the continuation of a limiting relationship with an ex-master.

Freedom did not restore the slave's heritage or family of origin. Unlike the *ingenuus,* the *libertinus* could not inherit his father's culture. If brought into Roman society from outside, he could not live out his culture's values in Roman society when he attained his freedom—at least not without incurring the stigma of being an alien. If born in slavery, he knew no other culture but his master's or that created by his fellow slaves. The lack of a socially acknowledged father was a source of dishonor that left the ex-slave vulnerable. A freedman might acquire wealth, the requisite of rank in Roman society, but his illegitimacy could always be used to shame him.[25]

> Let the right of (a father of) children, even of seven be given to you, Zoilus, as long as no one attributes a mother to you, no one a father.

> Ius tibi natorum vel septem, Zoile, detur,
>   dum matrem nemo det tibi, nemo patrem.
> (Mart. 11.12, cf. 1.81, 10.27)

As the object of ridicule, the freedman's position was reduced in relation to the man who laughed at him. His attempts to live within legitimate society are depicted by Martial, Juvenal, and Petronius as the mere aping of an outsider, and the values of the ex-slave who aspires to respectability are characterized as shallow.[26]

The freed slave also might experience difficulties in establishing a family of creation. The freedwoman who married after manumission at the legal age of thirty had passed her best childbearing years.[27] If the familial relations established in slavery continued after manumission, the marriage was not legally recognized as long as one of the partners remained a slave. A freedman with a slave wife had no legitimate children, for they were the property of the wife's master. A freedwoman with a slave husband had free children who were illegitimate and not in the *potestas* of their father. Husband and wife who both received their freedom had to leave any children born before their manumission in slavery. Even where the entire family was freed, the normal pattern of paternal domination was disrupted: children were not in the *potestas* of their father, and the ex-master had claims on wife as well as children. If the husband bought his family out of slavery, they legally became his *liberti;* only to him were they wife and children. Finally, jurists' concern with former masters' interference in the marriage of their freedmen and women suggests that attempts to control the family relations of ex-slaves recurred often enough to require regulation.[28]

Manumission did not end the relationship with the former master, the framework of the slave's powerlessness and dishonor. The former master, now patron, lost the right of life and death and total control of the freedman's economic productivity, yet the relationship gave the patron some control over the ex-slave's behavior. The grant of freedom by the master was a favor or kindness (*beneficium*) for which the freed slave was expected to show gratitude. The appropriate behavior was termed *obsequium;* more than proper respect, the term implies a compliance and accommodation to the will of another that is evident in the legal restrictions that *obsequium* imposed on freedmen in dealing with their patrons.[29]

Freed slaves acquired the physical integrity that slaves lacked *vis-à-vis* third parties but apparently never fully regained inviolability in relation to the person who once claimed their bodies. Instances where a patron used harsh words or even administered a "light beating," grounds for legal action by an *ingenuus*, were not severe enough to merit the action for injury by a freedman. According to Ulpian (*Dig.* 47.10.7.2), "the praetor should not endure the slave of yesterday, who today is free, to complain that his master has spoken abusively to him, or struck him lightly, or criticized him" (nec enim ferre praetor debet heri servum, hodie libertum conquerentem, quod dominus ei convicium dixerit, vel quod leviter pulsaverit vel emendaverit). Ulpian goes beyond simply defining the freedman's limited redress against the abuses of the patron; he justifies these limits by emphasizing the determinative effect of the freedman's servile past as property of the person whom he now claims has abused him.[30]

The balance of power lay with the patron, whom the legal system generally favored. Since *obsequium* was ultimately maintained by the threat of punishment administered by the patron[31] or, if necessary, by the state, to antagonize the patron was dangerous. The possibility of an arbitrary response arising out of a patron's ill-humor introduced an additional vulnerability in the freedman's position. Anger, often neither rational nor evoked for actual legal offenses, depended as much on the patron's self-control as on the freedman's behavior. Not surprisingly, fear enters the discussions of the relationship of patron and freedman; jurists pointedly cite it as well as excessive reverence in cases of freedmen's undue subjection to ex-masters.[32]

Patrons retained a claim to their ex-slaves' labor, especially through services called *operae* that were negotiated before manumission and confirmed by oath afterward. Jurists' attempts to modify the obligations of freedmen to work for their patrons suggest that they could become onerous.[33] In addition, since the loss of the slave's labor and the *beneficium* conferred by manumission had to be compensated, the patron, and in some cases the patron's heir, also had claims to the freedman's estate, depending on its size and the number of children instituted as heirs in the freedman's will. In effect, the limited continuance of the master's economic absorption of the slave extended to the products of the ex-slave's labor after the laborer's death.[34]

Freedmen, like *ingenui*, were not a class, all poorer or wealthier than the freeborn. Moreover, the freedman of an ordinary tailor must be distinguished from the emperor's freedman, who held a high post in the imperial bureaucracy. Freedmen's relations with patrons, too, varied: some were closely tied to their patrons, managing their property or working in their shops; others had no living patron, no obligations to the patron's heir, or were themselves their ex-master's heir. All freedmen, however, occupied that middle ground between slavery and the freedom of the *ingenuus*.

FORMAL NOMENCLATURE AND STATUS INDICATION: WHAT'S IN A NAME?

As in other cultures, Roman names functioned as an expression of individual existence and of incorporation into society.[35] Any study of Latin epitaphs must rely on the different name forms of freeborn citizen, slave, and freedman to determine the legal status of deceased and that of commemorator.[36] Since the concern here is also with the framing of identity, it will be useful to consider how names reflected not only legal condition but also relations to family and society. This is not to ignore how names individualize. Roman name forms in varying ways affirmed (or denied) individual identity, but this expression was inextricably embedded in the representation of social identity.

Formal nomenclature consisted of a name and status indication. The latter included a term of relationship that identified the individual as an inferior in an authority relationship (son/daughter, slave, freedman) and the name of the person with authority (father, master, patron). Together, name and status indication conveyed some of the essential elements of legal status discussed above: legitimate membership in Roman society or illegitimacy, identification with family or kinlessness. The free had a Roman family name, the nomen: for example, C. Turius C. f. Lollianus (Gaius Turius Lollianus, the son of Gaius, 9626) or T. Statilius T. l. Optatus (Titus Statilius Optatus, the freedman of Titus, 6273). Denied to free noncitizens as well as slaves, the nomen was the badge of membership in Roman society for the freeborn Turius as well as the freed Statilius. Filiation marked the legitimacy of the freeborn Turius; C. f. (son of Gaius) was evidence of his submission to the authority of a father, which brought with it a rightful place in society and marked him as an individual with a family of origin. By contrast, "libertination" revealed Statilius's assumption rather than inheritance of his nomen and registered the absence of a legal father and family of origin.[37] Thus, while the status indication T(iti) l(ibertus), the freedman of Titus, indicated a free citizen, it also displayed Statilius's lack of heritage and his relationship with a former master.

The slave's name was a badge of kinlessness and nonmembership in any legitimate social order. The slave had a single name (in effect, a cognomen) that included no reference to family, the chief feature of freeborn nomenclature: for example, Psamate Furiae (Psamate, (slave) of Furia, 9732) and Primigenius Q. Volusi Saturnini ser(vus) (Primigenius, slave of Quintus Volusius Saturninus, 7290). Legally, Psamate and Primigenius had no fathers from whom they could have taken a nomen even if their fathers in reality were free and had nomina; nor could they take their master's nomen, for they were not considered members of the master's family, although slaves were included in the family cult as members of the household. The master's name and an indication of his possession (genitive with or without the abbreviation ser.—slave) replaced filiation: name displayed ownership, not paternal relationship.

The very names that slaves were given and the process of naming by slave dealer or master also objectified the slave. In early Rome, the name of a male slave consisted of the genitive of his master's name and *puer* (boy): for example, Marcipor was Marci *puer* (Marcus's boy). Later, the Romans seem to have favored a few Latin or more commonly Greek names for slaves, whatever the slave's origin, and there are a group of names thought to be typically servile. Names like Eros (love), Fides (trust, good faith), Hilarus (cheerful), or Felix (lucky) seem to mark the slave with the master's fancy or expectations.[38] Varro's comment (*Ling.* 8.21) on the "voluntary derivation" of words is revealing of the naming process.

> So, when three men have bought a slave each at Ephesus, sometimes one derives the name (of the slave) from Artemidorus, the man who sold the slaves, and thus calls his slave Artemas; another names his slave Ion from the region Ionia, because he bought him there; the other names his slave Ephesius, because he bought him at Ephesus. So each man chooses a name from one source or another, however it seems right to him.

Sic tres cum emerunt Ephesi singulos servos, nonnunquam alius declinat nomen ab eo qui vendit Artemidorus, atque Artemam appellat, alius a regione quod ibi emit, ab Ion(i)a Iona, alius quod Ephesi Ephesium, sic alius ab alia aliqua re, ut visum est.

The same arbitrary quality of slave nomenclature is evident in documents confirming the sale of slaves that state the slave's nationality and name and add "or by whatever name he/she is known."[39]

If taken in war or a raid, the enslaved lost the name he or she was given at birth; sale or transfer to a new owner might also bring a new name. Emphasizing the importance of the change of name as a feature of the ritual of enslavement, Patterson notes that "the changing of a name is almost universally a symbolic act of stripping a person of his former identity. . . . The slave's former name died with his former self."[40]

ASSESSING LEGAL STATUS:
WHAT THEY DID AND WHAT WE CAN KNOW

In life, the men and women who appear in Roman inscriptions had formal names and, of course, a particular legal status, but in their epitaphs and dedications they did not always use formal nomenclature with status indication. In a sample of every fifth epitaph in *CIL* 6, the major collection of inscriptions from the city of Rome, Pertti Huttunen found that 31% of the deceased and only 13% of those commemorating epitaphs clearly noted their legal status.[41] A name in the absence of formal status indication leaves the modern reader with the problem of assessing an individual's actual status. The inscriptions that are the focus of this study raise two questions: (1) Did individuals with occupational title name their legal status? (2) Regardless of what they did, what can we observe about their actual legal condition? The first question must attend to the use of formal status indication; the second, to other circumstances of commemoration or dedication that suggest legal status—in effect, informal indications of actual legal condition.

The Use of Formal Status Indication

Table 2.1 shows the use of status indication in relation to an individual's role in an inscription. Fifty-one individuals who

Table 2.1   Use of Status Indication in Epitaphs and Dedications

Status Indication	Deceased	Commemorator	Dedication or Other	Total
Formal indication	466 (44.3)	100 (41.3)	52 (29.4)	618 (42.0)
Indication by term	30 (2.9)	14 (5.8)	7 (3.9)	51 (3.5)
No indication	555 (52.8)	128 (52.9)	118 (66.7)	801 (54.5)
Total	1,051 (100)	242 (100)	177 (100)	1,470 (100)

Note: Figures in parentheses are percentages.

lack formal status indication but whose status is indicated by a term of relationship have been placed in a separate category.[42] Over half the men and women with occupational title (58%, $N = 852$) did not use formal nomenclature in their epitaphs and dedications. They took only a part of assigned name forms:[43] 27.6% ($N = 405$) bear a single personal name without the genitive of a master's name; 30.4% ($N = 447$) have a nomen but use neither filiation nor libertination.

Thus, the inscriptions present two "uncertain" groups. The men and women with nomina were free citizens—either freeborn or freed. This is the group that Lily Ross Taylor labeled the *incerti;* here, they are called "uncertain freeborn."[44] The individuals with single personal names ("uncertain slaves") appear to have been slaves because they lack a Roman family name, although a single name is not as secure an indication of servile status as a nomen is of free status. Limited space, the pattern of naming young children, and the use of a name most familiar to the commemorator of an epitaph may account for the absence of nomen.[45] The label "uncertain" in both cases reflects our knowledge, not an actual legal status. The uncertainty arises from the different possibilities that are generated for us when one critical element of nomenclature, status indication, is missing.

Informal Indications of Legal Condition: The Circumstances That Suggest Legal Status

While formal nomenclature with status indication directly expresses aspects of legal condition, other information discloses circumstances associated with it. For example, the status indication of Doris Statiliae Mino[ris] *pediseq[ua]* (Doris, the slave of Statilia Minor, attendant, 9775) defines Doris's bond to her owner and indicates, at least potentially, that she belonged to a group of slaves owned by Statilia or her family, the Statilii Tauri, whose large *familia* (slaves and freedmen) was buried in a tomb on the Esquiline.[46] Nicepor *marmorarius* (marble mason, 6318), whose epitaph comes from this tomb, has no formal status indication that ties him to a specific owner, but his burial in a tomb reserved for the slaves and freedmen of an upper-class family points to his membership in the *familia,* which was defined by the bond of each member to the slaveholder and his family. Participation in a domestic *collegium* (self-help organization), certain name forms, and family relations function in ways similar to burial location and can be used to assess the actual proportions of freeborn citizens, slaves, and freedmen among those with occupational title.

Burial in a *columbarium* (chamber tomb) reserved for the staff of a single family and participation in a domestic *collegium* indicate membership in a large domestic household. Those with single names and no genitive were probably slaves; those with the appropriate nomen and no libertination, freedmen.[47] Without status indication, we cannot be certain of legal status; individuals with nomina and no libertination, for example, could have been the freeborn children of the household's freedmen and women. However, inclusion in a tomb reserved for the *familia* or participation in its *collegium* demonstrates a connection with the *familia*, most obviously as a slave or freedman. Further, we are concerned with individuals who used occupational title. They were not only buried in the tomb or simply members of the *collegium*; they worked for the household or its masters.[48] Consider the goldsmith Hilarus (9149) whose epitaph announces his membership in a *collegium* established in the household of Sergia Paullina ("collegium quod est in domo Sergiae L. [f] Paullinae"). His bond with a slave group is explicitly represented in his affiliation with the household *collegium*; his tie to his owner, Sergia Paullina, is implied. In the absence of status indication, epitaphs like Hilarus's and those from single-family *columbaria* locate an individual in a particular social group rather than designate a relationship with a particular master.[49]

Status indication conveys additional information, especially in the less defined situation of the *columbarium*. In the tomb reserved for the *familia* of the Statilii, it distinguishes the *dispensator* (steward) of Statilia (6272) from the *dispensator* of Corvinus (6273). The use of status indication to name employer is especially common for men and women in personal service and child care, whose work entailed close contact with masters and patrons.[50] In some cases, status indication reveals that master (or patron) and employer were different.[51]

Two additions to the name forms described above generally reflect aspects of servile or freed status: *natio* (origin), an indication of one's birthplace, and agnomen, an additional name indicating a former or current master.

Because of the equation of outsider with slave, foreign origin was closely associated with a servile past. Neither freeborn citizens nor freedmen who wished to hide their ethnicity would have used *natio* on their tombstones if it indicated a non-Italian place. For the few who did (N = 15) despite the stigma of alienness in Roman society, *natio* probably expressed a continued attachment or source of identity. L. Arlenus L. l. Artemidorus, a merchant of inexpensive clothing (*mercator sagarius*, 9675), for example, came from Paphlagonia (*natio Paphlago*); he had been enslaved, but by the time of his death had received his freedom. Yet, despite his status as a Roman citizen, he continued to identify himself as a native of Paphlagonia, that is, by the birthplace he had lost in slavery.[52] At death, at least, some made the claim to heritage and culture that had been disallowed, except as a personal idiosyncrasy, during their lives.

An agnomen, an extra cognomen usually ending in -*ianus*, was formed out of the nomen or cognomen of a previous master or of a current master if the latter was a slave.[53] Not every *vicarius* (slave of a slave) or slave who passed from one household to another used an agnomen. Its presence may signal either a particular distinction or a felt connection to a former master or household. Scirtus *symphoniacus* Cornelianus (6356) and Flaccus *faber tignuarius* Cornelianus (6365) were buried in the *columbarium* set aside for the *familia* of the Statilii and belonged, therefore, to that household. By their use of the agnomen Cornelianus they represented themselves as slaves (or former slaves) of Cornelia, daughter of Cornelius Sisenna and wife of T. Statilius Taurus, *triumvir monetalis*.[54] Whether the agnomen reflected a special bond with Cornelia (neither musician nor carpenter had an occupation that in itself would have brought him into close contact with her) or an attachment to a former *familia* is not clear, but it distinguishes them from other slaves in the *columbarium*.

An agnomen seems to have functioned this way for at least thirteen of the men and women with agnomina in this study (N = 21). They belonged to large households whose slaves came from diverse sources—birth, marriage, purchase, inheritance. In this setting there were not only more masters but also masters of diverse social and legal status—members of the *familia* itself as well as members of the owner's family. The agnomen indicated the subgroup to which one belonged or the source of one's membership in the *familia*.[55]

Because legal status ultimately determined a person's family rights and indeed the very structure of his or her family, the family relations depicted contain information about that status.[56] For example, Q. Haterius Evagogus, an official (*decurio*) in a carpenters' *collegium* (9408), has a nomen but no status indication. He and his wife, Iulia Arescusa, had a daughter, Iulia Euraesis, who has her mother's nomen, not her father's. At the time of their daughter's birth, Arescusa and Evagogus did not have a proper Roman marriage, so their daughter could take neither her father's nomen nor his status. Most likely, Evagogus, at least, was a slave at the time of his daughter's birth. Since Euraesis apparently took her nomen and status from Arescusa, it seems her mother was free (either freeborn or freed) when she was born.[57]

Our ability to deduce an individual's status from his or her relatives is limited by the type of relationship—mother, father, child, sibling—and by our knowledge of the actual status of the relative.[58] Moreover, in cases like Evagogus's, where wife and child also lack status indication, we are actually looking at a pattern of names rather than a pattern of statuses. The free family in which mother and father had different nomina and all children the nomen of their father establishes a reference point. Adherence to the appropriate pattern suggests free status; deviation, freed status. Despite the difficulties of interpreting patterns of names, especially those that include cognomina, they can reveal something of a family's structure and history.[59] In the example above, the indication of actual legal condition is fairly precise only for Evagogus; however, the names of husband, wife, and child clearly reflect the family's experience with slavery.

For men and women with job titles, ascertaining status from name patterns or the legal status of relatives is limited by the relatively small proportion of individuals whose epitaphs include family members other than a spouse (see

Table 2.2). Mothers and children, who most clearly reveal the status of children and parents, respectively, appear infrequently (2% [N = 26] and 5.5% [N = 73]). Moreover, the proportions of uncertain slaves (73.5%, N = 249) and uncertain freeborn (59.3%, N = 217) who have no family relations whatsoever is high, and 17.7% (N = 60) of the uncertain slaves and 25.1% (N = 92) of the uncertain freeborn have only a spouse. Nevertheless, in the absence of other evidence, name patterns and the legal status of relatives provide some information on the actual status of those in the uncertain categories.[60]

More generally, epitaphs reveal the family ties that existed regardless of their legitimacy. In Table 2.2, each percentage represents the proportion of the status group whose epitaphs mentioned a particular relative. There is some double counting in these figures, as some individuals included more than one family member in their epitaphs. The most dramatic contrast between the epitaphs of slaves and freedmen and those of the freeborn appears in the recurrence of parents and children. The epitaphs of the freeborn were considerably more likely than those of slaves or freedmen to mention a parent or a child.[61] However, there is little difference between slave and freeborn (and uncertain freeborn) in the recurrence of spouses. It is interesting that the epitaphs of slaves tend to include the names of spouses more often than those of freed slaves.[62]

These patterns provide a revealing contrast to the legal strictures on family rights. The comparatively more common occurrence of intergenerational family relations for the freeborn does mirror their potential for a legitimate family of origin as well as a family of creation; the mutual duties and the ties between parent and child are present in the epitaphs for the free in a way that they are not for slaves. However, the absence of any significant difference between slave and freeborn in intragenerational relations, especially marriage, is striking. Slaves did not have legal marriages any more than they had legitimate children or parents, yet the epitaphs reflect marital ties no less for them than for the freeborn (and uncertain freeborn) who had the right to contract a proper Roman marriage.

Scattered comments in the literary sources suggest that the relations of male and female slaves were not only per-

Table 2.2 Presence of Family Members and Legal Status in Epitaphs

Family Members	Legal Status					
	Slave	Uncertain Slave	Freedman	Freeborn	Uncertain Freeborn	Total
Spouse:	90 (33.0)	65 (19.2)	72 (22.0)	7 (30.4)	117 (32.0)	351 (26.4)
Certain	76 (27.8)	41 (12.1)	33 (10.1)	6 (26.1)	86 (23.5)	242 (18.2)
Possible	14 (5.1)	24 (7.1)	39 (11.9)	1 (4.3)	31 (8.5)	109 (8.2)
Mother	5 (1.8)	8 (2.4)	3 (.9)	4 (17.4)	6 (1.6)	26 (2.0)
Father	3 (1.1)	4 (1.2)	—	4 (17.4)	5 (1.4)	16 (1.2)
Sibling	11 (4.0)	12 (3.5)	9 (2.8)	1 (4.3)	10 (2.7)	43 (3.2)
Children	11 (4.0)	9 (2.7)	11 (3.4)	2 (8.7)	40 (10.9)	73 (5.5)
No family	162 (59.3)	249 (73.5)	237 (72.5)	12 (52.2)	217 (59.3)	877 (66.0)

Notes: Figures include relatives mentioned by term and not named and those whose names are obscured by breakage. Figures in parentheses are column percentages.

mitted but encouraged by slave owners. They increased the master's property when they resulted in the birth of children. But there is little comment on perpetuating relations between parent and child, much less of strengthening a nuclear unit of father, mother, and children. When Columella (*Rust.* 1.8.19) and Varro (*Rust.* 2.10.6–7) mention the relations of male and female slaves, they are generally concerned with sexual relations that produce children, not with the relationship of the couple.[63] When Columella (1.8.19) says that he manumitted slave women who had had more than three children, there is no mention of the father or family.

The bonds of the nuclear family would not have served the master's interest as effectively as slaves' attachment to the *familia* as a whole. Indeed, when Pliny (*Ep.* 8.16.2) says that the household is a kind of commonwealth (*res publica*) and a citizenship (*civitas*) for slaves, he emphasizes the tie to the entire household unit, not to a discrete group within it. A senatorial notion of *res publica*, too, would have assumed a ruling class, here a place filled by the master, while the ideal of the master as father of the household, specifically of the *familia*, precluded a vision of the individual male slave as *pater*.[64]

Indeed, the master's acknowledgment of a slave's family relations would have disrupted Pliny's household commonwealth. Strong, stable families would have created separate units within and apart from the *familia*.[65] Groups other than the *res publica* and bonds other than *civitas* obviated the ruler. The master's acknowledgment of a slave family appears as a special case: Varro (*Rust.* 1.17.5) and Columella (*Rust.* 1.8.5) grant family and children to the slave manager of an estate only as a privilege in order to strengthen his commitment to his job. In the master's eyes, as in Roman law, the union of female and male slave was not a marriage.

The pattern of family relations indicated in Table 2.2, then, may result from the difficulties experienced by the slave family. Slave parents did not have control of their children; sale and manumission divided the family. Yet, although sale affected marriages as well as relations of parents and children, the former were presumably easier to re-create. How these relations were perceived by slaves is another matter. Slaves used all the normal (i.e., freeborn) terms for husband and wife on their epitaphs.[66] Where the master saw sexual relations that produced more slaves, the slave saw marriage.

The factors and circumstances reviewed here not only aid in ascertaining the legal status of men and women with occupational title, they also describe their lives. Burial in a *columbarium* and participation in a domestic *collegium* conveyed membership in a social group composed of one's fellow slaves and ex-slaves; notation of office or membership in a domestic *collegium* placed pointed emphasis on one's role in a formal organization. *Natio* and agnomen described a man's or a woman's background: agnomen referred to one's past within slavery and *natio* to one's origin outside it. The dedication of epitaphs to and from family members reveal the ties between siblings, children and parents, and wife and husband. In the case of slaves, these indications implicitly made claims to what was denied by legitimate society— community, heritage, and family ties.

THE LEGAL STATUS OF
MEN AND WOMEN WITH OCCUPATIONAL TITLE

Table 2.3 shows the size of each status group when the informal indications discussed above are used as criteria for analyzing those in the uncertain categories. The representation of slaves and freedmen is very large compared with that of the freeborn: 60% of those with occupational title were slaves or freed slaves. Even if most of the uncertain freeborn

Table 2.3   Legal Status Groups Before and After
Consideration of Informal Indications

Legal Status	Before Analysis	After Analysis
Slave	302 (20.5)	469 (31.9)
Uncertain slave	372 (25.3)	205 (13.9)
Freedman	340 (23.1)	421 (28.6)
Freeborn	29 (2.0)	43 (2.9)
Uncertain freeborn	427 (29.0)	332 (22.6)
Total	1,470 (100)	1,470 (100)

Note: Figures in parentheses are percentages.

Table 2.4   Legal Status of Deceased in All Epitaphs,
Sepulcrales, and Occupational Epitaphs

Legal Status	In All Epitaphs (Huttunen)		In *Sepulcrales* Only (Huttunen)		In Occupational Epitaphs (Joshel)	
Slave	360	(5.8)	198	(4.9)	206	(19.6)
Uncertain slave	1,044	(16.9)	753	(18.8)	276	(26.3)
Freedman	1,613	(26.2)	544	(13.6)	270	(25.7)
Uncertain freedman	640	(10.4)	573	(14.3)	63	(6.0)
Freeborn	388	(6.3)	134	(3.3)	19	(1.8)
Uncertain freeborn	2,122	(34.4)	1,806	(45.1)	217	(20.6)
Total	6,167	(100)	4,008	(100)	1,051	(100)

Source: Huttunen 1974, 139, 189.
Note: Figures in parentheses are percentages.

actually were *ingenui*, they are still poorly represented in comparison with slaves and ex-slaves.

When the men and women with occupational title are placed within their immediate context—the entire extant epitaph material from Rome—their status pattern can be compared with that of all those who received named burial. Table 2.4 shows the status distributions of the deceased in all the epitaphs in Huttunen's samples, the deceased in epitaphs without occupational titles (*sepulcrales*) in his samples, and the deceased in the occupational inscriptions used in this study. In order to make comparisons with Huttunen's findings, I have given the figures for each status group, considering only formal status indication and terms of relationship, except in the case of freedmen whose status is indicated by other criteria (labeled uncertain freedmen).[67]

A comparison between the *sepulcrales* and the occupational epitaphs shows that the predominance of slaves and freedmen among those with occupational title is not characteristic of all who received named burial at Rome. Freedmen, slaves, and uncertain slaves are strikingly better represented in the occupational epitaphs. Most revealing are the figures for the clearly identified *ingenui* and the uncertain freeborn. While the former make a poor showing in both types of epitaphs, their numbers are larger among those without occupational title, as is also the case for the uncertain freeborn.[68] Even if this figure hides some ex-slaves, it points to a larger proportion of *ingenui* among the men and women undistinguished by title.

The correlation between the inscriptions and the actual population of the city is problematic. Although the epitaph material well reflects those who received named burial, it does not include all those who lived and died in Rome during the 200 to 250 years covered by Huttunen's study and this one. The unnamed men and women interred in the public cemeteries like that on the Esquiline, for example, are excluded: they lacked the means to pay for a tombstone or the connections to a large household that, in the absence of financial resources, provided the opportunity of named burial.[69] Huttunen argues that "probably 66 persons lived there for each burial known to us either directly or indirectly." This index of representation is better than Maier thought when he condemned the usefulness of nearly all statistics derived from inscriptions, but it is still poor and varies enough to include some systematic deviation like the omission of the population buried in the public cemeteries.[70]

This means, then, that the proportions of slaves, freedmen, and freeborn with occupational title do not necessarily correspond to the actual status structure of those who worked. Each individual with an occupational title must stand for too many people for these figures to reflect the complexion of the work force accurately. Further, in actuality, some in the *sepulcrales* had the same livelihoods as the men and women in the occupational inscriptions; they simply did not name their work at death. Huttunen has shown that, contrary to the assumptions of Tenney Frank and others, the occupational inscriptions and the *sepulcrales* do not represent different social strata in Roman society. The large percentage of slaves and freedmen among those with occupational title does not mean that freedmen and slaves dominated commerce and artisanry; they simply dominated the use of occupational title among those who received named burial.[71]

Whether the standard of comparison is the actual population (see app. 3) or the population recorded in the epitaphs, occupation and servile or freed status are closely associated. The proportions of slaves and freedmen suggest that this

identification by occupational title had a particular significance for men and women of servile origin.

TOWARD AN UNDERSTANDING OF
THE SIGNIFICANCE OF OCCUPATIONAL TITLE

Occupational titles gave slaves and freedmen varied identities, but it is work in general that frames these identities. A
theoretical perspective on work and legal condition will help
us to read the testimony of their epitaphs and dedications.

Work and Slavery

Whatever their stated theme, Roman writers who comment
on slavery include work as an essential element in the
slave's existence. The history of the slave system as it un-
folds in the ancient sources focuses on the use made of slave
labor in the countryside. The most direct correspondence
between slave and laborer recurs in the instructions on good
estate management offered by Cato, Varro, and Columella.
Seneca's advice on the proper actions of the truly good and
free man makes slaves part of the landscape, but he invariably locates them in particular employments or simply at
work in a nondefined sense. When an author's concern is the
behavior of slaves, his discussion usually describes them in
specific jobs. The vision of the slave as worker is not surprising; slavery is one form of dependent labor and was the
dominant institutional form of compulsory labor in Italy
during the first two centuries A.D.[72]

I do not mean that at Rome dependent labor totally defined the slave or that the slave's significance can be entirely
summarized by his or her work,[73] but, rather, emphasize just
how integrally Roman masters associated slave and labor.
When property was estimated for the census, the duties and
trades of slaves were supposed to be reported with other distinctive characteristics and *natio*. If a person had the right
to use a slave owned by someone else and to take what the
slave produced (*ususfructus*), the slave had to be used in a
way consistent with his or her training and usual occupation. One was not supposed to send a secretary to one's
country estate and force him to do carrying work; one could
not turn a musician into a hall porter. The labor of the slave
was part of the slave, even when the slave was sold or trans-

ferred. So completely undivided were slaves and their labor that in wills slaves could be identified by their jobs without their names. So total was the master's control that Varro (*Rust.* 1.17.1) could call the slave an *instrumentum vocale* (the tool that is able to speak).[74]

All this argues that the work of the slave was central to the master. However, as Table 2.5 shows, jobs were named in epitaphs primarily by slaves themselves or those close to them.[75] Although the deceased may have left instructions about his or her epitaph, the commemorator appears to us as its author and hence the person responsible for framing the deceased's identity. In only five cases (1.4%) was this individual specifically the master. More critical in the pattern of slaves' titulature are the commemorators of the epitaphs from single-family *columbaria*. These small plaques generally have little space for a commemorator's name, so we cannot always point to the specific person who gave the slave an occupational title. However, other epitaphs from these tombs that include commemorators' names indicate the general pattern: if the deceased did not arrange for his or her own epitaph, the commemorator was a relative, a fellow slave, or the *collegium* of the household's slaves and freedmen who administered the tomb. In the *columbarium* of the Statilii, for example, the epitaph of Aphrodisius, the curtain or awnings maintenance man, was written by his brother Eutychus, the bedchamber servant (*velarius, cubicularius,* 6258); Optata, the doorkeeper, was commemorated by her friends (*ostiaria,* 6326). Officials of the household's funerary *collegium* noted the employments of deceased members as well as their own (6215–19, cf. 7281–82). If the unnamed commemorators in the epitaphs from single-family *columbaria* are associated with those in the first four categories in Table 2.5, 74.4% (*N* = 267) of the deceased slaves will have received their job titles from themselves, their peers, or families. In short, while the master determined the slave's job and controlled the slave's labor, slaves themselves and their peers saw something essential for their own identity in their work.

The large proportion of slaves who used occupational title reflects the perspective of the slave, not the master. It is difficult to recover what slaves and their commemorators thought about work. A few epitaphs celebrate skills and

Table 2.5 Titling of Deceased and Self-Commemorators

| | Legal Status | | | | | |
Title Given by	Slave	Uncertain Slave	Freedman	Freeborn	Uncertain Freeborn	Total
Family member	80 (22.3)	22 (15.1)	37 (9.8)	14 (42.4)	42 (16.9)	195 (16.8)
Peer—friend or colleague	5 (1.4)	7 (4.8)	—	3 (9.1)	26 (10.5)	41 (3.5)
Peer—member of *familia*	29 (8.1)	—	4 (1.1)	—	—	33 (2.8)
Self	19 (5.3)	4 (2.7)	47 (12.4)	2 (6.1)	43 (17.3)	115 (9.9)
No commemorator, single-family *columbarium*	134 (37.3)	—	43 (11.4)	—	2 (.8)	179 (15.4)
No commemorator	71 (19.8)	100 (68.5)	201 (53.2)	11 (33.3)	99 (39.9)	482 (41.4)
Master, patron, etc.[1]	5 (1.4)	2 (1.4)	15 (4.0)	1 (3.0)	4 (1.6)	27 (2.3)
Other or unclear	16 (4.5)	11 (7.5)	31 (8.2)	2 (6.1)	32 (12.9)	92 (7.9)
Total	359 (100)	146 (100)	378 (100)	33 (100)	248 (100)	1,164 (100)

Note: Figures in parentheses are percentages.
[1] Includes nurses' charges and "employers."

moral qualities that make the deceased a valued person; however, the commemorators, the occupations praised, and the legal status of the deceased are so varied that general conclusions are difficult to draw.[76] We can observe only that slaves identified themselves by their occupations in particular situations and evaluate these acts against the background of their social and legal position. However, the association of slave and worker in law and literature sets any evaluation of the acts evidenced in inarticulate stone in a problematic context: why did slaves identify themselves by the element of their enslavement that was so important to their masters and so much within the master's control?

At a basic level, occupational title names the factor that determined the material conditions of the slave's life: physical comfort, control of property, social relations, and opportunities for manumission. Work's effects are most dramatic in the contrast between the slave laborer on a country estate and the slave artisan in the city. The former faced the possibility of chains and the estate's slave prison (*ergastulum*);[77] the latter could have had funds or property in his control (*peculium*), freedom of movement, and a more comfortable physical existence. Intelligence in his case was an asset: the epitaph of a young slave jeweler named Pagus (9437) boasts of his skills and records his master's favor.[78] For the slave in the countryside, however, intelligence was too often a fault. According to Columella (*Rust.* 1.9.4), viticulture required strong men and workers with mental acuity. But since this quickness of mind was generally a characteristic of troublemakers, these slave workers often ended up working in chains.

The future, too, differed for these two slaves. Columella's worker could look forward only to continual labor. By the evidence of the occupational inscriptions, Pagus, had he lived, could have expected manumission: twenty-three of the twenty-six jewelers in these epitaphs were free (eleven were clearly identified freedmen). Moreover, as the wealth of other jewelers attests, his work had the potential for financial success. Further, the city slave had a far better chance for named burial, a recognition that he had lived. Even Felix, an attendant in the Statilian household (*pedisequus*, 6333) in a city where there were many personal servants, was named; Columella's slave in the vineyard was not.

For Susan Treggiari and Marleen Boudreau Flory, slaves used occupational titles because of the status associated with their jobs.[79] They cite the frequent omission of job title by slaves and freedmen in large domestic households as evidence of the status associated with the titles that were used and, implicitly, of a hierarchy of jobs within the household. I take up the question of prestige in the next chapter and here only comment on its limits as an explanation for the predominance of slaves and ex-slaves among those with occupational title.

The observation that few had job title ignores the fact that it is an unusual element in all epitaphs. Only about 10% of the deceased in Roman epitaphs had occupational title, and this figure includes members of the emperor's *familia*, the imperial bureaucracy, senators, equestrians, soldiers, and performers in the amphitheater, circus, and stage.[80] Within the population defined by occupational title, slaves and ex-slaves were the predominant groups, indicating that something more than prestige was involved; the paucity of titles at least will not explain why slaves, in contrast to the freeborn, gave a more important role to work in the framing of an identity at death. Also, if there were a hierarchy in which servants had descending rank, the hierarchy itself would still have been an ordering of jobs, and kinds of labor would have been the scale of measurement.

The implications of job title (material conditions and prestige) can be comprehended within the larger framework of a society that defined the roles of slave and master. For an understanding of the importance of work in the slave's experience, Hegel's analyses of the relationship of lord and bondsman is a beginning point. As Orlando Patterson notes, Hegel "first explored in depth the dialectics" of the "political psychology of the everyday life of masters and slaves."[81] Especially important for this study, an ironic reversal emerges from the movement of Hegel's dialectic, focusing attention on the slave's work. His argument and Patterson's criticism of it help to clarify what may be reflected in the epitaphs of Roman slaves.[82]

According to Hegel, the master initially perceives his

own existence as for himself and not for another. He regards his slave as one who exists for his master, not for himself. "In other words, another person lives through and by him—becomes his surrogate—and the master's honor and power is [sic] thereby enhanced." In Hegel's scheme, the master's domination undermines his independence. He relies on the slave for recognition, but his own domination of the slave has made the latter only an extension of himself and therefore nonessential. "The slave cannot confirm his honor, cannot offer recognition, because he is not worthy."[83] The slave, however, does not suffer from such an existential crisis; he discovers independence through work that grounds him as it does not the master.

> Through work . . . the bondsman becomes conscious of what he truly is. . . . Work . . . is desire held in check, fleetingness staved off; in other words, work forms and shapes the thing. The negative relation to the object becomes its *form* and something *permanent*, because it is precisely for the worker that the object has independence.[84]

Patterson's criticism of Hegel focuses on two points. First, the equation of slave and worker is not a necessary one. Although "his slaveness, especially his natal alienation, made possible his effective exploitation as laborer in conditions where no other kind of laborer would do . . . , this does not in any way mean that slave necessarily implies worker." Second, slavery does not pose "an existential impasse for the master": the latter could and did gain recognition from other free persons who, even in most large-scale slave systems, were the majority in the population. In a hierarchical society such as Rome, clients, women, and children in paternal power served functions similar to Hegel's bondsman. Juvenal's poetic personae certainly accord with Patterson's observation that "the poorest free person took pride in the fact that he was not a slave. By sharing in the collective honor of the master class, all free persons legitimized the principle of honor and thereby recognized the members of the master class as those most adorned with honor and glory."[85] In addition, I would emphasize the effect of particular kinds of labor done by slaves. Many of the slaves with occupational title in Roman epitaphs did work that upheld and even created the social standing of their masters; their work required an orientation toward a specific other, which would not produce the "negative relation to the object" envisioned by Hegel.

That work was critical in the experience of the slave, even if not exactly in the way imagined by Hegel, suggests why occupational title as a mode of identification was more important to the slave than to the freeborn person. Lacking a heritage, socially acknowledged kin, a place in the social order, and even names of their own, slaves did have their work, even if that labor and its products were in another's control. In this light, slaves' use of occupational title stems from the poverty of their social position. The freeborn, at least the nonelite classes, also worked, but their other claims displaced work as an essential mode of identity.

Further, slaves' occupational titles may proceed from a perception of their social value, one that originates, ironically, in social poverty and natal alienation. Work of all kinds, especially the domestic jobs held by many of the slaves in the occupational inscriptions, was not a source of prestige in the ideology of the highest ranks of the freeborn. Yet Roman society required the production of goods and services. Upper-class slaveholders, especially, needed certain services for their material existence and social standing. Productive labor, although culturally devalued and not empowering for the slave, had social value, and Roman law and literature implicitly recognized this. Work carried with it a sense of importance. The predominance of slaves and ex-slaves among those who identified themselves as the producers of goods and services seems to bespeak slaves' awareness of the worth of their activities.

Occupational title, too, claims an active interaction with the world, contradicting Patterson's argument that the slave is "socially dead." According to Patterson, the slave's natal alienation evokes a particular response from the society in which he or she lives. "If the slave no longer belonged to a community, if he had no social existence outside of his master, then what was he? The initial response in almost all slaveholding societies was to define the slave as a socially dead person." In other words, the slave, although "desocialized" and "depersonalized," exists within the society of the master and must be incorporated in some way. The means used by most societies is "institutionalized marginality, the liminal state of social death." Patterson sees explicit expression of the slave's social death in the Roman ritual of enslavement and especially in Roman law: "the slave was *pro nullo.*"[86]

However, the slave is a "socially dead" entity only from the perspective of the slaveholder. For the master, slaves existed outside but on the border of the community to which they belonged as passive agents, conduits through which the master could act or be acted upon. But at the moment of real death, slaves with occupational title—these "socially dead" people (or their peers)—depicted themselves as active agents, summarizing their lives in terms of an essential social function.[87]

A consideration of the primary audience for this self-representation introduces a certain ambiguity surrounding the use of occupational title. Because job titles frequently identified slaves to their peers, we must ask about different systems of meaning. Should we read in these titles slaves' claims against the dominant value system? Did slaves, aware of their social contribution, see through the cultural values of the wider society that denigrated their work? Or are we observing another value system, a subculture of sorts with its own canons? Examining the audience for their occupational titles and the structure of master-slave relations suggests two reference points: the slave's immediate social circle and the legitimate social order. Commemoration by and among peers certainly indicates the value of work within a slave community, but slaves will have experienced in their relations with their masters, especially those from the upper classes, the cultural attitudes and material needs of the wider society.

Work and the Freed Slave

Interpreting the role of work in the life of the freed slave is more complex than it is in the life of the slave. A servile past in which work figured so importantly as a means of identification must be balanced against a free present in which the claims to membership in the legitimate community and to socially acknowledged kin were possible.

The view of legitimate society associated the freedman with work. In literature, commercial activities appear central to the ex-slave, who is often depicted as rich and annoying in his pretensions to social standing, which traditionally belonged to the gentleman landowner.[88] In law, the significance of the ex-slave's labor is expressed directly in workdays (*operae*) and indirectly in the patron's claims on the freedman's estate. Detailed regulations concerning the timing, location, conditions, and specific requirements of *operae* show the depth of patrons' concern with the labor of their former slaves. Yet, such regulations also divide freedmen and women from their work. Considerations like the ex-slave's personal physical maintenance, the freedman's capacity to earn a living and support children, and the freedwoman's ability to devote herself to her husband mark out the boundaries that gave ex-slaves an existence independent of their patrons and their own labor. So, too, did children's claims to the estate of a freed father.[89]

Although the state's intrusion into the relations of patron and freedman distinguished slave and freedman in terms of their labor and its products, neither the potential control of the patron nor the importance of the ex-slave's labor should be minimized. Patrons' demands had been sufficiently excessive to merit intervention in the republic, and legislation as well as the opinions of jurists indicates a continued need for regulation in the empire. Courts and judicial officials set limits on patrons' authority, attributing to ex-slaves a claim to their own labor; they made the burdens of freedmen in some sense negotiable between ex-master and ex-slave. But at no time was the patron's right to the labor of his former slave denied.[90]

In addition, despite the separation of the freedman from his or her labor that is implicit in law, we find the good freedman equated with the good "worker" in epitaphs authored by former masters. In commemorating their freedmen, patrons did not distinguish the deferential behavior required from the freedman from the labor rendered to the patron or the productive relations between freedman and patron.

To the departed spirits of Marcus Canuleius Zosimus. He lived twenty-eight years. (His) patron made (this) for a well-deserving freedman. In his life he spoke ill of no one. He did nothing without the accord (goodwill) of (his) patron. A great weight of gold and silver was always in his possession. Out of that, he never desired anything. As to skill, he conquered all (prevailed over all) in the Clodian style of engraving.

```
                    D  ·  M
     M     ·    C    N    U    L    E    I
                 Z O S I M I
     V  I  X  ·  A  N  N  ·  X  X  V  I  I  I
                   F E C I T
     P   A   T   R   O   N   U   S   ·   L   I   B
     B   E   N   E  ·  M   E   R   E   N   T   I
     HIC · IN · VITA · SUA · NULLI · MA
     LEDIXIT  ·  SINE  ·  VOLUNTATE
     PATRONI  ·  NIHIL  ·  FECIT
     MULTUM        ·        PONDERIS
     AURI  ·  ARG  ·  PENES  ·  EUM
     SEMPER · FUIT · CONCUPIIT · EX · EO
     NIHIL · UMQUAM · HIC · ARTEM · CAELA
     TURA  ·  CLODIANA  ·  EVICIT  ·  OMNES
                              (CIL 6.9222)
```

In the eyes of his patron, Zosimus—compliant, honest, and skillful—was deserving both as freedman and as engraver. His compliance in speech and action receives special attention. Zosimus bent himself to the will of his patron; he displayed *obsequium*. Skill made Zosimus a superior engraver; compliance, proper freed behavior, made him a superior employee or perhaps an investment.[91] Similarly, when Cossus Cornelius Lentulus Gaetulicus, son of the consul A.D. 26, dedicated a tomb to Atimetus, his father's freedman and "very faithful manager" (*procurator fidelissimus*) and his own "very faithful manager and most dutiful guardian" (*procurator fidelissimus et nutricius piissimus*, 9834), he described a productive relationship along with a personal one of dependence: here, trustworthy, devoted *procurator* and good freedman were virtually synonymous.[92]

The respective points of view of patron and freedman require consideration. In these two epitaphs, the patron or his son defines the ex-slave in terms of the work that belonged to the relationship with a former master. As in law and literature, the importance of work in the freedman's life appears as an extension of a servile past. Yet the free present allowed freedmen to describe themselves as citizens and as family members. Why, then, if freedmen had these other modes of identification, do they figure so importantly among those who in epitaphs defined themselves by work?

The pattern of commemoration for freedmen does not reveal as often as for slaves precisely who noted an individual's occupation, but we can observe the group of people among whom the ex-slave (or whoever commemorated the epitaph) used occupational title. Only 34.7% ($N = 131$) of the freedmen (compared with 74.4% of the slaves) received their titles from peers, family members, or self-commemoration (see Table 2.5). The relatively larger proportion of slaves who were commemorated by a family member is striking. However, freedmen with family relations are hidden among those who wrote their own epitaphs (many in this category had family tombs) and those whose epitaphs have no stated commemorator. Of the 201 freedmen in the latter situation, 46.8% appear with family members ($N = 45$) or fellow ex-slaves ($N = 49$). In effect, although we cannot name the person who identified the freedman by his or her occupation, we know that job title was used in the context of family and peers.

The experience of slavery should not be discounted in determining why freedmen used occupational title. Weaver has shown that, except for cases of "pathetic" manumission of young slaves on their deathbeds and of early manumission *matrimonii causa*, manumission at age thirty, the legal age established by the Lex Aelia Sentia (A.D. 4), was the general rule.[93] Freedom came in adulthood, after years of work that often began in childhood.[94] An attitude toward work based on experience had been engendered in the formative years of the ex-slave's life, and manumission in adulthood would not immediately have altered the now freed slave's valuation of work.

Where the relations formed in slavery were maintained, the former slave continued to associate, if not live and work, with the person who had had total control of his or her labor or with those to whom he or she had been a fellow worker. The epitaphs of 25.6% ($N = 104$) of the freedmen show continued relations with former masters or fellow ex-slaves. The specific conditions varied with occupation and patron. The freed slave who became his patron's *procurator*, like Atimetus, or remained in the household as a domestic servant, could identify himself as a citizen, but the conditions in which labor had been central to his identity had not significantly altered. His job, even when it involved some promotion, still defined him in terms of the *familia*, and he continued to experience the value of his labor in relation to his ex-master. The freed artisan who worked with his or her fellow freedmen (*colliberti*) in their own or their patron's shop was linked to others by shared work as well as a shared past.[95]

In a more general sense, the freedman's second-class membership in Roman society gave the use of occupational title a meaning that it did not have for the freeborn. The relationship with a former master restricted the freed citizen's legal recourse, physical integrity, and honor. Freedmen's ineligibility for office, senatorial or equestrian rank, and other inabilities in public law placed them outside the company of the freeborn. While few freeborn citizens had the financial or social qualifications for office or rank, they were not disqualified solely on the basis of birth. Even though capable of legitimate kin relations, the freedman never recovered a family of origin; servile birth was a permanent stigma. Outsider status and the loss of paternity left ex-slaves vulnerable to the freeborn who possessed the means to denigrate them. Any success was viewed as usurpation or, as in Juvenal (1.101–111; 3.60–80), a foreign invasion, an incursion of those who literally came from outside Roman society. Like ex-slaves in most slave societies, the Roman freedman occupied what Patterson sees as a marginal position:

> Freedman status was not an end to the process of marginalization but merely the end of the beginning—the end of one phase, slavery. . . . Freedman status began a new phase: the ex-slave was still a marginal, but the process was now moving toward demarginalization socially, and disalienation in personal terms.[96]

In view of this marginality, occupational title has a particular force. It shifts attention from birth and honor to productive activities and relations. From this perspective, the freedman with an occupational title no longer appears at the edges of Roman society. His or her claim to labor asserts a kind of centrality in the face of marginality. Further, while freedmen lacked the paternity necessary for social rank, those in lucrative occupations had the opportunity to acquire the pecuniary resources that formed the basis of any claim to standing. Occupational title named the means that provided "marginal" freedmen with the material base of high-ranking insiders. Although the freedman's wealth was not and could not be accompanied by the social standing conveyed by office, it was an avenue for his descendants. Even moderate financial success, when secured by children who countered a patron's claims, established an outpost on the inside.

· III ·

THE MEANINGS OF WORK

ZENA
COCUS

Zena, cook.

(*CIL* 6.6249)

C CLODIUS·C·L·EUPHEMUS
NEGOTIATOR · PENORIS
ET · VINORUM
DE·VELABRO·A   IIII·SCARIS   [*sic*]
ARAM · POSUIT · SIBI
CONSECRAVIT
DEDICAVITQUE
LIBERISQUE · SUIS
POSTERISQUE · EORUM

Gaius Clodius Euphemus, the freedman of Gaius, dealer in food and wines in the Velabrum at (the fountain of) the Four Scauri, set up this altar, made it holy, and dedicated it for himself, his children, and their descendants.

(*CIL* 6.9671)

WHEN THE SLAVE Zena (6249) and the freedman C. Clodius C. l. Euphemus (9671) called themselves cook and dealer in food and wines on their epitaphs, they identified their trades by the names also given in literature. The same term is used in two different "genres," each with its own "language" in the sense defined in chapter 1, and by individuals positioned differently in Roman society. In writing, the men who controlled labor, or at least did not work, named. They also claimed, assigning meanings to specific occupational titles or types of work: the cook, for instance, becomes a subservient pleaser, the tradesman a servile flatterer. Yet, in the absence of explicit testimonials, how do we read the claims represented in Zena's and Euphemus's use of "cook" and "tradesman"? The task of interpretation involves a critical assessment of the meanings attributed to work and worker in literature; accordingly, I begin with attitudes voiced there. Next, in order to assess the kinds of work named in Roman inscriptions, I examine the occupational structure formed by the use of titles, emphasizing, on the one hand, the needs of Rome's upper classes and, on the other hand, the naming of occupations by the men and women who practiced them. Finally, I evaluate the meanings produced in literature against those that might be claimed by individuals who worked but did not write.

NAMING AND CLAIMING: ATTITUDES TOWARD WORK IN LATIN LITERATURE

Derogatory attitudes toward work are a well-known feature of Latin literature.[1] Moreover, the denigration of work lies not only in what is said but also in occupation as a vehicle for other purposes. In reference to senators and emperors, for instance, it formed part of the vocabulary of political invective. For Juvenal and Martial, and perhaps for Petronius, attacks on tradesmen belonged to a larger critique of a society in which, from their perspective, wealth now determined social priorities. These attitudes engender and in turn reinforce stereotypes that constitute a vital element in satire: lying, cheating, vulgar tradesmen are stock figures along with rich, obnoxious freedmen, greasy foreigners, decadent nobles, needy clients, insensitive patrons, and unchaste women.[2]

The negative portrayal of work embodies certain patterns. Professional, servant, and tradesman are viewed as dangerous or more often simply as offensive. Doctors kill their patients, and teachers corrupt their students. Waiters ignore the poor freeborn client at his patron's table; the steward (*dispensator*) treats him with disdain. Business-men always cheat, and rich auctioneers are usually crass. Men who make their living in commerce are materialistic, and they will try to use their wealth to claim precedence.[3] These stereotypes implicitly attribute some power to doc-tor, teacher, servant, and tradesman, but the ability to offend is undermined by the very nature of their occupations. Their activities are dirty, their talents and skills base. The servant may insult the poor client, but he himself is compelled to please his master. The tradesman may achieve financial suc-cess, but his work is sordid or vulgar.[4]

The terms in which the tradesman is evaluated refer to the imagined experience of the domestic slave. The success-ful were depicted as adept at flattery, a form of pleasing that required a willingness to do what others wanted one to do or to be what others wanted one to be; the pleaser covered his "true" desires and sentiments. For the freeborn author, such behavior evoked the image of the slave, who had no choice but to please. The lack of real volition in turn pro-duced what was viewed as duplicity.[5] For a poor man to suc-ceed, according to these views, he had to act like a slave. The foreigner, alien, and little Greek could do so; Juvenal's freeborn narrator could not (3.41ff.). From this perspective, alien and slave are linked; thus, distinguishing foreigner from slave or ex-slave was unnecessary for Juvenal.

Reference to occupation (or, more often, occupation linked with legal status) then becomes the means of dis-honoring the wealthy tradesman and undermines any claim he is imagined to assert. The fictional parvenu can buy a privileged seat in the theater, equestrian status, or the honor of giving games; but since he was originally an auc-tioneer, barber, or shoemaker, he remains lowly, despite the external badges of prestige.[6] The limits of the wealth acquired by artisan and merchant are always emphasized: the money spent by them for approbation becomes the butt of a joke.

> A shoemaker gave you a show (i.e., of gladiators), cultivated town of Bononia, a fuller gave one to Mutina. Now where will the innkeeper give his?

Sutor cerdo dedit tibi, culta Bononia, munus,
   fullo dedit Mutinae: nunc ubi copo dabit?

(Mart. 3.59, cf. 99)

Martial is brutally direct: shoemaker, though you try to be more than a common person, you are no more than your trade—no person at all.

The man who uses wealth to compensate for alien origin or a servile past is equally the object of humor. Juvenal's freedman pushes praetor and tribune out of his way before his patron's door (1.101–6). Well aware that the alien origin betrayed by his pierced ear disqualifies him in the wider society and can be used to dislodge him from first place, he asserts that no senator's stripe could do more for him than his five shops that bring in 400,000 sesterces. In effect, he tries to alter the basis on which precedence can be claimed: the money earned in commerce replaces the claims given by birth.

But the satirists invent the snob's claim to precedence based on wealth only to disallow it. Money can never replace birth: it cannot buy the freedman a birthday or a legal father. Moreover, for Juvenal or Martial, any freedman who relies on his wealth for status has simply replaced one discrediting characteristic with another: money earned in the marketplace means duplicity and servility. The stigma of the marketplace only reinforces the stigma of servile origin. Thus, the wealthy freed merchant is ridiculed not only for his origin and occupation but also for the way in which he deals with them, in Erving Goffman's terms, for how he manages the social information conveyed by the signs of stigma.[7]

Occupation functions similarly in political invective. The archaic perspective of the aristocracy placed artisans and merchants among the lowly. Since the aristocratic claims to privilege depended on birth and wealth derived from land, contempt could be expressed by the accusation that one's family descended from shoemakers and fullers rather than consuls and conquerors. Octavian's family was maligned on all sides in this way: his paternal grandfather, Antony claimed, was a banker, and his great-grandfather not only a rope maker but a freedman; the maternal great-grandfather kept a perfume shop, then a bakery. Cassius accused him of being the grandson of a money changer and a baker. Responding to Cicero's attack on Antony, Q. Fufius Calenus denigrated the orator by calling his father a fuller, an accusation that dirtied Cicero, since fullers collected and used human urine to do their washing.[8]

Whether in political invective or as part of a critique of upward mobility, the standards of assessment are based on a simple polarity of "good" or "bad," honorable or dishonorable. In this process, all work becomes something like the fuller's trade—dirty(ing). Skills can be lauded in objects or adapted to metaphors. The fabulously wealthy Seneca (*Ep.* 15.4), who employs labor as a philosophical trope, uses the fuller's activity as a derogatory name for a physical exercise for the Stoic in training. Productive relations and the subjectivity of the worker do not enter consideration. Like Cortés in the face of Aztec civilization, Roman authors reserved their admiration for objects but did not "acknowledge their makers as human individualities to be set on the same level as [themselves]."[9]

Cicero's (*Off.* 1.150–51) well-known catalog of trades (*artificia*) and occupations (*quaestus*) brings together these standards of assessment by reviewing which livelihoods are considered respectable (*liberales*) or base (*sordidi*).[10] Collectors of harbor dues (*portitores*) and moneylenders (*faeneratores*) are objectionable because they incur the ill-will of others. Wage earners (*mercennarii*) are base because they sell their labor, not their skills. So, too, are retail merchants, for in reselling goods they must lie in order to make a living. Since the workshop (*officina*) is unsuitable for the freeborn, all artisans engage in vulgar activities. Finally, trades that satisfy sensual desires rank as the least respectable: Cicero cites Terence's list—fishmongers, butchers, cooks, poulterers, fishermen (*cetarii, lanii, coqui, fartores, piscatores*)— and adds perfumers (*unguentarii*), dancers (*saltatores*), and all those involved in a low form of song-and-dance entertainment (*totumque ludum talarium*).

Cicero next turns to more respectable activities. Professions like medicine, architecture, and teaching receive more favorable consideration because they benefit society or require intelligence. But their respectability is limited: they are honorable (*honestae*) not for *ingenui* as such but for those to whose social rank they are suited (*quorum ordini conveniunt*). Although retail trading is vulgar, commerce on a large scale that involves importing and wholesale distribution, if not entirely respectable, ought not to be extensively criticized. It does not require deceit and, like medicine, architecture, and teaching, has social utility. Most important, wealth gained in commerce can be invested in agriculture, which merits Cicero's highest respect. At that point, the merchant has become a landholder and engages in the enterprise appropriate for the free man.

Thus, honorable occupations can be distinguished from dishonorable by a specific set of criteria: the behavior required in a given job; the degree of dependence; the nature of the workplace; the degree of service to a specific person; the amount of intelligence required; and social utility. In these terms, the *mercennarius* ranks as the lowliest. Not only did he do manual labor, he also worked for another, hiring out his labor rather than entering into a contract to produce a specific object or service. By selling his labor, then, the *mercennarius* sells himself, for, regardless of the legal distinctions, the laborer was not separated from his labor. Hiring out his labor potentially reduces him to the state of something owned—an animal, inanimate object, a slave. That is why Cicero adds that the wages of *mercennarii* were the reward of slavery.[11]

The retail merchant's disgrace lies in the falsity required in trade—a servile trait, as we have seen. Furthermore, some of those involved in food production and sales and perfuming were retail merchants or small-scale producers, yet Cicero places them in a separate category with entertainers, emphasizing their fulfillment of sensual desires. In a general social context, pleasing another, especially at this basic level, was associated with servile activities. Thus, a connection with other men's appetites assimilates the cook, butcher, entertainer, and unguent dealer to the position of the slave. In addition, by grouping small tradesmen with stage performers, Cicero links merchant and producer with those whose disreputable occupations resulted in reduced civil rights.[12]

Although Cicero's text appears to establish gradations, his description of each trade works with two poles—honorable and dishonorable. His standards delineate what is respectable for the freeborn citizen. Cicero finds unrespectable any trade whose characteristics had servile associations—falsity, pleasing, dependence. Free men should not engage in such activities. In effect, the polarity between honorable and dishonorable becomes the polarity between slave and free. Appropriately, the dichotomy honorable/dishonorable is broken by the intrusion of a qualified honor (*quorum ordini conveniunt, honestae*), just as there exists a middle stage between freeborn and slave—the freedman.

Cicero's catalog also participates in a discourse that attempts to distinguish modes of accumulation. Proper wealth came from land and was increased by intelligence, diligence, and thrift, characteristics associated with self-control.[13] Devotion to commercial moneymaking was often associated with greed, a lack of self-discipline. Favorinus and his circle agree with Sallust (*Cat.* 11.3) that avarice made a man's body and soul effeminate. From the point of view of one of Petronius's freedmen (43.1), it can lead a man to pick up a coin from a manure pile with his teeth. Martial (11.66) dirties the trader (*negotiator*) by associating his moneymaking activities with those of the fellator. Such sentiments rely on a sense of impurity—a collapse of proper distinctions: the male body becomes female; the money-hungry man stains his mouth with excrement; the tradesman is assimilated to one whose mouth is dirtied by genital contact. The dichotomy pure/impure informs the metaphors that speak of the odor of money.[14]

The dirt of commercial moneymaking is connected with the heterogeneity created by merchants and producers. In Martial's Rome (7.61), peddlers, shopkeepers, barbers, innkeepers, cooks, and butchers spilled into the city's streets before Domitian's edict: the city did not exist; it had become one huge undifferentiated shop. Cicero (*Rep.* 2.4.7–10) explains that maritime cities suffer corruption because foreign ways and luxury flow in with trade goods and mix together. From the point of view of Juvenal's narrator (3.62–65), the Syrian river Orontes pours into the Tiber, carrying with it foreign tongues, mores, music, and prostitutes. Horace's (*Odes* 3.6.21–32) adulterous matron answers the call of a salesman or the captain of a Spanish ship.

Although this discourse separates the goodness and purity of Roman practices from foreign ones, the dirt of trade and tradesman expresses facets of Roman imperial society itself.[15] All things flowed to Rome, but not simply because of trade. In a circulation much vaster that that of commerce, imperialism brought goods, money, and foreigners to Rome in the form of booty, taxes, and slaves. As the ruler of vast territories, the city drew in provincials and foreigners on administrative and diplomatic business. Imperial expropriation, large-scale slavery, and the centralization of power in a world-state are displaced symbolically onto the dirty body of the tradesman and the stain of commerce.

OCCUPATIONAL STRUCTURE: THE WORK NAMED IN ROMAN INSCRIPTIONS

Yet men and women in Latin epitaphs profess the same titles that literature denigrates. In fact, a functional categorization of those with occupational title shows a concentration in service work, which would be judged as most servile (see Table 3.1). Before assessing the meanings that these titles may have had for those who used them, I want to look more closely at the kinds of work noted in Roman inscriptions.

Just as the inscriptions do not accurately depict the status structure of the city, neither do they necessarily reflect its actual occupational structure. The 800,000 to 1,000,000 residents of the city had to be fed, housed, clothed, and supplied with articles of daily use, yet 42.6% ($N = 627$) of those who named their work filled none of these needs. Rather,

Table 3.1   Occupational Groups of Men and Women with Job Title

Occupational Group	Men	Women	Total
Building	112 (8.9)	—	112 (7.6)
Manufacture	282 (22.3)	49 (23.6)	331 (22.5)
Sales	99 (7.8)	9 (4.3)	108 (7.3)
Banking	42 (3.3)	—	42 (2.9)
Professional service	101 (8.0)	19 (9.1)	120 (8.2)
Skilled service	40 (3.2)	35 (16.8)	75 (5.1)
Domestic service	235 (18.6)	86 (41.3)	321 (21.8)
Transportation	55 (4.4)	—	55 (3.7)
Administration	296 (23.5)	10 (4.8)	306 (20.8)
Total	1,262 (100)	208 (100)	1,470 (100)

Note: Figures in parentheses are percentages.

they kept house, served as personal attendants, cooked, and served food, or they managed the property and finances of wealthy men and women, kept their records, and wrote their letters.[16] Moreover, while many individuals made or sold products consumed by a wide range of Rome's population, a substantial proportion dealt in expensive goods whose consumers would have been relatively few. In fact, the trade in precious metals, jewelry, fancy furniture, fine clothing, and unguents and perfumes accounts for the work of 31.7% ($N = 139$) of the artisans and distributors. In general, the tradespeople in Rome's epitaphs and dedications tend to be concentrated in a few areas. Distributors were more likely to have sold food products (42.6%, $N = 46$) or unguents and perfumes (32.4%, $N = 35$) than other goods. Artisans most frequently made and sold metalware (26.9%, $N = 89$) and clothing (27.5%, $N = 91$). Those in cloth production and treatment (16.6%, $N = 55$) complement the latter.

Notations of occupational *collegia* indicate that other needs were met and that the actual proportions of builders, artisans, and distributors, especially those outside the trade in luxury goods, were larger than these figures reveal. *Collegia* of carpenters, marble masons, interior workmen, and stonecutters point to the existence of more builders than appear in the city's inscriptions. *Collegia* of metal artisans, lime producers, fullers, ragmen, tailors of cheap clothing, shoemakers, butchers, and bakers reveal larger numbers of artisans producing food, clothing, and articles of daily use as well as luxury goods.[17] *Collegia* of distributors point primarily to a larger number of men and women involved in the sale of foodstuffs: four of the five who belonged to *collegia* dealt in wine, oil, salted provisions, and fish sauce.[18]

Collegia are mentioned more often in production and distribution ($N = 32$) than in the service fields ($N = 12$), and the *collegia* in administration ($N = 10$) were composed of grain measurers, jailers, and those connected with the public or imperial warehouses (*horrea*).[19] The existence of *collegia*, therefore, suggests not only larger numbers of producers and distributors but larger proportions of them relative to domestic servants and administrators, financial agents, and secretaries.

Also, the proportion of distributors would have been even larger than the number recorded, since the socially prominent in large-scale distribution and overseas commerce were not likely to record their activities with an occupational title. Huttunen suggests that this was also the case for men whose success in business gained them a position among the *apparitores* (the assistants to the magistrates), many of them honorary posts requiring little of their holders: "just as the senatorial and equestrian epitaphs almost entirely ignore activity in business life, so the dedications of *apparitor* businessmen usually mentioned only their activities in public service."[20] The number of distributors, too, was supplemented by artisans like L. Helvius L. l. Gratus, a tailor at the Aliarian crossroads (*vestiarius a compito aliario*, 9971), whose indication of a shop address suggests that he sold the clothing he made. Of the artisans, 24.5% ($N = 81$) mentioned a shop address and therefore combined the activities of making and selling. This is especially important because nearly half (42.6%, $N = 46$) of the men and women in distribution dealt exclusively in food products.

In the occupational inscriptions, men and women in the service fields, especially domestic servants and administrators, are considerably better represented than builders, artisans, and distributors. Of the artisans and distributors who appear, many dealt in luxury goods. The accident of epigraphical survival will not account for the social factors that inform the kinds of work named in inscriptions: the needs of the city's residents and how those who met them used occupational title. The existence of certain jobs responds to the demands of society, especially the section of it with money, power, and slaves. Yet job titles, in contrast to jobs, exist because, as we shall see, men and women actually called themselves foot servants, financial agents, silversmiths, and jewelers.

OCCUPATIONAL TITLES AND THE NEEDS OF ROME'S ELITE

Luxury Trades: The Display of What Money Can Buy

The luxury trades obviously depend on a population with money to spend and a desire for fine clothing, fancy furniture, jewelry, and silver or gold vessels. Significant in that population were the empire's social elite. Senators and equestrians made up less than 1% of the empire's population, but in Rome, the political and administrative center of the empire in this period, the proportion of senators in the population will have been larger. In any case, their wealth and the fact that they set the standards for those who wished to appear high-class were more determinative than their number.[21]

Wealth, at least technically, never constituted the primary mark of status: birth, office, and service to the state did. Yet, in the republic, wealth characterized the political elite and was necessary for attaining prominence. Standing was exhibited in generosity to the Roman populace in games, feasts, and buildings, and in the elegance of private houses, gardens, villas, and precious objects.[22] Under the principate, wealth took on increased significance as a distinguishing characteristic of the elite. Office still conveyed rank but no longer led to political ascendancy because the princeps monopolized the resources of power—the army, the provinces, and access to office itself. The ability to display wealth, however, remained, and despite Tacitus's (*Ann.* 3.55) assertion that Vespasian's reign inaugurated greater simplicity, luxury continued to be a favorite target for satirist and moralist.[23] The stereotypical quality of Juvenal's and Martial's complaints and the dual preoccupation with things and status highlight the close connection drawn between social position and possessions: the man of standing or the man who desired to be thought one expressed his prominence through the objects that he owned. This mode of expression became the subject of criticism when practiced by the socially unworthy or abused by patrons who should by definition be generous.

The invitation to an unpretentious dinner, a trope in the literary sources, illustrates the social dynamics of objects or their absence. The invitation emphasizes the simplicity of food, plate, and service.[24] The host self-consciously sets aside his claims to status: the dinner takes place among equals; guest and host can be at ease with one another. Pliny (*Ep.* 1.15) admonishes Septicius Clarus for preferring elaborate dinner parties to a simpler meal at his house: "you can dine more sumptuously at many houses, but nowhere more light-heartedly and in a freer and more unguarded manner" (potes adparatius cenare apud multos, nusquam hilarius simplicius incautius). The lack of elaborate accoutrements levels Pliny and Clarus, making them peers.

A person who aspired to social standing wanted distance between himself and others. In a hierarchical social order, silver and gold plate, jewels, fine clothing, fancy furniture helped to distance the haves from the have-nots. Competition among the haves, like the admiration of the have-nots, served to reinforce a man's sense of prestige.[25]

The elite's demand for luxury goods is reflected in the occupational inscriptions by the relatively large proportion of independent tradesmen and not by artisans working directly for the upper classes. Only a few artisans in the luxury trades belonged to large domestic households: a slave goldsmith of Sergia Paullina (9149: *aurifex*), a slave silversmith of Caecilia Metella (37381: *argentarius*), and a slave mirror maker or glass artisan of Q. Volusius Saturninus (7299: *specular(ius)*).[26] Many luxury items or the raw materials for their production, in fact, were imported. The socially prominent or pretentious evidently purchased these goods in the marketplace from artisans and distributors whose labor they did not directly control.[27]

Services: Living Nobly and the Display of Slaves

The elite's presence in Rome also informs the large proportion of individuals in the service fields. Since 21.4% (N = 255) of all the epitaphs come from *columbaria* set aside for the domestic staffs of prominent members of Roman society and since Rome was the primary residence of many others whose household tombs are now missing, it is not surprising to find their servants in the occupational inscriptions. However, their particular activities and numbers require comment.

Service workers enabled a wealthy man or woman to live nobly. A person of substance did not keep accounts, handle disbursements, or deal with the day-to-day management of property: accountants, secretaries, or agents took care of these matters. Waiters, wine pourers, cooks, provisioners, attendants, bedchamber servants, hairdressers, and masseurs saw to personal needs. When an important man went out in the city, servants as well as clients accompanied him. When he traveled, an entourage of attendants traveled with him. Whether it is the man of standing who is embarrassed by a lack of appropriate service or the parvenu who is ridiculed for deriving his sense of self-importance from a horde of waiters and maids, the assumption is the same: the person of substance requires servants.[28]

The wealthy could meet the social necessity of living nobly by the direct control of the labor of their slaves and ex-slaves. Indeed, 73.8% (N = 346) of the slaves with occupational title can be associated with wealthy households, and nearly a third of all individuals with title (31.6%, N = 465) worked for the upper classes. These men and women were involved primarily in service activities.[29] They carried litters, did hair, kept records, administered property and monies, provisioned the household, cooked, took care of children, attended in the bedroom, poured wine, waited tables, or simply waited (see Table 3.2).

The occupational inscriptions confirm the literary picture of noble living and suggest that the canons of standing described or implied by Roman authors were indeed meaningful. Only the *columbarium* for the household staff of the Statilii offers a fairly detailed picture of a single private household (see Table 3.2). Because the tomb was in use from Augustus to Nero, and few of the epitaphs are datable, we cannot know how many bedchamber servants, attendants, cooks, or porters served the family at any one moment. However, as Treggiari has observed in her study of Livia's household, the job titles themselves, apart from their bearers, give us an idea of the number and types of "distinguishable functions."[30] Men and women in the noncommercial service fields (professionals, hairdressers and entertainers, domestics, transport workers, and administrators) name forty-seven discrete employments, and their titles register extensive personal, child care, housekeeping, administrative, and secretarial services. Admittedly, the Statilii were special—powerful and enormously wealthy,[31] yet the individuals in the noncommercial fields who can be assigned to a particular household name ninety-eight employments and reveal the same range of services. The activities denoted in job titles suggest that those who could afford it and who had considerable control of slave labor had nearly all the needs of personal and domestic maintenance met.

Yet something more than living nobly is involved; the sheer numbers of servants must be connected with the significance of slaves as a constituent of wealth.[32] Trimalchio's army of waiters, decuries of cooks, crowd of bath attendants,

Table 3.2   Service Occupations in the Large
Domestic Household

Occupation	Household of the Statilii		All Households in Occupational Inscriptions	
	Individuals	Distinct Job Titles	Individuals	Distinct Job Titles
Teachers	—	—	2	2
Architects and surveyors	1	1	4	3
Doctors and midwives	3	2	22	2
Barbers and hairdressers	3	1	11	2
Masseurs and oilers	7	1	8	1
Readers and entertainers	3	2	10	7
Bath attendants	1	1	4	2
Child nurses and attendants	5	3	34	5
Bodyguards	10	2	10	2
Room servants	19	4	57	11
Table servants	1	1	2	1
Cooks	3	1	9	1
Provisioners	2	2	11	4
Caretakers	10	4	22	10
Gardeners	4	3	5	3
Social organizers	1	1	9	4
Animal tenders	2	2	7	6
Runners and bearers	16	2	26	3
Financial agents	7	3	54	8
Administrators	11	6	50	15
Secretaries and copyists	7	5	28	6
Total	116	47	385	98

band of runners, and litter bearers had a function beyond attending to his physical existence. They demonstrated that he was wealthy. Servants alone did not mark the man of standing: his importance was measured by the number of his attendants or litter bearers.[33] Unlike the artisans and distributors discussed above, some of these servants did not simply deal with objects; as slaves, they were in a real sense "things." Further, the performance of their assigned tasks made them *visible* as wealth to guest, onlooker, and master. Like precious inanimate objects, they distinguished the haves from the have-nots and evoked the latter's deference, real or feigned. Without being directly exploited, poorer citizens behaved in a way that acknowledged the rank of the wealthy and socially prominent.[34] Human property helped to secure this acknowledgment.

In Juvenal (esp. 5.24ff.), human "things," like inanimate objects, not only create distance between a wealthy man and others but also function as "middlemen" in the relations of patron and client. The least attractive and most inappropriate slaves are assigned to poor clients; the patron's special attendants disdain to serve such guests. This use of servants puts the client in his place and allows the patron to express his standing without direct involvement in the client's humiliation. Equally, the slave allows the client to express his frustration without a direct confrontation with a patron he cannot afford to alienate. The tensions in the relationship are vested in the servant.

The material and social needs of the upper classes are better represented in the occupational inscriptions than those of any other group: presumably their purchasing power and direct control of labor provided livelihoods for those in the luxury trades and determined the jobs of their slaves and freedmen. The importance of certain goods enriched tradesmen and artisans, providing them with the resources for named burial. The social necessity of the elite to live nobly and to make an impressive display of their wealth and position informs the concentration of men and women in service work.

NAMING AND CLAIMING: COMMERCIAL SUCCESS AND PROFESSIONAL PRESTIGE

While the wealthy may have had a large role in determining the kinds of occupations that appear in inscriptions, they did not entirely control the use of occupational title. For 43.2% of the deceased ($N = 503$; 58.6%, $N = 682$, if the epitaphs from single-family *columbaria* with named dedicators are included), we know or can infer the commemorator—that is, the person who recorded an individual's livelihood (see Table 3.3). In only twenty-seven cases (2.3% of all the deceased) was that person a master or patron who had a direct claim to the individual's labor.[35] As pointed out in chapter 2 and evident from Table 3.3, title primarily depends

Table 3.3   Titling of Deceased and Self-Commemorators in Different Occupational Groups

Title Given by	Occupational Group									Total
	Building	Manufacture	Sales	Banking	Professional	Skilled Service	Domestic Service	Transportation	Administration	
Family member	6 (6.9)	32 (11.5)	15 (16.1)	7 (18.4)	33 (31.7)	15 (22.4)	41 (15.2)	3 (6.5)	43 (23.6)	195 (16.8)
Peer—friend or colleague	24 (27.6)	5 (1.8)	1 (1.1)	—	3 (2.9)	1 (1.5)	5 (1.9)	1 (2.2)	1 (.5)	41 (3.5)
Peer—member of *familia*	—	5 (1.8)	—	—	1 (1.0)	2 (3.0)	14 (5.2)	2 (4.3)	9 (4.9)	33 (2.8)
Self	7 (8.0)	39 (14.0)	22 (23.7)	6 (15.8)	9 (8.7)	2 (3.0)	11 (4.1)	3 (6.5)	16 (8.8)	115 (9.9)
No commemorator, single-family columbarium	17 (19.5)	27 (9.7)	—	—	10 (9.6)	8 (11.9)	61 (22.7)	20 (43.5)	36 (19.8)	179 (15.4)
No commentator	30 (34.5)	146 (52.5)	43 (46.2)	19 (50.0)	35 (33.7)	32 (47.8)	106 (39.4)	13 (28.3)	58 (31.9)	482 (41.4)
Master, patron etc.[1]	—	3 (1.1)	—	—	1 (1.0)	1 (1.5)	15 (5.6)	—	7 (3.8)	27 (2.3)
Other or unclear	3 (3.4)	21 (7.6)	12 (12.9)	6 (15.8)	12 (11.5)	6 (9.)	16 (5.9)	4 (8.7)	12 (6.6)	92 (7.9)
Total	87 (100)	278 (100)	93 (100)	38 (100)	104 (100)	67 (100)	269 (100)	46 (100)	182 (100)	1,164 (100)

Note: Figures in parentheses are percentages.
[1] Includes nurses' charges and "employers."

on commemoration by self, family, or peers. Ultimately, the proportion of individuals in each occupational group is a product of how they, their peers, and their families constructed their identities at death.

Consideration of who used occupational title shifts attention from the requirements of consumers, especially those with money, power, and direct control over the labor of others, to the perceptions of the producers of goods and services. From this point of view, the relative size of the occupational groups in Roman inscriptions indicates the kinds of labor claimed by the men and women for whom work was most significant.

I examine two kinds of claims, each suggested by the literary sources: the tradesman's commercial success and the prestige value attributed to professional service and administration. Roman authors give us the crass, materialistic tradesman, and their texts establish criteria for the professional's and administrator's sense of self-importance. In each case, however, the inscriptions suggest other frames of reference. The discussion focuses on the deceased with occupational title (and living commemorators who included themselves in a tomb) in order to compare individuals in the same position.

The Demonstration of Commercial Success: The Problem of the Rich Freed Tradesman

In literature, wealthy tradesmen use their money to purchase the external badges of prestige. Clothes, accoutrements, and servants cover some flaw, social or personal. Freed tradesmen, especially, rely on their success. Like Juvenal's wealthy freedman with five shops, they make claims to standing based on what they have.[36] Or, like Petronius's Trimalchio (77.6), they believed that "you have a penny, you're worth a penny; you have something, you'll be considered something" (assem habeas, assem valeas; habes, habeberis). Trimalchio's more modest guest Hermeros best articulates the satirist's vision of the successful freedman's claims of self-worth.

> I am a man among men. I walk with my head uncovered. I owe no man money. I never had a court summons. No one has said to me in the forum, "Pay what you owe." I have bought small pieces of land and acquired little plates of metal. I feed twenty

bellies and a dog. I bought the freedom of my *contubernalis*, so no one could wipe his hands on her front. One thousand denarii I paid for my own freedom. I was made a *sevir* without charge.

Homo inter homines sum, capite aperto ambulo, assem aerarium nemini debeo, constitutum habui numquam, nemo mihi in foro dixit, "redde quod debes." Glebulas emi, lamellulas paravi, viginti ventres pasco et canem. Contubernalem meam redemi, ne quis in sinu illius manus tergeret. Mille denarios pro capite solvi. Sevir gratis factus sum.

(Pet. 57.5–6)

In the epitaphs, we can read tradesmen's relation to money only through their burial arrangements and presentations at death. For some, the use of occupational title appears to be connected to the control of material resources, some of which were spent on tombs dedicated before their own deaths. I take as an example the distributors (23.7%, $N = 22$), artisans (14%, $N = 39$), and bankers (15.8%, $N = 6$) who commemorated themselves, for this pattern of commemoration recurs considerably more often for them than for the men and women in the service fields and construction. Generally, they had family tombs that included themselves, family members, and often freedmen. Q. Caecilius Spendo, for example, a producer of inexpensive clothing (*sagarius*, 9865: uncertain freeborn; cf. 13780) dedicated a tomb to his wife, himself, and eighteen of his ex-slaves. Spendo had evidently done quite well: the freedmen and women reflect property once held in slaves as well as his continued claim on their labor. Including those implied in the epitaph's formulas, the tomb probably was intended for twenty-three people. The precise cost of Spendo's tomb is not indicated, but presumably the more numerous the individuals included in a tomb the larger the tomb and the higher its cost.[37]

In comparison with other occupational epitaphs, Spendo's names an unusually large number of freedmen, yet artisans, distributors, and bankers tend to claim freedmen more frequently in their epitaphs than do other commemorators in these inscriptions. The epitaphs of only 11.4% ($N = 133$) of the deceased and self-commemorators mention their former slaves by name or include them in the tomb with the formula *libertis libertabusque posterisque eorum* (for their freedmen and freedwomen and their descendants). Few ($N = 19$) had more than three freedmen. By contrast, 55.2% of the artisans, distributors, and bankers who commemorated themselves used the formula *libertis libertabusque* alone ($N = 27$) or named freedmen individually ($N = 10$).

These tradesmen also had larger tombs than individuals in other occupational groups. Outside the *columbaria* (where epitaphs usually name only one person), epitaphs in which the bearer of a job title is among the deceased regularly record no more than two individuals (79.1%, $N = 623$; 64.9% have only one deceased), and the median tomb size is 1.3. By contrast, of the tombs of the artisans, distributors, and bankers considered here, 44.6% ($N = 25$) include four to six people, and 28.6% ($N = 16$) between seven and ten people (median tomb size is 5.3). It is interesting that, although the luxury trades were among the more lucrative, the epitaphs of such tradesmen do not include appreciably more individuals than those of other tradesmen; however, they did claim their freedmen more frequently.[38]

Many of those who commemorated themselves, then, were propertied. Others should be included in this group: (1) those whose spouses or children dedicated the tomb and mentioned freedmen, for these reflect family resources, and (2) men whose offices in *collegia* required expenditures (see chap. 4). Although material prosperity will account for their tombs, something more than named burial is at issue here, because these men chose to identify themselves by their occupation. To our eyes, epitaph and tomb enshrine a financial success that is associated with its source—trade. Although occupational title in these circumstances apparently involved a level of self-consciousness, I am wary of readings that make these individuals into some version of satire's materialistic tradesmen. Such readings omit other perspectives on materiality.

Take the exaggerated case of the baker Marceius Vergilius Eurysaces (1958: uncertain freeborn), much wealthier than the individuals considered here. His large elaborate tomb is a monument to his trade: its friezes depict the activities of baking, and its vertical and horizontal columns may represent grain measures. The epitaph of Eurysaces's wife, Atistia, calls the tomb (or perhaps her ash urn) a breadbasket (*panarium*).[39] Where political invective lumps baking with perfuming and money changing as sources of stigma, erasing work as an active interaction with the world, Eurysaces distinguishes his particular trade, emphasizing its skills, processes, and equipment. If the baker intended to exhibit his wealth, he might be seen only to acknowledge its fundamental importance in Roman society. Yet Eurysaces's practice differs from the elite's display of accoutrements and servants. Wealth drawn from land tilled by slaves and tenants was made visible indirectly in what money could buy and in human beings focused on a master's needs; the practice flaunts the owner's leisure and makes invisible the labor that permits it. Eurysaces effected no displacement: his tomb features a direct connection to labor. By calling her resting place a breadbasket, his wife identifies herself with her husband's (and perhaps her own) product.

Freedmen show no greater tendency than the freeborn or uncertain freeborn toward propertied status, but they figure significantly among the self-commemorators with larger tombs and claims on ex-slaves. Freedmen dedicated seventeen of the twenty-five (68%) artisans' and distributors' tombs that include four to six people (53.7%, 44/82, of the tombs of all deceased and self-commemorators outside *columbaria*) and eight of the twenty (40%) tombs that include over seven people. Half of the artisans and tradesmen who indicated claims on their freedmen by formula alone (51.9%, 14/27) were themselves freedmen, as were seven of the ten who named their freedmen individually. The tendency is similar where a family member dedicated the tomb.

The pattern evokes the stereotypical freedman of Roman satire who thinks that one is what one owns. The epitaph of a freed clinical doctor, surgeon, and oculist from Assisi would seem to confirm the stereotype more articulately than the epitaphs under consideration here.

> Publius Decimius Eros Merula, freedman of Publius, clinical doctor, surgeon, oculist, *sevir*. In return for his freedom, he gave 50,000 sesterces. In payment for his sevirate, he gave 2,000 sesterces to the community. For the purpose of putting up statues in the temple of Hercules, he gave 30,000 sesterces. For the purpose of paving streets, he gave 37,000 sesterces to the municipal treasury. On the day before he died he left an estate of . . . sesterces.

P·DECIMIUS·P·L·EROS
MERULA · MEDICUS
CLINICUS·CHIRURGUS
OCULARIUS · VI · VIR
HIC · PRO · LIBERTATE · DEDIT · HS · I˞˞
HIC · PRO · SEVIRATU · IN · REM · P
DEDIT · HS · ↀↀ
HIC · IN · STATUAS · PONENDAS · IN
AEDEM · HERCULIS · DEDIT · HS IIIII IIIII IIIII
HIC · IN · VIAS · STERNENDAS · IN
PUBLICUM · DEDIT · HS IIIII IIIII IIIII I˞˞ ↀↀ
HIC · PRIDIE · QUAM · MORTUUS · EST
RELIQUIT · PATRIMONI
HS . . .

(*CIL* 11.5400)

All of these expenditures indicate a man of considerable means. If his estate can be restored as 800,000 sesterces, he had twice the fortune required for an equestrian and nearly that required for a senator.[40]

The contrast of wealth and low birth made the situation of the wealthy ex-slave ambivalent; he mixed social categories. In him, according to Finley, "criss-crossing categories . . . generated tensions and conflicts in the value system and the behavior pattern."[41] Implicitly, work was the means of this heterogeneous collapse of categories. The stereotype of the wealthy freedman cannot function without lucrative livelihoods as avenues to success. Perhaps at the heart of the denigration of artisanry and trade lies an apprehension of the potential of work to produce wealth—the source of standing.[42] Ironically, work, so fundamental to the existence of the natally alienated slave, becomes the means to achieve the necessary resources of a high-ranking insider.

Money enabled the wealthiest freedmen to live like those in the higher ranks of a social order in which the ex-slave had only second-class membership. Living on incomes converted into loans and estates, they could be served by elaborate household staffs and surrounded by the accoutrements that signaled the wealth and cultivation appropriate to a man of class. Petronius's Trimalchio may lack good taste as well as honorable birth, but he differs not at all from his consular creator in the sources of his income and his luxurious life-style.[43] Wealthy freedmen, too, could spend money to improve their communities. Eros Merula's expenditures at Assisi compare with Pliny the Younger's bequests to his native Comum (*ILS* 2927). The difference in their gifts was one of scale and, of course, the social standing of the giver. Yet presumably the rewards of giving for consul and freedman were the same—prestige and the approbation of their respective communities.[44] In his life-style and benefactions, the wealthy freedman could adopt the code of the society into which he had been "reborn." Yet, from the perspective of the freeborn, the attempt appears a misguided imitation of patron and social betters; the behavior of the ex-slave is never genuine.[45] In Eros Merula, the satirist could see only a Trimalchio.

The impression given by Juvenal, Martial, and Petronius of the ubiquitous rich ex-slave should be distrusted, and the wealth of freedmen should not be exaggerated. As a stereotype of satire, the rich freedman, like decadent noble, heartless patron, or poor freeborn client, speaks of his creator's perceptions and fears. Moreover, the context in which the fiction appears is revealing. Rarely simply descriptive, it often functions to make some moral point on the pretensions associated with wealth or the perversion of the social order that wealth has created. What is documented about Roman incomes suggests that rich ex-slaves were neither ubiquitous nor among the top ranks of the wealthy. Duncan-Jones's list of the fortunes noted in literature shows few fabulously wealthy freedmen compared with members of the elite, and of the few on the list, four were imperial freedmen. Even the wealthiest freedmen about whom we have information, the Augustales from outside the city, do not have wealth that compares with the fortunes of senators like Cn. Cornelius Lentulus (HS 400 million), Seneca (HS 300 million), Eprius Marcellus (HS 200 million), or even Pliny (c. HS 20 million).[46] Yet, a few freedmen like Eros Merula may have been enough to attract the freeborn author's attack, for they embodied the contradictions of the society. Or, perhaps, poet and satirist simply needed Eros Merula's stereotypical, fictional counterpart. They could vest in this figure the ambiguities of the social order and affirm their own and their audience's experience as insiders.

The freedmen under consideration here were not as wealthy as Eros Merula, or at least their epitaphs do not reflect similar incomes and expenditures. They were propertied but not rich. Only a few of those who are clearly iden-

tified as freedmen spent their money on their communities
or *collegia.* Perhaps the rest did not have the means to do
so. More important, as we shall see, there is a tendency
for those who did to omit status indication altogether (see
chap. 4).

The freedmen in these epitaphs find a comparable fictional counterpart in Petronius's Hermeros, not his fabulously wealthy Trimalchio. Yet I hesitate to turn the ex-slaves
in Roman epitaphs into any of satire's freed characters. That
their epitaphs record some modest financial success can be
read as something other than the conviction that a man
was what he owned. The family tomb, often including freed
slaves, does reflect the significance of the prosperity that
lay behind it in a particularly appropriate way: it is a concrete record of the freedman's establishment of a socially acknowledged family whose descendants, unlike the freedman
himself, belonged to the legitimate social order by birth. The
inclusion of freedmen signals the establishment of his own
household, an image of independence. For those manumitted after the peak childbearing years (likely if the couple
had been *conservi* and the husband was not freed until age
thirty) or those who had lost children, ex-slaves may have
been included in a familial way; at times they became the
future occupants of the tomb, as in the case of the freedmen
and women of L. Lepidius L. lib. Hermes, the freed dealer in
copper ware and ironware (*negotiator aerarius et ferrarius*),
and his wife Obellia Threpte (9664), whose son and daughter
died at age eight and five, respectively.[47] Perhaps occupational title was Hermes's way of claiming a position as the
head of a household; it may emphasize that the resources
that permitted this achievement were earned in the trade
noted by his title.

Occupation, then, was not only the source of some prosperity but also the means by which the male ex-slave could
create a normal order in his social life. The use of conventional language in the epitaphs often conveys this normality.
The freed pearl setter C. Ateilius Serrani l. Euhodus (9545:
margaritarius) says that he was good, compassionate, lov-
ing, and poor.[48] Since his tomb, his freedmen, and his ability
to include some of them in the tomb indicate money and
property, we could too easily assume that his words are
empty formulas. From the point of view of the satirist, Eu-

hodus made a vain show of adopting an upper-class diffi-
dence toward wealth and the Roman tradition that associated poverty with the virtues of simplicity and self-control.[49]
The pearl setter was simply being disingenuous—claiming
poverty while displaying material success. Yet we might
take the intent of his words quite literally and read in their
conventionality his desire to construct a normal household.
He did not claim material success. The tomb and freedmen
do not so much belie a pretense of poverty as portray him as
a modest head of household, certainly not a grubbing, duplicitous foreigner.

Prestige, Status, and the Sense
of Self-Importance

Among professionals as well as administrators, financial
agents, and secretaries, different patterns of commemoration and less evidence of an association of work and material
success raise questions about the use of occupational title
as a response to the attitudes voiced in literature and to the
positions, real and imagined, offered by these occupations.
In these fields, where family members had a larger role in
naming the deceased's occupation, we do not find quite the
same tendency to indicate propertied circumstances. Those
who commemorated themselves had tombs (median tomb
size for professionals is 4.5; for administrators, financial
agents, and secretaries, 3.3) comparable with those of the
artisans and tradesmen discussed above, and individuals in
professional service had comparable claims to freedmen
(55.6%, $N = 5$). However, where a family member gave the
individual an occupational title, there is little indication of
property in the epitaph. Most of the professionals (75%,
$N = 24$) and those in administration, finance, and secretarial service (85.7%, $N = 30$) were buried in tombs intended for no more than three people. For both groups, the
median tomb size was 1.2.

The comments of various authors about these occupations would seem to provide the grounds for a sense of self-
importance. Cicero (*Off.* 1.151) praises the activities of
teaching, architecture, and medicine; ideally, their practitioners were well educated. Secretaries, often highly trained,
were valued by those they served.[50] The steward (*dispensator*) and manager (*procurator*) had to be literate and in

wealthy households needed the acumen to handle considerable property and funds. All are depicted in literature with certain capacities. The complaints about doctors killing their patients and teachers corrupting their students do not belittle these professionals; quite the reverse, they indicate some fear about what the doctor or teacher could do. The figure of the pompous steward (*dispensator*) who controls his master's purse reflects an apprehension about the position in which a job placed its practitioner.[51] The stereotypicality of these complaints points to a degree of control that these individuals had or were imagined to have had in the practice of their occupations.

A few epitaphs express pride in skills, ability, or excellent performance. The epitaph of a *grammaticus* (teacher of literature and grammar, here probably at an elementary level) and *procurator* (manager) stresses his moral responsibilities and implies his power to prevent the moral corruption of his student and charge. Pudens, the freedman of M. Aemilius Lepidus, consul A.D. 6 (9449), took care of his patron's daughter, Aemilia Lepida, the wife of Germanicus's son Drusus. According to Tacitus (*Ann.* 6.40), Lepida was accused of adultery with a slave after her father's death; without making a defense, she killed herself. In light of Lepida's disgraceful end, Pudens defends himself and disavows any negative influence on his part: "I guided her morals [character]. While I lived, she remained the daughter-in-law of Caesar."[52] Implicit in his defense is a claim to control, the fear of which is so central to the stereotype.

For the most part, of course, the motives of the families who dedicated the epitaphs of professional people are not articulated, but literature's evaluation of their work fills the silence, leading historians to consider status consciousness. Susan Treggiari and Marleen Boudreau Flory have observed that slaves and freedmen used job titles for their prestige value. In her study of Livia's domestic staff, Treggiari argues that the slaves and freed slaves with job title represent a "cross-section of the upper and middle grades of domestics": "scrubbers and scullions" are rare. In Treggiari's view, the many slaves and freedmen without title "had no particular reason to be proud of their jobs, or . . . could not afford a grander inscription."[53] Stressing the absence of titles naming menial work and the records of job title for only about half of Livia's slaves and freedmen, Flory suggests that "the slaves and freedmen without titles had no clearly defined work or their job designations did not qualify as status symbols worthy of commemoration on a tombstone."[54]

Some of these assumptions merit reevaluation. Flory's contention that those without job title lacked defined work or had several tasks instead of a single job is undermined by an observation made by Treggiari and confirmed by literary texts: the standards of organization made specialization and clearly defined duties normal in wealthy households. For instance, the lack of proper order informs one of Petronius's jokes about Trimalchio's domestic staff. His servants perform tasks inappropriate to their assigned duties: a porter (ostiarius) shells peas (28.8), and a litter bearer (lecticarius) sweeps up the trash (34.3).[55] Contrary to Treggiari's suggestion about job title and prestige, the jobs named by slaves include employments like attendant (pedisequus) and litter bearer (lecticarius) that were not prestigious, although it is, of course, possible that they were ranked in some hierarchy from which "scrubbers and scullions" were excluded.

The concept of prestige itself is not neutral and requires a consideration of perspective. What sort of ranking system, if any, did the slaves who used occupational title have? Did the secretary's literacy, the cook's skills, or the steward's peculium determine "place"? To the outsider, the steward appears more important, even more powerful, yet the spinner (quasillaria), whom Petronius (132.3) ranks among the lowest in the familia, also noted her occupational title. Because the literature so powerfully identifies different types of work as either honorable or dishonorable, reliance on its canons invariably makes the use of occupational title a function of pride or shame, measured on a scale established by those who did not work. And its standards assimilate the imagined aspects of work to servile behavior or condition.

Even if the literary sources are dismissed as prejudiced, the very terms of their discourse enter interpretation. If women or men called themselves hairdressers or cooks, trades that are denigrated in literature, we might assume that, contrary to the standards established by others, hairdressers or cooks felt proud. But this interpretation bears an uncomfortable similarity to the satirist's depiction of the haughty servant whose self-importance is part of his vulgarity. Although the names of occupations may figure in both literature and epitaphs, we need to entertain the possibility that the claims associated with them differed in each context.

A comparison of those in administration, finance, and secretarial service, on the one hand, and domestic servants and transport workers, on the other, is instructive. In literature where administrative, financial, and secretarial work is specially regarded, domestic service is stigmatized because the domestic servant catered to the material needs of others. Moreover, domestic servants often simply form part of the scenery; litter bearers (*lecticarii*) usually exist only as numbers. Even where the waiter has a role, he only offends his master's poorer guests. Unlike the negative characterization of the domestic servant, that of the steward (*dispensator*) assumes his importance: the haughty man withholds wages or the patron's handouts.

In Roman epitaphs, the individuals in all these fields share status and work setting: slaves and uncertain slaves predominate in each field, and many can be associated with specific elite households.[56] At first glance, the epitaphs seem to reflect the values expressed in literature. They suggest a more advantageous position for administrators, financial agents, and secretaries than for domestic servants and transport workers. The dedications of *dispensatores* (9320–22) indicate that they had certain material resources at their disposal that domestic servants and transport workers lacked. In part, this will account for the latter's simpler epitaphs: more often than slaves in administration, finance, and secretarial service (32.2%, $N = 50$), slave domestic servants (47.2%, $N = 60$) and transport workers (65.6%, $N = 21$) appear alone. For all slaves, family relations existed as a privilege granted by the master, but slaves in domestic service and transportation show less evidence of this privilege than slaves in administration. The slaves in domestic service (69.3%, $N = 88$) and transportation (84.4%, $N = 27$) appear without family members more often than those in administration (59.2%, $N = 90$).

Yet work defines *dispensator*, no less than *pedisequus* and his labor was no more his own than that of the *pedisequus*, however much better the material conditions of his life. Indeed, the pattern of who named whose job raises suspicions that neither pride nor shame provides an adequate explanation for the use of job title. If the epitaphs from household *columbaria* without named commemorators are omitted, administrators, financial agents, and secretaries would receive their titles from family, peers, and themselves considerably more often than transport workers or domestic servants. Yet exclusion of these plaques omits aspects of commemoration that are not evident in the text of an epitaph—aspects that affect the pattern of naming jobs and hence our conclusions about prestige. As noted earlier, space in these tombs often prohibited specification of the commemorator; other epitaphs from these tombs suggest that, if the workers did not in fact write their own epitaphs, a fellow member of the *familia* did. Men and women whose simple plaques include only a name and job should be associated with those whose epitaphs were composed by clearly identified peers, for the latter group often included fellow freedmen (*colliberti*) and fellow slaves (*conservi*). Commemoration of this type, common for domestic and transport workers, explains the absence of family and peers as those who named their work.

If the epitaphs without named commemorators in household *columbaria* are taken into consideration, the proportion of domestic servants and transport workers who received their titles from themselves, their families, and their peers is less out of line with those in other occupational groups. The proportion of domestic workers so titled is still smaller than those in professional service and administration. But since the proportion of transport workers, primarily litter bearers and grooms, is at least slightly larger than the more educated and privileged architects, doctors, teachers, accountants, administrators, and secretaries, it is difficult to see stigma as an explanation for a smaller proportion of domestic servants. Litter bearers and grooms did not have any more worthy employments than domestic servants, and, no less than domestic servants, they reflected the substance of those they served.

The epitaphs of the litter bearers in the tomb set aside for the *familia* of the Statilii tell a relevant story. The lives of Aba, Laetus, Medus, and Trucunda (6302, 6309–10, 6313: slaves) are condensed into a single name and a job; Philiros (*sic*, 6311: slave) may have added his place of birth. The epitaphs of Bithus and Potamo (6307, 6312: slaves) note a master's name, and the former, like Alcimus and Ascla (6304–5: slaves), has an age at death of forty. Even if the repetition of forty signals a formulaic approximation, we can still observe the records of a relatively long period of carrying, assuming the work of a *lecticarius* began as a young adult. Named commemorators make T. Statilius Tauri l. Spinther, a supervisor (*supra lec(ticarios)*: freedman, 6301), Agatho, Astragalus, and Iucundus (6303, 6306, 6308: slaves) appear in terms of their relations to family and *familia* and provide the context for the other litter bearers.[57] Two of Agatho's (6303) commemorators, Callista, his *vicaria* (slave of a slave), and Philologus, also composed the epitaph of Iucundus (6308). The situation suggests a subgroup within the *familia* that revolved around the litter bearers. If so, job title functioned like agnomen to delineate relations.

Callista and Philologus had special reasons to remember "Iucundus, slave of Taurus, litter bearer" (Iucundus Tauri *lecticarius*): "As long as he lived, he was a man and acted on behalf of himself and others. As long as he lived, he lived honorably."[58] His name, Iucundus (agreeable, pleasant), common among slaves, seems to mark a master's expectation: could the noble Taurus read his bearer's epitaph literally— "he was the agreeable slave of Taurus, a litter bearer"? Assuming job title signals a servile assessment of prestige, we can say only that despite, or even in the face of, the upper-class denigration of his work and his master's point of view, Iucundus was proud to have been a litter bearer. It seems to me that prestige value and pride do not adequately account for what is inscribed here and what may be suggested for the other men who performed the same labor. We can set out other meanings by reading the description of the man in terms of his work. He may have been the slave who lugged around the master, but that did not make him a pack animal subject to a driver's whip. "He was a man," able to defend himself and others. His name labels him as agreeable; his slave commemorators' description marks a limit to subjection. Was the strength of the litter bearer applied to other purposes? Could we read "because of his job, he was strong"? Callista and Philologus shift the claim of an integrity associated with citizenship to a claim of manhood associated with the defense of self and others. Whatever he did for work, or even because of it, "he lived honorably"—an impossible assertion in terms of Cicero's catalog.

Despite the disadvantages of domestic servants and transport workers, their occupations do not appear to have been a source of stigma, at least as far as they and their peers in the *familia*, who had so significant a role in writing their epitaphs, are concerned. The dishonor implicit in roles that made them an expression of another's standing did not inhibit them from naming their jobs. In a complex way, servants' job titles asserted their importance to the master who, in a way, required their dishonor. Without domestic servants and litter bearers, the man of standing could not appear as a person of rank: without them, he could not live nobly and had no living demonstration of his wealth. What the servant claims with occupational title must account for its use within the *familia*. The importance of the household as the context in which domestic servant or transport worker is identified suggests a reference point other than prestige, pride, or honor—the community in which an individual has an identity as the practitioner of a particular occupation.

· IV ·

WORK IN ITS
SOCIAL CONTEXT
The Question of Community

*Thus, after three years spent in the country, roughing it in the
field, and experiencing all sorts of hardships, I was again permitted to return to Baltimore, the very place of all others, short
of a free state, where I most desired to live. . . . I rapidly became an expert in the use of calkers' tools, and in the course
of a single year, I was able to command the highest wages paid
to journeymen calkers in Baltimore. . . . I sought my own employment, made my own contracts, and collected my own
earnings. . . . Here, then were better days for the Eastern shore
slave. I was free from the vexatious assaults of the apprentices
at Gardiner's, free from the perils of plantation life.*
(Frederick Douglass, Life and Times of Frederick Douglass)

IN THE STORY of his life as a slave, Frederick Douglass
recounts changes in his occupation and in his workplace.
The move from country to city meant something more than
a shift from field to shipyard. Different workplaces involved
different social contexts. In the city Douglass worked independent of master and fellow slaves, participating in the
practices that organized nineteenth-century wage labor. On
Freeland's farm, he and his "brother slaves . . . never under-
took anything of any importance which was likely to affect
each other, without mutual consultation. We were generally
a unit, and moved together." Earlier, on the Lloyd planta-

92

tion, Douglass had inhabited "a little nation by itself, having its own language, its own rules, regulations, and customs."[1]

Especially for modern readers, Roman occupational inscriptions lack the fullness of Douglass's narrative. The social contexts of the men and women in them are generally far less accessible to us because, aside from having a different perspective, we usually cannot see an epitaph in its setting. We might have a different appreciation of a job title if we were to see it in a *columbarium* that was festooned with wreaths and littered with the remains of a banquet. If we participated in the ceremonies that regularly occurred in the tomb, we might gain an altered sense of a plaque that reads "Plecte, spinner" (Plecte *quasillaria*, 6344). Then, perhaps, we would glimpse from the slave's point of view Plecte's place in what Douglass calls "a little nation by itself" or understand the force of the identity "spinner" for a "unit" that "moved together."

Yet the location of epitaphs and the text of inscriptions themselves suggest the social contexts that we can no longer experience in settings and rituals. In the place of Douglass's articulate accounts of different worlds of work are fragmented signs, almost gestures, of lived social realities in which the trades named in inscriptions were carried on. I divide the diverse epigraphical information into two categories that broadly defined social worlds: the private environment of the large domestic household headed by an upper-class master and the public world outside it. The evidence of a private world reflects personal bonds or the household unit: burial in a single-family *columbarium*, participation in a domestic *collegium*, notation of occupational rank, reference to an upper-class master, patron, or employer.[2] Burial in a single-family *columbarium* ($N = 278$) points only to the deceased's membership in a *familia*. Participation in a domestic *collegium* ($N = 26$) denotes a role or even a position of leadership in a formal organization.[3] Occupational ranks like *supra lecticarios* or *supra cubicularios* ($N = 4$) usually describe the supervision of a group of servants (here, of litter bearers and bedchamber servants).[4] The notation of an upper-class master or patron ($N = 143$) names relations with a slaveholder whose social standing would require servants of a particular kind and number.[5]

The assessment of public contexts relies on the forms of

occupational title or on the information accompanying it: notation of a business address ($N = 146$), association with an occupational *collegium* ($N = 91$), participation on a public staff ($N = 13$),[6] and indications of public posts ($N = 12$).[7] Each of these elements delineates relations or rank in public organizations and the legitimate social order. Even if an individual belonged to a large *familia* or maintained close ties with master, patron, *conservi*, or *colliberti*, the context of occupational title or the title itself displays engagement in the society at large, either as a member of a public institution or as a producer in the marketplace.

While these signs do not eliminate the possibility that an artisan who was buried in a single-family *columbarium* may have worked outside the household in the marketplace,[8] most often they define either the physical location of work or conditions that cannot be divorced from it. For example, the job of Menander, a freed porter in the Statilian amphitheater (6227: *ostiarius ab amphitheatro*), took him outside the confines of the domestic space, but his burial in the tomb reserved for the slaves and freedmen of the Statilii indicates his ties with that aristocratic family and its staff. His job depended on those ties, and his fellow custodians (6226, 6228), slaves in the same *familia*, had different but parallel attachments to the same masters.

TWO OCCUPATIONAL STRUCTURES AND THE MOVEMENT BETWEEN TWO WORLDS

When occupational titles are considered in light of social contexts (see Table 4.1), it is clear that we have two occupational structures. In the private sphere, the size of the service groups increases because of the large number of workers needed to meet the requirements of their upper-class owners. The proportion of builders, artisans, salesmen, and bankers decreases. Conversely, in the public sphere, the overrepresentation in domestic service and administration disappears. In transportation and administration, finance, and secretarial service, individuals who located themselves in public contexts named different employments from those attached to elite households. Skilled service workers outside the domestic setting practiced certain trades exclusively. For those in the unknown category, the evidence for assessing orientation is missing. However, some jobs make

Table 4.1   Occupational Structures in Private
and Public Social Contexts

Occupational Group	Private	Public	No Information
Building	32 (6.8)	39 (14.8)	41 (5.6)
Manufacture	46 (9.8)	123 (46.6)	162 (22.0)
Sales	2 (.4)	35 (13.3)	71 (9.6)
Banking	—	23 (8.7)	19 (2.6)
Professional service	28 (6.0)	4 (1.5)	88 (11.9)
Skilled service	33 (7.0)	8 (3.0)	34 (4.6)
Domestic service	160 (34.1)	—	161 (21.8)
Transportation	33 (7.0)	4 (1.5)	18 (2.4)
Administration	135 (28.8)	28 (10.6)	143 (19.4)
Total	469 (100)	264 (100)	737 (100)

Note: Figures in parentheses are percentages.

little sense outside the domestic setting: nurses, child attendants (*paedagogi*), bedchamber servants (*cubicularii*), table servants, provisioners, and many caretakers. When individuals in these fields disclosed a social context, it was a private one.[9]

In construction and artisanry, where the household did use such labor, context is more problematic. Although artisans with occupational title were more likely to locate themselves in the public sphere (37.2%, $N = 123$), some were attached to domestic households (13.9%, $N = 46$). By contrast, men in construction were more divided between private (28.6%, $N = 32$) and public (34.8%, $N = 39$) worlds.

Some artisans and builders used different titles in different settings. Outside the household, tailors used the title *vestiarius;* inside, they called themselves *vestificus/a* and perhaps *sarcinatrix.*[10] *Faber* occurs frequently in a domestic environment (76.9%, $N = 10$); *faber tignuarius*, a title used by men in the public world, appears infrequently (13.3%, $N = 6$). Also, artisans in large households were comparatively more concentrated in certain activities—baking, cloth production, and clothes making. More than specific titles, however, legal condition differentiates artisans in private and public settings. Most artisans in the domestic sphere were slaves (84.8%); outside it, they were freeborn (4.1%), uncertain freeborn (39.8%), or more often freedmen (55.3%).

Almost half of the 147 freed artisans (49%, $N = 72$) lack any indication of their social context; however, few (4.8%, $N = 7$) belonged to a large domestic household, and many (46.3%, $N = 68$) placed themselves in a public world. The domestic artisan's opportunities for manumission seem to have been limited, although the use of job title and status indication by slaves and freedmen in this setting makes this difficult to assess (see below, pp. 101–105).

Although artisans freed by upper-class masters rarely appear in continued service to their former masters, patterns traced by senatorial names suggest the domestic origins of some artisans located in the public sphere. Such patterns depend on a slave artisan who, on manumission, received the praenomen and nomen of his senatorial patron and then passed the name on to his own children and freedmen. Senatorial nomenclature can only outline possible events, but it recurs often enough among artisans whose trades had domestic practitioners to suggest a movement from the large domestic staff into the marketplace in certain fields.[11]

Marcus Iunius Pudens, a baker who sold a special type of bread in large quantities (*pistor magnarius pepsianus*, 9810), exemplifies how artisans with their skills could pass into the society at large by a process of birth and manumission. Pudens's occupational title indicates a large-scale operation, and he apparently headed his own establishment, for the family tomb, dedicated by his wife Claudia Earine, included their freedmen. However, Pudens's nomenclature, particularly in light of Earine's, traces his genealogy to a freedman of the Iunii Silani, some of whose *familia* were buried in a tomb on the Via Appia (7600–7643). Earine bore the nomen of families closely connected with the Iunii Silani by blood and marriage—the imperial family and the Appii Claudii. No baker appears among the slaves and ex-slaves in the tomb on the Via Appia, but large households normally had their own bakers, one of whom may have been Pudens's father, grandfather, patron, or patron's patron manumitted by a Marcus Iunius Silanus.[12] The praenomen and nomen (Marcus Iunius) could have been preserved by passage from father to son, patron to freedman, or some combination of these. With the name perhaps passed the trade of baking. The transition between household and marketplace depended on occupation: attendants and bedchamber servants lacked the skills for independent work and would find no consumers for their services outside the domestic setting.

In construction, too, the status pattern differs markedly between private and public settings. However, freedmen are well represented among the household's builders, as they are not among its artisans: thirteen domestic builders (40.6%) were freedmen; nineteen (59.4%), slaves. Over half (53.3%) of the freed builders left no indication of their social context, but a substantial group (43.3%) clearly did belong to large households. In this field, in contrast to artisanry, slaves who gained their freedom continued to work for the household or at least to identify with it. Outside the domestic setting, men in construction depicted themselves as members and officers of *collegia*, not as freedmen or freeborn citizens (see below, pp. 114–20).

Nonetheless, some, if they were not freedmen, had freed ancestors in large domestic households. Their histories resemble Pudens's: freedmen of upper-class families left the households, set up their own businesses, or passed on their occupations to sons or freedmen. The process can be observed with T. Statilius Onesimus, T. Statilius Isochrysus, and Isochrysus's son, T. Statilius Hiero (9405), members of the tenth decury of the carpenters' *collegium*, who were buried at the expense of its president L. Cincius L. f. Martialis. The men lack proper status indication, but the free status of Isochrysus makes it very likely that Hiero, at least, was freeborn. The distinctive nomen and praenomen connect Onesimus and Isochrysus with the Statilii, whose urban staff included a comparatively large number of construction workers,[13] but their burial outside the household tomb and dependence on Martialis mark a separation from the *familia*.

The connection with the household would originate with a patron or father (patron's patron or grandfather) manumitted by the Statilii. Although the carpenter T. Statilius Tauri l. Antiochus (9414: freedman) cannot be directly connected with these men, he serves as a good example of their antecedents. Antiochus's clear identification of his patron associates him with the household of his former master, yet his burial outside the household *columbarium* and acquisition of a plot measuring twelve by twelve Roman feet indicate distance from the *familia* and the control of some material resources.

Antiochus, Isochrysus, and Hiero signal a movement between two worlds: occupation and skills passed from the freedman in the large domestic household to his children or freedmen and then to their children or freedmen. Antiochus, I believe, occupied a position midway between the domestic setting and the public world: his relationship with his patron was important enough to note carefully, yet his burial points away from the household. His son or freedman (someone like Isochrysus) would have been one step removed from the household. Hiero, who took up his father's trade, represents a further stage in the process.[14]

WORK, STATUS, AND COMMUNITY: HOUSEHOLD, SHOP, AND *COLLEGIUM*

A consideration of social context suggests that slaves, freedmen, and the uncertain freeborn found occupational title especially important in specific but generally different circumstances. Only four (.9%) slaves and two uncertain slaves (.9%) give evidence of a public context.[15] The vast majority of slaves with occupational title (73.8%, $N = 346$) were attached to large households. These slaves, like most of the slaves (66.3%, $N = 311$) and uncertain slaves (65.4%, $N = 134$), regardless of indicated social context, were domestic servants or administrators, financial agents, and secretaries. The large representation of service workers, especially in the latter fields, and the considerable presence of slaves among the population with occupational title are brought together in the large household. Further, this is the setting in which women were most likely to name their work, usually as domestic servants of various kinds (especially nurses) and skilled service workers (especially *ornatrices*, hairdressers and maids).

By contrast, only 25.9% ($N = 109$) of the freedmen with occupational title associated themselves with a domestic staff (see Table 4.2). Freed slaves in domestic service, transportation, and administration are usually connected with a household, often as nurses, managers (*procuratores*), and supervisors.[16] A third (34.3%, $N = 107$) of the other freedmen clearly placed themselves in the public world, mainly as bankers (15.9%, $N = 17$), salespeople (11.2%, $N = 12$), and—especially—artisans (63.6%, $N = 68$).[17] There, shop location appears as an important definition of context.

Table 4.2   Social Contexts of Different Status Groups

| | | | | Legal Status | | | | | |
Social Context	Slave		Uncertain Slave		Freedman		Freeborn		Uncertain Freeborn
Private	346 (73.8)		3 (1.5)		109 (25.9)		1 (2.3)		10 (3.0)
Public	4 (.9)		2 (.9)		107 (25.4)		22 (51.2)		129 (38.9)
No information	119 (25.4)		200 (97.6)		205 (48.7)		20 (46.5)		193 (58.1)
Total	469 (100)		205 (100)		421 (100)		43 (100)		332 (100)

Note: Figures in parentheses are percentages.

Freedmen are the major group among individuals with a shop address (62.3%, N = 91), and they (29.2%, N = 91) are more likely to have an address than the freeborn (9.5%, N = 4) and the uncertain freeborn (15.5%, N = 50). These patterns are especially characteristic of artisans, bankers, and skilled service workers.[18]

Not surprisingly, only 2.3% (N = 1) of the freeborn and 3% (N = 10) of the uncertain freeborn with occupational title indicated attachments to large households (see Table 4.2). Aside from the few in child care (3) and one *nomenclator* (announcer) whose duties gave him a public function, they were architects, doctors, or teachers, whose domestic affiliations seem to have enhanced their positions, and, for doctors, defined their patients.[19] Most of the freeborn (52.4%, N = 22) and the uncertain freeborn (40.1%, N = 129) outside the large domestic household placed themselves in the public sphere. In general, like freedmen, they appear in the nonservice fields, although they are better represented among builders than their freed counterparts.[20] Participation in the city's occupational *collegia* figures as a particularly significant context for the freeborn and especially the uncertain freeborn, as shop does for freedmen. Of those in *collegia*, 67% (N = 61) were free but lack any indication of status; 17.6% (N = 16) were freeborn. Actually, if we rely solely on formal status identification, 76.9% (N = 70) were uncertain freeborn, and 8.8% (N = 8) freeborn. And the freeborn (38.1%, N = 16) and uncertain freeborn (18.9%, N = 61) were more likely to present their occupations this way than freedmen (4.5%, N = 14).

More than simply the contexts of occupational title, household, shop, and *collegium* refer to particular associations of individuals. Viewed as communities, they give occupational title a social reference point.

The Large Domestic Household

The slave or freedman in the large domestic household was a member of a group, the *familia*, that the legitimate social order defined by its attachment to the slaveholder.[21] Freeborn citizens, too, had ties to a specific individual and were defined by their membership in certain groups, but with quite different implications. The nomenclature of the freeborn Roman citizen identified him or her in terms of a father; this definition was the basis for membership in society. Family certainly determined the freeborn citizen's position; however, that position, even if a lowly one, was at least within the social order.

In the domestic context, a tie to a master or patron removed the servant from the legitimate social order. The worker was defined in terms of a particular person, his or her needs, desires, and material existence, and the restriction of work to one individual or family grounded the worker in a circumscribed setting. Each household formed a private community bound to its master and separated from Roman society as a whole. For the men and women whose occupations had commercial potential, the master's household perhaps offered indirect entry into society, but the *cubicularius* (bedchamber servant) and *pedisequus* (attendant), unless they changed employments, needed someone to serve. Slaves still in the household had entry into legitimate society only as extensions of their masters.

Nevertheless, membership in a *familia* did not preclude communal interaction. As Flory has shown, slaves and exslaves in the *familia* identified each other as members of a community; familial and extrafamilial ties brought them together as a social unit.[22] Domestic *collegia* reflect associations within large *familiae*. Yet the integrity and composition of this community existed by the will of the master; however members experienced their participation, continued membership ultimately depended not on citizenship in the community but on the person who had power over it.

Treggiari's observations on the use of status indication and job title in the household of Livia, wife of Augustus, are useful for interpreting the strikingly different proportions of slaves and freedmen who used job title in this community. According to Treggiari, in the Monumentum Liviae (the *columbarium* reserved for Livia's staff), the number of slaves with status indication $(N = 41)$ is nearly equal to the number of freedmen with clearly indicated status $(N = 43)$, although, as Treggiari points out, these proportions are misleading since "probably many slaves used the cheapest form of memorial which mentioned neither job nor status nor owner" (see Table 4.3). The actual number of slaves, therefore, would have been larger.[23] My own figures for Livia's staff in the Monumentum Liviae—which include all those

Table 4.3   Occupational Title and Legal Status
in the Monumentum Liviae

| A. Naming of Jobs by Slaves and Freedmen[1] | | | |
	Slaves	Freedmen	Total
With job	36 (87.8)	21 (48.8)	57 (67.9)
Without job	5 (12.2)	22 (51.2)	27 (32.1)
Total	41 (100)	43 (100)	84 (100)

| B. Status Indication for Slaves and Freedmen[2] | | | |
	Slaves	Freedmen	Total
Status indication	28 (58.3)	20 (90.9)	48 (68.6)
No status indication	20 (41.7)	2 (9.1)	22 (31.4)
Total	48 (100)	22 (100)	70 (100)

Note: Figures in parentheses are percentages.
[1] Figures include only those with status indication. Data for pt. A are drawn from Treggiari, "Jobs in the Household of Livia," *PBSR* 43 (1975), 59, Table D: Comparison of Slaves' and Freedmen's Practice in Naming Jobs.
[2] Figures include only those with job title.

with occupational title, regardless of status indication (excluding those who name a master or patron other than Livia)—show more than twice as many slaves ($N = 48$) as freedmen ($N = 22$).

These figures indicate a larger number of slaves with occupational title, not necessarily a larger number of slaves in the household. They point to the special importance of job title for Livia's slaves, as do Treggiari's own figures for the staff with status indication: 87.7% ($N = 36$) of the slaves, as compared with 48.8% ($N = 21$) of the freedmen, have a job title. Treggiari suggests and then rejects this conclusion on the grounds cited above. Instead, she argues that slaves and freedmen simply emphasized different aspects of their lives in their epitaphs.

> Once a slave had reached a certain position of comparative wealth and importance, he will mention his job, as well as personal details, such as the names of family or friends. Freedmen, on the other hand, will emphasize their position as those given freedom by an Augusta or a *diva*.[24]

The evidence of other *columbaria* and the pattern among all slaves and freedmen with occupational title, with and without status indication, lead me to stress the relative significance of job title for slaves in large households. In this study, 68.3% ($N = 136$) of the slaves whose epitaphs come from *columbaria* lack status indication. Moreover, while about half of the slaves owned by men and women of Livia's class noted their legal status, they were less likely to do so inside single-household *columbaria* (31.7%, $N = 63$) than outside these tombs (96.9%, $N = 95$). Within the community mirrored in the *columbarium*, slaves who used work to construct an identity at death found that work more memorable than their legal condition.

The precedence of occupational title over legal status characterizes many of the men and women whose nomenclature (single names without family nomina) immediately suggests servile status. Although 60.1% ($N = 405$) have no status indication, nearly half (49.4%, $N = 200$) were certainly slaves according to the evidence of other factors. Further, I believe that many of the slaves and possible slaves whose epitaphs lack signs of social context did, in fact, belong to large households. The pattern of their employments resembles that of slaves whose epitaphs confirm their membership in upper-class *familiae:* concentration in the nonprofessional service fields, especially domestic service and administration (see Table 4.4).[25]

Contrary to Treggiari's assumption that slaves who mention a job had probably attained importance or wealth, 18.6% ($N = 64$) of the slaves attached to large households were workmen, spinners, personal or table servants (excluding *cubicularii*), grooms, litter bearers, and runners.[26] Another 19.2% ($N = 66$) were cooks, those who cared for specific objects, doorkeepers, and bedchamber servants, not all of whom will have been either skilled or charged with special responsibilities.[27] These figures are conservative, for they exclude slaves in professional, skilled, and administrative services, menders, child attendants, and nurses. The epitaphs of only a few reveal any material resources: most (86.9%, $N = 279$) appear in epitaphs that name only one deceased, and, for nearly half (48.9%, $N = 156$), we have no evidence of family or other social relations.

The use by some freedmen manumitted by upper-class masters of both status indication and occupational title suggests that these ex-slaves had more to record than a job, namely, their membership in the legitimate social order; yet

Table 4.4 Occupations of Slaves and Possible Slaves Inside and Outside Large Domestic Households

Occupational Group	In Household			Outside Household or No Evidence		
	Slave	Possible Slave	Total	Slave	Possible Slave	Total
Building	2 (1.1)	17 (11.0)	19 (5.5)		7 (3.2)	7 (2.1)
Manufacture	10 (5.3)	29 (18.7)	39 (11.3)	12 (10.6)	26 (12.0)	38 (11.5)
Sales	1 (.5)	1 (.6)	2 (.6)	1 (.9)	5 (2.3)	6 (1.8)
Banking	—	—	—	—	—	—
Professional service	5 (2.6)	4 (2.6)	9 (2.6)	2 (1.8)	15 (6.9)	17 (5.1)
Skilled service	15 (7.9)	13 (8.4)	28 (8.1)	8 (7.1)	13 (6.0)	21 (6.4)
Domestic service	56 (29.6)	51 (32.9)	107 (31.1)	20 (17.7)	79 (36.4)	99 (30.0)
Transportation	16 (8.5)	12 (7.7)	28 (8.1)	3 (2.6)	12 (5.5)	15 (4.5)
Administration	84 (44.4)	28 (18.1)	112 (32.6)	67 (59.3)	60 (27.6)	127 (38.5)
Total	189 (100)	155 (100)	344 (100)	113 (100)	217 (100)	329 (100)

Note: Figures in parentheses are percentages.

the importance of status for upper-class freedmen should not be exaggerated. As Treggiari suggests, Livia's freedmen appear to have had a special interest in status indication. My own figures for slaves and freedmen with job title in the Monumentum Liviae show that 90.9% ($N = 20$) of Livia's freedmen (including those without status indication or notation of another patron) properly indicated their legal status, compared with 58.3% ($N = 28$) of her slaves. But freedmen of other elite patrons did not claim their legal condition as frequently (53%, $N = 44$), and they used formal status indication no more often than the slaves of this class.

The simultaneous notation of occupational title and status indication would imply service to a specific individual. Of the freedmen attached to large households, 43.1% ($N = 47$) were, in fact, in domestic service. Perhaps, then, the relatively small proportion of freedmen with occupational title whose epitaphs indicate a private social context means that freedmen tended to record their employments less often than slaves, and, as Treggiari suggests, preferred to emphasize their free condition. When they did use job title, their work was focused on a particular person (see chap. 5).

There is, however, an explanation other than Treggiari's for the small proportion of freedmen with occupational title who locate themselves in the domestic setting. As pointed out above, some freedmen apparently left the household on manumission, and their exodus reduces the number of freedmen we can observe there. Their movement out of the household can be glimpsed in the burial circumstances of the uncertain freeborn whose names connect them with upper-class *familiae* like that of the Statilii. Some had property or control over the labor of others; lacking any articulated attachment to a large *familia*, they appear to have established their own households, run their own businesses, or simply worked independently. If these uncertain freeborn with distinctive names were freedmen, they had either left the household or preferred to omit their relationship to it; if freeborn, they were the descendents of those who had left.

It is primarily the slaves of the upper classes who claimed their work in a community of fellow slaves and ex-slaves. The urban staff (*familia urbana*) of a slaveholder is supposed to have been more privileged in living conditions, manumission, and family opportunities. In the next chapter, I look at the other side of these privileges in terms of slaves' working conditions and their perspective on the master's needs. Here, I would stress another aspect of slaves' viewpoint: unlike agricultural workers, urban slaves lived in the midst of varied employments that both distinguished them from and connected them to each other. Since the *familia* in essence was a group of individuals who worked for a specific person or family, job title registered a specific role in this community and expressed a bond that tied the *familia* together. In linking peers, it also may have complemented the pattern of strong intragenerational family relations. When Plecte, a slave buried in the *columbarium* of the Statilian *familia*, called herself (or was called) *quasillaria* (spinner), she associated herself with seven other slave women who were also *quasillariae* (6339–46). Perhaps, too, her title identified relations with others in related work—weavers (6360–62), fullers (6287–90), seamstresses, and tailors (6373, 6348–51). Shared work, rather than kin relations, was the stated connection among the spinning women. Occupational title, then, expressed particular social relations within the *familia*, for the reality named by title must have involved physical proximity, cooperation or competition, interactions, and conversations around shared tasks.[28]

The Shop

For 146 men and women, the location given with occupational title named a place of business, most commonly a shop. Separating an individual from the domestic setting, a shop address in a particular street or area of the city located him or her in the marketplace, within the community of other tradesmen and artisans in the same locale. Where address referred to a small shop with living quarters, it marked an identification with a neighborhood in a fuller sense of the term.

An address, however, does not necessarily denote a propertied person. The typical shop in Pompeii or Ostia, excluding fulleries and bakeries, was small. In those that included living quarters, the shopkeeper, his or her family, or fellow workers inhabited and worked in the same space, generally a cramped one; and most often the shop would have been rented, not owned.[29] Although some shopkeepers (29.4%, $N = 43$) had freedmen and therefore a claim to the labor of others, 26% (N = 38; 40.7% of the freed shopkeepers) had ties to a patron, fellow ex-slaves, or both, relations that point to the claim that someone else had on their own labor. In some cases, their situations reflect, not their own property, but the wealth of others.

Shop location recurs most commonly among artisans (28.4%, N = 81), bankers (50%, N = 21), and salesmen (26.4%, N = 28).[30] Jewelers, ivorists, and craftsmen in related materials (50%, N = 18), metalworkers (23%, N = 20), and those who produced clothing (37.5%, N = 30) show the highest concentration of artisans in this setting (figures are for those outside the large domestic household).[31] In general, especially for jewelers and tailors of fine clothing (*vestiarii tenuiarii*), the locations associated with the sale of luxury goods are better represented: twenty-nine artisans with an identifiable address (42.6%) placed themselves in the elegant shopping areas of the city—Via Sacra, Vicus Tuscus, and Velabrum.[32]

For half of the bankers (50%, N = 21), an address seems to have been an integral part of occupational title, functioning frequently to indicate a specific clientele. An elegant location mattered little, and only one of the twenty-one bankers with an address did business in the city's fashionable areas (*de Velabro*, 9184). Most frequently (N = 11), they mentioned an area of intense commercial activity, especially those like the Forum Vinarium (9181–82).[33]

Salespeople (here used interchangeably with distributors), like bankers, did not generally use shop address to express an association with the elegant shopping areas of the city, although, as with artisans, there are a few instances where it was appropriate. Of the six who noted a fancy address, at least four sold luxury goods.[34] Since most of the men and women sold foodstuffs (60.7%, N = 17), a location of this type was not important or related to their activities.

The social relations that recur with shop location distinguish artisans and bankers from distributors. Artisans' and bankers' relations with fellow ex-slaves and former masters were associated especially with a shop location: the shop defined the boundaries within which work and the social relationships originating in slavery and manumission were intertwined. These men and women are often represented as members of productive associations framed by ties to an ex-master, fellow ex-slaves, or both. For distributors, the relationship between ex-master and ex-slave was equally important, but these individuals tend to appear as patrons rather than as freedmen, at the heads of such associations rather than as members. In terms of social relations and position, therefore, distributors with an address depicted themselves differently than their counterparts in artisanry and banking.

Among artisans, the recurrence of groups of *colliberti* (fellow ex-slaves) or patrons and freedmen all with the same occupational title in single epitaphs explains the comparatively large percentages of shopholding jewelers (*margaritarii* and *gemmarii*, 63.6%, $N = 14$), shoemakers (57.1%, $N = 4$), tailors (*vestiarii* only, 59.4%, $N = 19$), and ironsmiths (83.3%, $N = 10$). We find five *gemmarii* (jewelers, 9435) freed by the same two patrons, ten *ferrarii* (ironsmiths, 9398) freed by the same two or three patrons, four *vestiarii* (tailors, 33920) who appear to have been *colliberti*, and three *vestiarii tenuiarii* (tailors of fine clothing, 37826), a freedman, his patron's patron, and his patron. Occupational title and shop location applied to the group as a whole or to each man and woman in it. Whether the freedmen had separate shops or worked in the same shop is not clear, but in each case the artisans appear as one group. Beyond a simple explanation of percentages, these groups reveal one pattern of productive relations: the organization of work followed the lines of relationships between patron and freedman and among *colliberti* (see chap. 5).

The social relations that joined the people in these groups recur in the epitaphs of many artisans (37.9%, $N = 96$) outside the large domestic household (with and without shared occupational title; see Table 4.5). But these relations, especially with patron and *colliberti*, more often characterized the lives of artisans located in a specific shop; 53.8% had such ties, 51.2% ($N = 22$) of whom appear in groups where a shared trade was explicitly noted. The recurrence of these social relations should be connected with the larger concentration of freedmen in the shop setting relative to other status groups, especially the free. In effect, this form of organization characterized not artisans in general, but those of servile orgin.

The naming of shop location counterbalances the implications of the formal indication of status used by most freed

Table 4.5   Artisans' Relations with Patrons, *Colliberti*, or
Freedmen, and Business Address

| Relations with | Use of Business Address | | |
	With Address	Without Address	Total
Freedmen	14 (17.5)	23 (13.3)	37 (14.6)
Patron or *colliberti*	28 (35.0)	27 (15.6)	55 (21.7)
Freedmen or *colliberti?*	1 (1.3)	3 (1.7)	4 (1.6)

Note: Figures in parentheses are column percentages only for artisans in epitaphs.

shopkeepers (87.9%, $N = 80$). The latter implicitly signaled an attachment to a former master, and the articulated social relations of many confirmed that bond or emphasized the continuation of relations formed in slavery. Shop address, however, separated these workers from the material needs of a patron in the domestic household, demonstrating that the artisans produced for anyone who could purchase their products in the marketplace.

For bankers, too, shop location seems to name a work-place in which individuals were linked by the relations originating in slavery and manumission. Three epitaphs feature bankers connected by a common trade and a shared servile past or the ties between patron and freedman. These epitaphs increase the number of freed bankers, especially those with shop location: seven freedmen, patrons, and *colliberti* with shop location (9181–82) and three *colliberti* without shop location (9170).[35] As with artisans, these social relations characterize other bankers whose *colliberti* or patrons lack occupational title: 45% ($N = 18$) of the bankers had ties with freedmen, patrons, or *colliberti* that are reflected in their epitaphs (see Table 4.6). The recurrence of bankers whose relations included their freedmen but not their *colliberti* does not vary with the notation of shop; however, those attached to specific locations more frequently displayed relations with *colliberti* and patrons than bankers without a business address.

Salespeople differ from bankers and artisans in the type of social relations associated with the notation of an address. As among bankers and artisans, groups of *colliberti* or of patrons and freedmen all with occupational title recur in

Table 4.6 Bankers' Relations with Patrons, *Colliberti*, or Freedmen, and Business Address

| | Use of Business Address | | |
Relations with	With Address	Without Address	Total
Freedmen	4 (21.1)	4 (19.0)	8 (20.0)
Patron or *colliberti*	6 (31.6)	3 (14.3)	9 (22.5)
Freedmen or *colliberti*?	—	1 (4.8)	1 (2.5)

Note: Figures in parentheses are column percentages only for bankers in epitaphs.

the epitaphs of salespeople, but, unlike bankers and artisans, no sales group mentions a specific place of business. Common for distributors in general, the recurrence of these social relations varies with shop location, but primarily for those with freedmen (see Table 4.7). The proportion of distributors with *colliberti* or patrons decreases with the notation of an address, and the representation of those who name relations with their freedmen increases more substantially than for artisans and bankers. Further, salespeople with a shop address appear more frequently with their own freedmen and less frequently with *colliberti* or patrons than artisans or bankers.

The legal status of shopholders does not account for this pattern. The presence of freedmen among shopholding distributors (42.9%, $N = 12$) is smaller than among artisans (67.9%, $N = 55$) or bankers (76.2%, $N = 16$), so there would seem to have been fewer men and women who would have had ties with patrons or *colliberti*. However, only a single clearly identified freeborn salesman (3.6%) appears among the shopholders, and the uncertain freeborn (50%, $N = 14$) are not significantly better represented than freedmen. Rather, clearly identified freed distributors did not reveal relations with *colliberti* and patrons as often as their counterparts in banking and artisanry, nor did the freed salespeople whose lack of status indication places them among the uncertain freeborn.

Why freed artisans and bankers articulated these relations and freed distributors did not is explained by the way artisans, bankers, and salespeople presented themselves. Salespeople in general constructed a different image of them-

Table 4.7   Distributors' Relations with Patrons, *Colliberti,*
or Freedmen, and Business Address

Relations with	Use of Business Address		
	With Address	Without Address	Total
Freedmen	8 (29.6)	14 (20.3)	22 (22.9)
Patron or *colliberti*	4 (14.8)	13 (18.8)	17 (17.7)
Freedmen or *colliberti?*	—	3 (4.3)	3 (3.1)

Note: Figures in parentheses are column percentages only for distributors in epitaphs.

selves than artisans and bankers. Many artisans and bankers with shop location appear in circumstances that suggest someone else had claims on their labor; distributors with shop location, on the other hand, more frequently emerge as either those who were free of such claims or those who could make them.[36]

In examining the notation of business address by distributors, we must take into account the activities signaled by specific titles. By definition, the activities of the *negotiator* or *mercator* could extend beyond retailing. Indeed, the use of shop location varies considerably if *mercatores* and *negotiatores* are separated from distributors whose titles name only a product. Sellers of foodstuffs (40.7%, $N = 11$) more frequently noted a shop location than *mercatores* (22.2%, $N = 2$), *negotiatores* (29%, $N = 9$), and others, most of whom dealt in perfumes, unguents, and related products (12.5%, $N = 5$).[37]

Although the titles *negotiator* and *mercator* could refer to large-scale commercial activities, some *negotiatores* and *mercatores* were simple tradespeople. Abudia M. lib. Megiste *negotiatrix frumentaria et legumenaria ab scala mediana* (9683: freedwoman), for example, appears to have been a greengrocer.[38] In such cases, the title *mercator* or *negotiator* may have elevated the stature of the individual who used it.

For *negotiatores* and *mercatores*, address covered a wide range of commercial activities, from retail trading to wholesale distribution.[39] Most of the *mercatores* and *negotiatores* with a business address appear as individuals with at least some property, but their marriage patterns suggest a fairly humble social context for their prosperity. In general, these dealers married within their *familiae*. Megiste, the greengrocer, was the freedwoman of her husband. Successful individuals, but without social pretensions, they evoke Petronius's Hermeros (57.6), who reclaimed his wife (*contubernalis*) from slavery, becoming her patron so that no one could shame her.[40]

By contrast, the activities of *negotiatores* and *mercatores* without business address involved extensive trading, including importing. The scale of their activities distinguishes them from the dealers who located themselves in a specific place.[41] Their prosperity, too, reflects a different social level. All had achieved some financial success. Some, like P. Clodius Athenio, dealer in salted provisions, president of the association of merchants of Malagan fish sauce (*negotians salsarius, q(uin) q(uennalis) corporis negotiantium malacitanorum*, 9677: uncertain freeborn), or L. Scribonius Ianuarius, wine merchant and shipowner, *curator* of an organization of shippers in the Adriatic (*negotians vinarius item navicularius cur(ator) corporis maris Hadriatici*, 9682: uncertain freeborn), probably were quite wealthy: their diverse business interests, offices in *collegia*, and inclusion of freedmen in their tombs signal considerable means.[42] In contrast to dealers with shop addresses, these men married outside their *familiae*, and their wives, regardless of their actual legal status, appear as free women whose relationship with their husbands originated in marriage, not slavery and manumission.[43] Further, the standing of the most successful free or freeborn men and those involved in large-scale commerce is revealed by the way they or their relatives presented their occupations. They named a public post or an important role in a *collegium* that, as noted below, reflected their claims to standing.

In summary, while shopkeepers could and did present themselves as the heads of their own establishments, they appear to have lacked extensive material resources and aspirations to some sort of rank. By contrast, the wealthier *mercatores* and *negotiatores* did not name a place of business; the most prosperous emphasized their public position rather than their role in the marketplace.

The Collegium

The ninety-one men associated with occupational *collegia* (9.1% of those outside the domestic setting) have a different mode of identification from a simple occupational title or even a title embellished by shop location, and perhaps even a different sense of place.[44] T. Statilius Tauri l. Antiochus *fab(er) tig(nuarius)* (9414: freedman) identified himself as a carpenter; L. Cincius L. f. Suc. Martialis *quinquevir* (9405: freeborn) appears as an official of a *collegium* of *fabri tignuarii;* Sex. Iulius Aprilis (9405: uncertain freeborn), as a member of the same *collegium.* Where Antiochus's title specifies a trade, the titles of Martialis and Aprilis speak of their roles in officially recognized organizations and thus their place in the society as a whole. Association with an occupational *collegium,* then, seems to be in direct contrast to the signs of a private social context that signified one's removal from legitimate society.

The implications of this form of title depend on an individual's role in an inscription and on the position he held in his *collegium.* Half of the men in *collegia* made dedications to the organization itself, individuals, or deities important to the *collegium,* or were themselves honored by other members. In general, these dedications resulted from their positions and duties as officials (87%, $N = 40$). Six *magistri* (presidents) of the fullers' *collegium* (268: uncertain freeborn), for example, made a dedication to Minerva, the patron deity of fullers, as the chief officers of an organization of her artisans, not as individuals or as fullers per se. Chronicling interactions with the gods, state, and authorities, these inscriptions were public documents, and their authors memorialized their activities in the public sphere.

Epitaphs record place and achievement rather than particular actions. What is registered differs for deceased and dedicator, member and officer. With a single exception (9186), when the deceased was a member, he was buried by his *collegium* or given space in a tomb by one of its officers. In these circumstances, membership associated him with an organization constituted outside the domestic setting, and the epitaph reflects his social life and the bonds among the members of the *collegium.* He participated in meetings, feasts, and other activities that engendered more than casual contact and had responsibilities to other members. In general, officers set up their own epitaphs or were buried by their families. Office rather than occupation represented their own and their families' perception of their positions; epitaph commemorated their distinction for descendant and passerby and testified to their material resources.[45]

Although there were *collegia* in every field except professional, skilled, and domestic service, the representation of different employments is quite limited. Those associated with occupational societies were primarily builders ($N = 39$) and artisans ($N = 34$).[46] Most in construction were carpenters; even without an epitaph that names twenty-three *fabri tignuarii* (9405), *fabri tignuarii* still account for most of the builders in *collegia* (13/16). The activities of artisans included cloth making and treatment ($N = 6$), the production of clothing ($N = 11$), metalwork ($N = 7$), food preparation ($N = 8$), and the lime trade ($N = 2$). Although the inscriptions name eleven different groups of artisans, the presence of the clothiers is exaggerated by the evidence from one tomb. Five ragmen (*centonarii*), all L. Octavii (7861, 7863–64), came from a *columbarium* used by those who apparently belonged to the same *familia*.[47]

The L. Octavii are important in two respects. First, although their social relations would seem to have excluded any standing in society, they explicitly claimed one. As in the cases of *colliberti* whose occupational title included a shop address, a public orientation coexisted with the relations originating in slavery and manumission. The burial and nomenclature of the ragmen made clear these bonds, yet they identified themselves as officers of a public organization with all the implications of rank. Whether in separate shops or in one business, they achieved the prosperity that enabled them to hold high office in the city's *collegium*.[48] Second, this claim to rank is made by artisans whose trade itself would have precluded claims to standing.

On this point, *centonarii* must be seen in terms of fullers, butchers, and bakers, men in potentially discrediting trades who also show a marked preference for noting their official positions, usually the highest offices in their *collegia*.[49] At first glance, the preference for office rather than occupational title as such seems to have been a response to stigma.[50] The connection with a vulgar trade was not denied but transposed: in Goffman's terms, a "prestige symbol" replaced a job title that in these trades would have been a "stigma symbol." C. Lollius Faustus *magister fontani* (268: uncertain freeborn) was not a fuller collecting urine from the public latrines, stomping about in his tubs, cleaning other people's soiled clothes; he was president of a publicly constituted association, albeit of fullers. The context for the notation of *collegium* affiliation, however, limits inferences along these lines: for all the fullers, butchers, and bakers, one *centonarius*, and ten *fabri tignuarii* appear in dedications connected with their offices; and it is apparently their duties as officials, not stigma, that account for this form of identification.

Despite these tradesmen's preference for noting office and the varied artisanal societies reflected in the inscriptions, there is no concentration of artisans in *collegia* (10.3%, $N = 34$), nor does the notation of affiliation recur with any frequency in other employments except construction (34.8%, $N = 39$), where one inscription inflates the proportion of builders in *collegia*. The majority of these men (62.6%, $N = 57$; without 9405, 80.9%, $N = 55$) held offices whose duties and expected donations were costly.[51] Few fullers, tailors, or builders would have achieved the necessary prosperity, so the relative proportions of men whose livelihoods are identified by their association with *collegia* are small. In general, therefore, most of the men with this form of occupational title would have been among the wealthier practitioners of their trades.

The evidence of burial and dedication certainly reveals their financial success. The presence of their freedmen points to property once held in the form of slaves, and comparatively larger tombs and the provisions for the burial indicate the funds at the disposal of these men and their families.[52] The erection of honorary inscriptions to public officials, emperors, and the imperial family, and the dedication of altars, shrines, and images often will have been expensive, although in cases of joint dedications, like that made by the *magistri* of the fullers' *collegium* (268), the cost to the individual officer would have been less. Where the details of the dedication are given, the donation is impressive. For example, L. Sextilius Seleucus (9254: uncertain freeborn), *decurio* of the ragmen's *collegium*, dedicated some structure, probably an altar, with a marble base and two copper candlesticks bearing an effigy of Cupid holding baskets, and he deposited 5,000 denarii in the treasury of the *collegium* so that a yearly stipend from the interest would be paid out on the birthday of Augustus.

Although records of gifts like Seleucus's (1625b, 9224, 33883, cf. 148) involved activities solely within the *collegium*, the inscriptions put these acts into the public record. Dedications made to gods, the emperor, and his family depicted *collegia* officers in interactions outside the circle of their fellow tradesmen. Indeed, the resources of men like Seleucus permitted them to act on behalf of *collegium* members and thus gave them an official capacity in the public sphere, beyond the marketplace. As intermediaries between their fellow tradesmen and the state as well as the gods, these men dealt with government authorities when necessary, thanked and honored them when appropriate, and maintained a *pax deorum* much as Roman magistrates did for the Roman people.[53] These interactions were necessary because of the government's capacity to affect trade, distribution, and working conditions. Fullers relied on an adequate water supply; bakers, on reasonable grain prices. Imperial construction programs employed builders. Duties and governmental intervention influenced distributors of imported goods; and market regulations, provision of commercial space, taxes, and imperial policy helped or hindered retail merchants and wholesale dealers. Ultimately, too, prosperity required the goodwill of the appropriate deities.[54]

The preference for noting a public role is not a pattern for the people in this study: with few exceptions, they had none. Yet, in identifying themselves as officials, the officers of occupational societies follow the pattern of senator, equestrian, municipal magistrate, and *apparitor* (magistrate's assistant). In Roman inscriptions as a whole, standing within the community is most often conveyed by an association with the state. In Huttunen's samples, which include senators, equestrians, members of the imperial bureaucracy, *apparitores*, and those with occupational titles as such, twice as many deceased and three times as many dedicators were involved in public rather than private activities: they held a magistracy or worked for the imperial or civil authorities.[55] The standing of men like Seleucus depended on a position among their fellow tradesmen and on commercial success rather than birth, magistracy, or municipal office; nevertheless, *collegium* offices functioned like the records of senatorial, equestrian, or municipal careers on another social level, for they, too, registered standing in a community. *Collegium* officers articulated their distinction to society as a whole and especially to the community of their fellows, one defined by occupation, not citizenship. Their records of office implicitly make a claim to rank in a hierarchy, if not in the Roman social order as a whole.

For men like Seleucus, there was an intimate connection among rank, wealth, and occupation. Dedications like his augmented prestige, for the gift made the donor a benefactor and technically earned him the gratitude of donees. The ability to give implied a certain ascendancy as did Pliny's contributions to his native Comum, and placed Seleucus above those who received.[56] Unlike Pliny's, Seleucus's ability to give depended on success in his trade. Holding office and donating an altar and money to his *collegium* translated success into rank. Office, then, involved these men in a system of acquiring honor.

For the men who noted their offices in *collegia*, occupation was significant since it was inextricably intertwined with recording rank. A wealthy consular like Petronius would not have regarded these men as persons of standing. His distinction in the social order did not include an indication of his livelihood; indeed, notation of magistracies and priesthoods signaled an absence of occupation. But in order to claim prominence, the officials of *collegia* had no choice but to name their trades, the source of the material resources on which rank depended. Yet they did so in a way that separated them from ordinary men. In their terms, office put them above others who could not afford to hold the position.

Significant in this respect is the close connection between an affiliation with an occupational *collegium* and the absence of proper status indication. In a period when the use of status indication declined, the association with a *collegium* (most often as an officer) appears as almost a substitute for formal legal status as a mode of identity. While 54.5% of all those with occupational title lack status indication, the proportion rises to 78% for those associated with occupational *collegia*. To some extent, particular circumstances explain the reference to an affiliation with a *collegium;* it expressed the relationship between dedication and dedicator, as legal status did not.

Yet these circumstances do not account for the additional omission of formal status indication. Whatever the actual legal condition of the uncertain freeborn, the freeborn citizens among them as well as those freedmen who did not identify themselves as ex-slaves emphasized their attainment of office or membership in a particular community rather than their occupations. At the same time, while their nomina demonstrated their free status and citizenship, they omitted notation of its source. Membership conveyed a kind of belonging; office signaled one's elevation above one's fellows. Perhaps belonging and standing, even at this modest level, were especially significant at a time when citizenship no longer determined privilege. Status was omitted, either because it was unimportant compared with membership or office or because the freedmen among this group did not wish to intrude an element that would disturb the claims of legitimacy and honor implicit in this form of identification.

Q. Haterius Evagogus, a *decurio* of the carpenters' *collegium* (9408), illustrates how office was used at the expense of status indication. Evagogus appears as a man of standing among his fellows and as the head of his own establishment. His wife Iulia Arescusa recorded his position in the carpenters' association, but not the origin of his freedom, although the name pattern within the family points to Evagogus's status as a freed slave.[57] The family tomb, which included freedmen, displays his prosperity. His office marks the rank he had attained among his fellow carpenters. Freed status indication, which at least implied a limiting relationship with a former master, would have disrupted this picture, and what it conveyed paled in importance next to Evagogus's position within the community of carpenters.

Evagogus's nomen illustrates another recurrent pattern for men distinguished by their role in occupational *collegia:* the appearance of senatorial and imperial nomina (with appropriate praenomina) in a group of men with some notation of rank, but without filiation. While names cannot provide precise biographical information, they suggest an association, even long past, with an elite household. Considered together, the nomina of Evagogus and his wife Arescusa point to a background in the *familiae* of the political elite. The orator Q. Haterius, *cos. suff.* 5 B.C., had connections with the imperial family; he may have married a daughter of Agrippa and Marcella Minor and apparently had good relations with Livia.[58] The manumission of Evagogus and Arescusa by Q. Haterius and Livia (i.e., Iulia Augusta) respectively would indicate links between their *familiae* and perhaps a closer relationship between the consular and Livia than has been assumed. Alternatively, the marriage between Evagogus and Arescusa may simply reflect Haterius's marital alliance with the imperial family and their own association with these households or some past tie to Haterius's and Livia's freedmen.

The recurrence of well-known senatorial names is especially interesting where the *collegium* member or officer had an occupation that was practiced by slaves and ex-slaves in large domestic households, like the free carpenters with the name T. Statilius discussed above.[59] Since the representation of clearly identified freedmen strongly suggests the freeborn status of most of the uncertain freeborn, they probably were not the freedmen of the nobles whose names they bore. Senatorial names, however, were passed on in ways other than from senator to freedman. The senator's freedman transferred the nomen and praenomen to his own sons and freedmen, and the T. Statilii indicate that the uncertain free with senatorial names may well have been the sons or grandsons of freed slaves.

In light of this pattern, the frequent absence of status indication among these men is intriguing. We would expect them to use the filiation denied to their fathers or grandfathers, but rank and membership in an organization took precedence over clear notation of freeborn citizenship. Nomen sufficed to mark membership in the legitimate social order. Officeholders' standing and prosperity distinguished them more effectively than the origin of their citizenship, both within the immediate community—that of their fellow tradesmen—and, perhaps, in comparison to men whose circumstances resembled their own—free, unprivileged members of society who practiced some trade.

In summary, household, shop address, and *collegium* delineate particular communities whose memberships were defined differently. In the large domestic household, belonging depended on bonds with the slaveholder, although the slaves in this community more frequently articulated their connections to fellow slaves and ex-slaves who shared this bond. Nonetheless, in the terms set out in law and literature, the tie to a specific individual and the compulsion that bound members to the group separated this community from the legitimate social order. Shop address and occupational *collegium* refer to the larger society, although the nature of the public connoted by each should be distinguished. Address located an individual in the marketplace; where it referred to a small shop with living space, it placed a man or woman in a particular physical area and linked him or her with others living and working in the neighborhood. Frequently associated with the shop was a social unit founded on the ties between patron and freedmen and among *colliberti*. As in the large domestic household, the cohesion of the group originally involved a degree of compulsion, although the group's work life was directed outward toward the marketplace. With *collegia*, public is defined by an official organization.[60] For the men in occupational *collegia*, community rested on a common trade, but, unlike *colliberti* with the same title, the association of *collegium* members depended on the voluntary participation of those in the same trade.

Despite the different implications of household, shop, and *collegium*, occupational title in each situation made special reference to community, identifying individuals as members or distinguishing them as persons of rank. For slaves in the large household and for the free in *collegia*, occupation and community were linked in a particularly intimate way. In the domestic setting, the predominant role of peers in naming the occupations of their fellows means that the claims to labor emanated from the household community. Title registered one's part in that community, especially where it named employments in domestic service and administration, which made little sense outside the household. For the free in *collegia*, reference to community was embedded in title itself. For officials, distinction was measured in terms of fellow tradesmen and could not be communicated without reference to their livelihoods.

Ironically, in the legitimate social order, free as well as

slave needed occupational title either as a mode of identity
or as a form of distinction. Slaves had no rights, acknowledged kin, honor, or legitimate standing in society apart
from their masters. Those in large domestic households, especially the men and women whose jobs located them physically within the house, were exiled even from a public
sphere defined as the marketplace. In the absence of normal
forms of identification and direct reference to public activities, work has a special dimension in the expression of identity. Perhaps work's significance was enlarged by its role in
maintaining a class whose rights of ownership cut the slave
off from the wider society but whose social standing, or at
least a demonstration of it, relied on the slave's labor (see
chap. 5).

In possession of rights and socially acknowledged kin,
free men could claim citizenship and family as husbands,
fathers, and, if freeborn, as sons. But despite this ability to
frame a normal identity, the means of distinction were limited, at least compared to those available to the privileged
orders. Ordinary citizens did not hold magistracies or state
priesthoods, sit in the Senate, or serve as imperial legates,
although they were not disqualified by birth as were freedmen. Their residence in the city of Rome itself also limited
their opportunities at least compared to their counterparts
in the municipalities, because the political institutions of
city and state were not distinguished at the highest level. On
the other hand, *collegia* offered them a hierarchy for rank.

Certain aspects, of course, differentiate the slaves in
domestic settings and the freeborn in *collegia*. In the first
place, these slaves used title as a mode of identity. For the
free, whose nomina already defined them as citizens and,
at least potentially, as members of families, title served as
a means of distinction. Second, the men in *collegia* have
transposed occupational title. Although notation of office or
membership in a *collegium* indicates a man's livelihood, it
depicts him not as a worker or tradesman but as an official
or a citizen of a community. Still, it should be acknowledged
that slaves may have read the simple job titles of their peers
in a similar fashion. Finally, most slaves in the large domestic household labored for others: they were workers in our
sense of the word. Few owned property or had claims on the
labor of slaves and ex-slaves, at least on the evidence of their

epitaphs. Although some free members of *collegia* worked for others, many officers controlled labor, and their epitaphs reflect material prosperity.

Occupational title defined the slave Bassus, a builder (*faber*, 6283), and L. Cincius L. f. Suc. Martialis, a freeborn official of the carpenters' organization (9405), within their respective communities. Bassus was buried in the *columbarium* reserved for the staff of the Statilii and commemorated by a simple plaque with his name and job; Martialis provided burial space in his tomb for thirty-two people, including members of his *collegium*. Property or its lack, the communities to which the title referred, and their respective roles in those communities separate these builders, yet they are parallel in their use of occupational title.

THE RE-FORMATION OF
WHAT WAS GIVEN

My first beginning was as a gardener, and then I came to the city of Louisville, where I was put at the barber's trade. I served my apprenticeship of seven years, and then kept shop for myself one or two years, and then I was one year steam-boating up the river. . . . As I had been raised a barber and among freemen, it always seemed to me that I was free; but when I was turned over to another man, who kept me close round, I saw I was not a freeman; that all the privileges were taken from me.

(Isaac Throgmorton, former slave, interviewed 1863, Canada)

I was not free born. I didn't feel that any body had a right to me, after I began to think about it. . . . I was learnt the black-smith's trade. . . . I can't say that I experienced any hard treatment . . . , but I worked hard, and got nothing for it. I thought that was hard, when I got to be about 22.

(George Ramsey, former slave, interviewed 1863, Canada)

My oldest brother fell to one of the oldest sons, who sold him to a millwright, and he learned him the millwright's trade. After serving seven years, he was emancipated, and taken into partnership by the miller, and in the course of two years saved considerable money, which he gave to two of my sisters to purchase their freedom.

(A. T. Jones, former slave, interviewed 1863, Canada)

LIKE MANY OTHER former slaves in North America, Isaac Throgmorton, George Ramsey, and A. T. Jones tell stories of laboring lives.[1] The barber details the relations among work, the master's proximity, and the slave's sense of self. The blacksmith records his resentment at not benefiting from his own hard work. The field hand recounts his brother's rise from slave apprentice to partner and his ability to accumulate the money to liberate his siblings. Their words set in high relief the muteness of the Roman testimony that is the subject of this chapter—the epitaphs of freed artisans and slave domestic servants. The inscriptions freeze the lived experience articulately described by Throgmorton, Ramsey, and Jones into the stark circumstances of burial. Yet, if we cannot construct individual biographies full of movement and sentiment, we can observe the effects of occupational title in framing an identity at death.

My project in this chapter is to bring the preceding discussion to bear on the most typical freedman and slave in the occupational inscriptions: the freed artisan outside the domestic setting and the slave domestic servant in the large elite household. In each case, occupational title modifies the conditions established by individual masters, patrons, and the legitimate society as a whole: in Paul Willis's terms, it re-forms and reapplies "what is given." Despite their silence, these epitaphs provide the grounds on which to entertain stories other than those told by the Roman slaveholder and the satirist.

THE QUESTION OF PREDOMINANCE

Questions about work and status arising from the inscriptional evidence have tended to be phrased in terms of predominance: did slave, freedman, or freeborn citizen dominate a particular productive activity relative to other status groups?[2] Originally, this approach responded to remarks made by Roman authors. The large number of freedmen in the city's epitaphs, especially the occupational inscriptions, was seen to confirm the complaints of Juvenal's narrator (3.21ff.) that foreigners controlled the city's commercial and professional activities, or the observations of Tacitus's senators (*Ann.* 13.27) that freedmen outnumbered the freeborn. Yet these remarks belong to explanations of society's perceived corruption or an experience of powerlessness inappropriate to freeborn author, his persona, or characters. The processes of stereotyping shape their formulation.[3]

Although the occupational inscriptions reveal the relative predominance of particular status groups in different employments, the information they provide on the structure of the Roman work force requires qualification. From Table 5.1, it would appear that builders were generally of uncertain free status; that artisans were freedmen; and that domestic servants and administrators, financial agents, and secretaries were slaves. But this observation does not consider the setting of work discussed in the last chapter. In the large domestic household, for example, artisans were slaves, not freedmen.

More important, the question of predominance cannot be answered definitively for Roman society from these inscriptions because they represent individuals who attached a special significance to work. The inscriptions tell us about the men and women who made claims to particular kinds of labor, not about all those who labored. The figures of Gummerus and Kühn continue to be used to discuss the predominance of freedmen in artisanry,[4] yet, in fact, they and Table 5.1 show only that, of the individuals for whom the role of artisan was an integral part of an identity at death, it was most meaningful to freed slaves. Similarly, the representation of slaves in domestic service and administration measures only their importance among those who named these jobs. When we analyze the proportions of slaves, freedmen, and freeborn citizens in particular fields of employment, we can speak most accurately about the status pattern of individuals for whom a particular kind of work was significant in different settings. This sort of reassessment of the epigraphical evidence prevents us from equating predominance with the control of production and from attributing a power to slaves or ex-slaves that they did not have. Workers often did not choose their trades, although some used them to frame an identity at death.

Table 5.2 shows which occupations were most often named by slaves, freedmen, and the freeborn, comparing their claims to different kinds of labor. For the reasons noted above, this approach cannot explain where every person, slave and free, worked. Used comparatively and in light of social context, Table 5.2 suggests the differences determined

Table 5.1 Status Patterns in Different Occupational Groups

Legal Status	Occupational Group									Total
	Building	Manufacture	Sales	Banking	Professional Service	Skilled Service	Domestic Service	Transportation	Administration	
Slave	19 (17.0)	52 (15.7)	3 (2.8)	—	15 (12.5)	37 (49.3)	129 (40.2)	32 (58.2)	182 (59.5)	469 (31.9)
Uncertain slave	7 (6.3)	25 (7.6)	5 (4.6)	—	11 (9.2)	12 (16.0)	77 (24.0)	11 (20.0)	57 (18.6)	205 (13.9)
Freedmen	30 (26.8)	147 (44.4)	46 (42.6)	28 (66.7)	35 (29.2)	13 (17.3)	85 (26.5)	8 (14.5)	29 (9.5)	421 (28.6)
Freeborn	10 (8.9)	8 (2.4)	8 (7.4)	1 (2.4)	5 (4.2)	2 (2.7)	2 (.6)	1 (1.8)	6 (2.0)	43 (2.9)
Uncertain freeborn	46 (41.1)	99 (29.9)	46 (42.6)	13 (31.0)	54 (45.0)	11 (14.7)	28 (8.7)	3 (5.5)	32 (10.5)	332 (22.6)
Total	112 (100)	331 (100)	108 (100)	42 (100)	120 (100)	75 (100)	321 (100)	55 (100)	306 (100)	1,470 (100)

Note: Figures in parentheses are percentages.

Table 5.2 Occupations of Slaves, Freedmen, and Freeborn

	Legal Status					
Occupational Group	Slave	Uncertain Slave	Freedman	Freeborn	Uncertain Freeborn	Total
Building	19 (4.1)	7 (3.4)	30 (7.1)	10 (23.3)	46 (13.9)	112 (7.6)
Manufacture	52 (11.1)	25 (12.2)	147 (34.9)	8 (18.6)	99 (29.8)	331 (22.5)
Sales	3 (.6)	5 (2.4)	46 (10.9)	8 (18.6)	46 (13.9)	108 (7.3)
Banking	—	—	28 (6.7)	1 (2.3)	13 (3.9)	42 (2.9)
Professional service	15 (3.2)	11 (5.4)	35 (8.3)	5 (11.6)	54 (16.3)	120 (8.2)
Skilled service	37 (7.9)	12 (5.9)	13 (3.1)	2 (4.7)	11 (3.3)	75 (5.1)
Domestic service	129 (27.5)	77 (37.6)	85 (20.2)	2 (4.7)	28 (8.4)	321 (21.8)
Transportation	32 (6.8)	11 (5.4)	8 (1.9)	1 (2.3)	3 (.9)	55 (3.7)
Administration	182 (38.8)	57 (27.8)	29 (6.9)	6 (14.0)	32 (9.6)	306 (20.8)
Total	469 (100)	205 (100)	421 (100)	43 (100)	332 (100)	1,470 (100)

Note: Figures in parentheses are percentages.

by status among those to whom occupation was meaningful, albeit for different reasons. And, if, for slaves and often for freed slaves, work was externally determined, the table indicates what work they themselves chose to claim and what work they claimed relative to others. Because this perspective focuses on how those with different sets of rights, powers, and positions in the legitimate social order identified themselves, it reveals more clearly what different status groups did with what was given. It puts into question how recording work alters the representation of slave and ex-slave.

THE FREED ARTISAN: FRAMING A FREE PRESENT

In the occupational inscriptions, the freedman outside the large household is most often an artisan (44.9%, $N = 140$), and freedmen (49.1%, $N = 140$) are the largest group among nondomestic artisans (although the status pattern in particular kinds of artisanry varies; see Table 5.3).[5] Freed artisans outside the household are typical in another respect. Indication of a shop address and of the relations originating in slavery and manumission that form the context for freedmen's use of occupational title are particularly characteristic of their epitaphs; 39.3% ($N = 55$) gave a shop address with their occupational title, and 38.9% (51/131) of those who appear in epitaphs had clearly defined relations with a patron, *colliberti*, or both, frequently in the context of shop location. Another 13.7% ($N = 18$) had their own freedmen outside of any stated relations with *colliberti* or patron. Many *colliberti* and some patrons and freedmen in these epitaphs bear the same occupational titles.

Groups of freed artisans and their presence in the marketplace raise the specter of the satirist's Rome, where ex-slave and foreigner control economic activities. This vision must be readdressed before we can analyze the epitaphs of freed artisans, for how we read their epitaphs depends on how we understand the literary portrait of the freedman in the marketplace.

Juvenal is concerned with the freedman because of the shopkeeper's role in the plight of the poor freeborn Roman. The poverty of Juvenal's *ingenuus* (3.147–53) makes him an object of ridicule. He has become a victim (3.190–202, 234–48, 282–301), and the satirist's irate description of the "denizens of the marketplace" (3.21ff., 153ff.) shows how

Table 5.3 Occupations and Legal Status of Artisans Outside the Large Domestic Household

Artisan (Material or Product)	Legal Status					Total
	Slave	Uncertain Slave	Freedman	Freeborn	Uncertain Freeborn	
Jewelry	2 (8.3)	1 (4.2)	10 (41.7)	1 (4.2)	10 (41.7)	24 (100)
Metalware	3 (3.4)	5 (5.7)	53 (60.9)	2 (2.3)	24 (27.6)	87 (100)
Ivory and glass	—	—	8 (66.7)	—	4 (33.3)	12 (100)
Cloth	2 (5.7)	4 (11.4)	13 (37.1)	—	16 (45.7)	35 (100)
Clothing	2 (2.7)	10 (13.7)	38 (52.1)	3 (4.1)	20 (27.4)	73 (100)
Footwear	1 (14.3)	—	2 (28.6)	1 (14.3)	3 (42.9)	7 (100)
Leather	—	1 (25.0)	3 (75.0)	—	—	4 (100)
Food	1 (5.3)	3 (15.8)	7 (36.8)	1 (5.3)	7 (36.8)	19 (100)
Other	2 (8.3)	1 (4.2)	6 (25.0)	—	15 (62.5)	24 (100)
Total	13 (4.6)	25 (8.8)	140 (49.1)	8 (2.8)	99 (34.7)	285 (100)

Note: Figures in parentheses are row percentages.

they contribute to the poor man's degradation. The shop-keeper, whose livelihood depends on sales, reserves his ci-vility for those with money to spend (3.86–108, 212ff., 5.132–37). His behavior reinforces the perception that money is king in Rome (3.126ff.), and his neglect of the poor *ingenuus* can only make the latter aware of his poverty. The buyer feels powerless, and the seller appears powerful.

In reality, the freeborn victim cannot remedy his poverty, but in satire the poet can attack those who demoralize the freeborn—namely, the tradesman who had once been a slave. The satirist denigrates the behavior of the shopkeeper by exaggerating it as crass materialism and portraying it as servile.[6] The poet undermines the capacity of the freed shop-keeper to wound the freeborn consumer by depicting the shopkeeper's behavior as characteristic of the slave, a being without physical integrity. He reminds him that he had been merely the extension of another's existence, a person with-out honor or place in society. Thus, the unsuccessful *inge-nuus* asserts power over the object of his jokes who, he imag-ines, has degraded him; in literature, legal status turns the supposed aggressor into the victim.

The freedman was perhaps too visible. If the inscrip-tional evidence reflects the typical pattern in the small shop, it suggests that when residents of the city purchased some-thing, especially food or a luxury item, had their hair done, or used the services of a banker or money changer, they of-ten dealt with a freed slave. The person on whom the shop-keeper was dependent was not always so present, nor did his social status make him vulnerable. D'Arms has argued that while members of the privileged orders were in fact in-volved in commerce, their "involvement was indirect and discreet," leaving men of lower station, especially freedmen, "in the foreground."[7] Although few freedmen in this study can be directly connected with members of the senatorial order, the situation described by D'Arms bears comparison with the freed shopkeepers here, for many of them were not independent entrepreneurs. Thus, the satirist launched his attack on the man he could see, who, conveniently for his purposes, was not protected by legal privilege or social standing.

Visibility must be distinguished from real power. The freedman's visibility, which Juvenal and others may have translated into commercial dominance, depended on bonds that the ex-slave could not escape. For freed slaves, especially artisans and bankers, the shop frequently defined the setting in which they were closely tied with patron or more often with *colliberti,* relations arising directly from their status as ex-slaves. Groups of *colliberti* or of patron and freedmen with the same occupational title show that these relations shaped work relations and determined membership in a productive unit. Ex-slaves' participation in the marketplace stemmed from their legal condition, not their control of commerce or production.

The epitaphs of freed artisans describe the other side of visibility, the side unseen in Juvenal. They offer freedmen's depictions of themselves, indicating how the claim to work affects the presentation of their identity and the appearance of relations with patrons and fellow ex-slaves. In addition, the use of occupational title in this context reveals some of the dynamics of work and status. The portrait that emerges from the epitaphs bears almost no resemblance to that offered by the Roman satirist.

Focusing exclusively on the relations between patron and freedmen and among *colliberti,* Table 5.4 divides freed artisans into four types:[8]

(1) those who appear with both their patron and *colliberti,*
(2) those who appear with *colliberti* but not their patron,
(3) those who appear with their own freedmen but not their patron or *colliberti,* and
(4) those who appear with their patron but not *colliberti.*

Philusa, Hilarus, Anteros, and Felix, tailors on the Cermalus, part of the Palatine Hill (33920), exemplify freed artisans whose epitaphs show relations with both *colliberti* and patron (Type 1: 7.6% [N = 10], 10.9% [6/55] of those with shop location).

P · AVILLIO · P · L · MENANDRO PATRONO
POST MORTEM LIBERTI FECERUNT ET
SIBI I QUI INFRA SCRIPTI SUNT
Θ AVILLIA · P · L · PHILUSA
P · AVILLIUS · P · L · HILARUS
P · AVILLIUS · P · L · ANTEROS
P · AVILLIUS · P · L · FELIX
VESTE///RI DE CERMALO MINUSCULO A ////S OBE//

Table 5.4   Freed Artisans' Relations with Freedmen, *Colliberti*, and Patrons

						Artisan (Material or Product)				
Relations with	Jewelry	Metalware	Ivory and Glass	Cloth	Clothing	Footwear	Leather	Food	Other	Total
Freedmen	2 (11.1)	6 (12.5)	2 (25.0)	1 (8.3)	4 (10.5)	1 (50.0)	—	—	2 (33.3)	18 (13.7)
Colliberti	5 (50.0)	15 (31.3)	—	5 (41.7)	8 (21.1)	—	1 (33.3)	—	—	34 (26.0)
Patron and *colliberti*	—	4 (8.3)	—	1 (8.3)	4 (10.5)	—	—	—	1 (16.7)	10 (7.6)
Patron	—	3 (6.3)	—	—	2 (5.3)	—	1 (33.3)	—	1 (16.7)	7 (5.3)
Freedmen or *colliberti*?	—	2 (4.2)	1 (25.0)	—	1 (2.6)	—	—	—	—	4 (3.1)

Note: Figures in parentheses are column percentages only for artisans in epitaphs.

For Publius Avillius Menander, the freedman of Publius, patron, after his death his freedmen made (this) and for themselves who are named below: Avillia Philusa, the freedwoman of Publius (dead); Publius Avillius Hilarus, the freedman of Publius; Publius Avillius Anteros, the freedman of Publius; Publius Avillius Felix, the freedman of Publius; tailors on the smaller Cermalus.

(*CIL* 6.33920)

Of the ten freed artisans characterized by these relations, seven belonged to two groups of *colliberti* with the same occupational titles. The Avillii *vestiarii* (above) provided a tomb for themselves and their patron Menander, whose occupation they did not name. Naevii Eleuther, Narcissus, and Thesmus, makers of copper vessels (*aerarii vascularii*, 9138), their patron's heirs, dedicated a tomb for themselves, their patron L. Naevius Helenus (without occupational title), and their own freedmen.[9]

In these epitaphs, where *liberti* rather than *patroni* framed their own and their patrons' identities, occupation receives emphasis. The Avillii and Naevii linked themselves by their shared labor, while their relations as fellow ex-slaves are only implied in the reference to their patron. Even if shared work characterized the servile past, it is the salient element from that past that commemorates them at death. The patrons' lack of occupational title only emphasizes the freedmen's own association as fellow tailors or copper vessel makers. Even if Menander and Helenus were not themselves artisans, their interest in tailoring or copper ware is marked by having had several slaves in these trades.

The freedmen in this group of inscriptions did not detail their relationships with former masters, but the relations appear familial in the very Roman sense of the son in paternal power who accedes to the position of his *paterfamilias* on the latter's death. In all but one case, the patron relied on his freedmen for burial, although only in the epitaph dedicated by the Naevii *aerarii vascularii* is it clear that the *colliberti* carried out a stipulation in the patron's will (*ex testamento eius fecerunt*). As his heirs, Eleuther, Narcissus, and Thesmus stepped into their patron's place, unlike the freedmen of senators like Pliny or Dasumius, who received legacies but could not accede to their patrons' position.[10] The tailors on the Cermalus noted the status of their patron Menander, identifying him as a freed slave like themselves.

Whether they were his heirs or not, they, too, at least potentially, could fill his place in society.

I emphasize the freedmen's representation of themselves and their patrons rather than the intimacy and affection between freedman and patron, because assumptions about the latter can be drawn only from the terms of commemoration. Technically, Menander had the rights of a patron—*officium*, *obsequium*, and *operae* that, as pointed out in chapter 2, involved an element of coercion (although so, too, did the rights of the *paterfamilias*). The freed tailors presented a patron who, like themselves, was potentially subject to the claims of his own patron and to the social stigma attached to servile origin, and the epitaphs of both the tailors and the coppersmiths feature ex-slaves who could occupy the social position of their former masters. The Naevii, at least, had been granted the financial means to do so, and, like Helenus, they had become *patroni* themselves.

More frequently (Type 2: 26% [$N = 34$], 32.7% [18/55] of those with a shop location), artisans were buried with or by their *colliberti* without mention of a patron, as in the epitaph of Babbia Asia, Babbius Regillus, Plotius Nicepor, Plotius Anteros, and Plotius Felix, jewelers on the Sacred Way (9435) who misspell both their job title and "street."

V · BABBIA · Ɔ · L · ASIA
V · C · BABBIUS · Ɔ · L · REGILLUS
Θ · Q · PLOTIUS · Q L · NICEPOR
V · Q · PLOTIUS · Q · L · ANTEROS
V · Q · PLOTIUS · Q · L · FELIX
GEMARI DE SACRA VIAM

Babbia Asia, freedwoman of a woman (living); Gaius Babbius Regillus, freedman of a woman (living); Quintus Plotius Nicepor, freedman of Quintus (dead); Quintus Plotius Anteros, freedman of Quintus (living); Quintus Plotius Felix, freedman of Quintus (living); jewelers on the Sacred Way.

(*CIL* 6.9435)

Like the Avillii and Naevii, many (76.5%, $N = 26$) belonged to groups of *colliberti* with the same occupational title and a shared tomb. Although name, status indication, and the circumstances of commemoration point to their relationship as *colliberti*, they identified themselves as fellow artisans, some of whom worked in the same location, like the freed jewelers in this epitaph.

Technically, there are two groups of *colliberti* here, the freedman and freedwoman of a woman called Babbia, and the freedmen of Q. Plotius. Shared labor and workplace link the ex-slaves within each group and bring the two groups together. While Babbia and Q. Plotius may have had no close association, the parallel of a group of freed ironsmiths (*ferrarii*, 9398) bearing the nomina Titius or Fannius/a—the freedmen of a man T. Titius, a woman Fannia, or both—suggests that Babbia and Q. Plotius held their freedmen and resources in common.[11] The joint patronage of a man and woman immediately suggests a married couple, and the epitaph would seem to reflect one-half of a family business made up of patrons and freedmen.

If the arrangements of death mirror their lived experience, the *colliberti* with shared occupation worked together after manumission. Babbia and Plotius's claim to the labor of their ex-slaves provided an external and coercive condition for the maintenance of the group. Yet the epitaphs set by the Avillii and Naevii demonstrate that other *colliberti* remained together after the patron's death. The inheritance of the patron's resources, as in the case of the Naevii, will have been one reason. In some fields, shared resources, the patron's or those produced by the *colliberti* themselves, were necessary for carrying on the freedman's trade. Dyeing, for example, required an extensive plant and expensive materials, and an individual dyer would have been inhibited from working on his or her own. Eight of the forty-four freed artisans whose relations include *colliberti* had their own freedmen, indicating the possession of property and potentially the control of a labor force such as they may have been for their patrons.[12]

The affinities and allegiances generated by working together could have been another factor in the group's continuing association. Although feelings are notoriously difficult to assess in epitaphs, we can track how work experience will have been reinforced by family and marital relations. Three groups of *colliberti* with shared occupation (9435, 9398, 33920) include both men and women. These *colliberti* named only their working relationship, but the epitaphs of other freed artisans point to multiple bonds. The latter, too, record relations with *colliberti*, patrons, or both; however, here it is clear that freed artisans also had relatives and spouses among their fellow ex-slaves.[13]

In this context, the marriage patterns among all freed artisans are very suggestive. Those with clearly identified spouses generally married their fellow ex-slaves or patrons. In cases where the spouse seems to be a *libertus/a*, he or she originally may have been a *conservus/a* whose freedom was purchased by his or her partner.[14] Seventeen freed artisans appear with a member of the opposite sex in circumstances that immediately suggest marriage. Here, too, the possible spouse was a fellow ex-slave, freed slave, or patron.[15]

It should be stressed that, although the latter epitaphs certainly describe shared lives, these partners were not claimed as spouses. Veturia D. l. Fedra, a freed dyer in the area of the Marian monuments (*purpuraria Marianeis*, 37820), defines the relationship with such a partner. Out of her own funds, Fedra paid for a tomb for herself, her patron, her *collibertus* Nicepor, and the freedman she shared with her fellow ex-slave.[16] She used a particular, though not uncommon, expression for marriage: "Nicepor fellow ex-slave lived with me twenty years" (Nicepor conlibertus vixit mecum annos XX).

Fedra's terms seem particularly appropriate for those fellow ex-slaves who bore the same occupational title, regardless of their technical familial ties. Perhaps they expressed their living together in shared work, or, for them, working together involved living together.[17] Their original constitution as a group lay in their ex-master's hands, yet shared work meant conversation, interaction, and cooperation as well as time spent together, and the shared activity and time are commemorated in their epitaphs and frame their identities at death.

M·SERGIUS · M·L	M·SERGIO · M·L
EUTYCHUS	PHILOCALO
AXEARIUS SIBI·ET	AXEARIO paTRON

Marcus Sergius Eutychus, the freedman of Marcus, axle maker, (made this) for himself and for (his) patron Marcus Sergius Philocalus, the freedman of Marcus, axle maker.

(*CIL* 6.9215)

Here, the axle maker M. Sergius Eutychus dedicates a tomb to himself and his patron, the axle maker M. Sergius Philocalus, himself a freedman. Eighteen freed artisans, like Philocalus, appear in epitaphs that name freedmen individually or by the formula *libertis libertabusque* (Type 3). Freed artisans with their own freedmen and without mention of *colliberti* shift attention to the freedman in the role of patron, to Philocalus rather than Eutychus. However, it is difficult to discuss Philocalus without Eutychus. Some patrons, like Philocalus, had freedmen with occupational title, and these freedmen $(N = 7)$ appear among artisans characterized by relations with patrons (Type 4). Since the latter represent the other side of the relationship of a freed patron and his or her freedmen, both types of relations are considered together.

In seven of the eleven cases where a patron's freedmen are named individually, the circumstances of death suggest a special tie between ex-master and ex-slave. Like the Avillii *vestiarii*, the ex-slave(s) (in one case acting with the patron's wife) buried their freed patron.[18] It is uncertain whether the artisan-patron lacked or had lost the family members who were normally responsible for commemoration, but the absence of such relations is conspicuous. No family is mentioned for five patrons; another (9547) is commemorated by spouse and freedmen; and the other (9971) appears with his young sons.

The freedmen, then, presented at death their freed artisan-patrons, and in doing so, they reformulated the relationship of patron and freedman. For all the freedmen-commemorators, the patron was an artisan and, like themselves, an ex-slave. Eutychus carried the identification with his patron even further. By noting his own occupational title as well, he presented his patron as he presented himself—an ex-slave with a particular livelihood, the same as his own. Perhaps Eutychus inscribes in the language of death the skeleton of a story not unlike the one A. T. Jones tells of his brother, the slave apprentice who became a partner in his ex-master's millwork business.

While patronal claims should not be discounted, these epitaphs of artisan-patrons commemorated by their freedmen record a different context for the relations of patron and freedman than that of the tailor T. Statilius T. l. Hilarus

(6373, Cor(vini) *vest(iarius)*) and his patron Taurus Statilius Corvinus, consul A.D. 45.[19] Hilarus, buried in the Monumentum Statiliorum, worked for his consular patron; manumission could never make him Corvinus's equal. Eutychus and Philocalus lived in a social world where the ex-slave never had Trimalchio's problems in becoming what his patron was. In the occupational epitaphs, work, not simply legal status, critically alters the representation of the relationship of patron and freedman. At death, shared occupation and legal condition make them social peers. What is displayed, too, suggests a different productive relationship: ex-master and ex-slave practiced the same trade whether as partners or as employer and employee.

Like the commemoration made by Cameria Iarine (below), epitaphs that include the artisan's own freedmen and women as well as his or her *colliberti*, patron, or both reveal the potential for these working relations to extend over generations of manumission.[20]

*cameri*A L · L IARINE · FECIT
*l. cam*E R I O ·L·L·T H R A S O N I·P A T R O N O
et L · C A M E R I O · L · L · A L E X A N D R O
PATRONO · EIUS ET
*l. c*A M E R I O · O N E S I M O · L I B · E T
*vi*RO · S U O · POSTERISQUE · OMNIBUS
*vest*IARIIS · TENUARIIS · DE · VICO · TUSC

Cameria Iarine, freedwoman of Lucius, made (this) for (her) patron Lucius Camerius Thraso, freedman of Lucius, and for his patron Lucius Camerius Alexander, freedman of Lucius, and for her freedman and husband Lucius Camerius Onesimus and for all (their?) descendants. Tailors of fine clothing on Tuscan Street.

(*CIL* 6.37826)

Cameria Iarine dedicated a tomb to her patron (Camerius Thraso), her patron's patron (Camerius Alexander), and her own freedman and husband (Camerius Onesimus). The men all shared a trade and a workplace. While it is not clear whether they made and sold fine clothing in the same shop on the Vicus Tuscus, Iarine joined them as a group. Whatever the particular arrangements, occupation passed from patron to freedman to freedwoman's freedman; slavery and manumission by a particular master determined occupation and perhaps inclusion in a productive unit.

The presentation of these artisans, however, has implications other than the patron's control of his freedman's labor. Although Iarine clearly articulated the respective ranks of Alexander, Thraso, and Onesimus, she gave patron and freedman the same social identity—freedman and tailor of fine clothing. And, in fact, the epitaph makes it clear that Thraso had become what Alexander had been, a freed tailor on the Vicus Tuscus with his own freed slave.

Ten freed artisan-patrons (or their spouses) commemorated their ex-slave(s) or included them in the tomb with the formula *libertis libertabusque*.[21] Where freed patrons commemorated themselves and dedicated tombs that included their freedmen by formula, they portrayed themselves as the head of some establishment. In all ten cases, however, the evidence of death shows households composed primarily of patron, spouse, and freedmen, and only infrequently family beyond a spouse.[22]

The epitaph dedicated by Pompeia Memphis (37781) indicates the shape of these establishments and suggests the background of the Babbii and Plotii *gemmarii:* a household composed of artisan, spouse, and freedmen (his, hers, and theirs) who were involved in their patrons' business.

POMPE*ia mem*PHIS · FECIT · SIBI · ET
CN · POMPEIO · IUCUNDO · CONIUGI
SUO · AURIFICI · VIXIT · ANNOS · XXXV · ET
CN · POMPEIO · FRUCTO · LIBERTO · SUO
AURIFICI · VIXIT · ANNOS · XXXX · ET · LIBERTIS
LIBERTABUSQUE · SUIS · POSTERISQUE · EORU

Pompeia Memphis made (this) for herself and for her husband Gnaeus Pompeius Iucundus, goldsmith, (who) lived thirty-five years, and for her freedman Gnaeus Pompeius Fructus, goldsmith, (who) lived forty years, and for her freedmen and freedwomen and their descendants.

(*CIL* 6.37781)

The shared nomen of wife and husband points to their relation as *colliberti*. By the time of Iucundus's death, the couple had their own freedmen, one of whom was named apparently because of his timely death. Fructus, the freedman of Memphis, was a goldsmith like his patrona's husband, and their occupational titles associate Memphis, wife and patrona, with the productive activities of husband and freedman.

Married artisans with their own freedmen outline situations parallel to that of Memphis, Iucundus, and Fructus and point to the missing patrons of the Babbii and Plotii *gemmarii*. There are sixty-three couples of free status (freed, freeborn, and uncertain freeborn) where one or both partners were artisans (regardless of other social relations). In twenty-three cases, one or both spouses made a claim to freedmen. Most frequently (12), the individual with the occupational title made the commemoration, and the freedmen named individually or by formula refer to his or her patronage, although in the example of Veturia D. l. Fedra noted above, the freedman owed his manumission to both spouses. When the artisan's spouse (usually a wife since most entitled artisans were men) dedicated the tomb, the claim to the freedmen in the formula is hers, as in the case of Memphis and Fructus. Dedications by or to both partners give both a claim to the freedmen.

The case of the ivorist P. Clodius A. et Clodiae l. Bromus (*eborarius*, 9375) reflects the configurations of the household businesses of artisan-patrons. His status indication tells us that Bromus was freed by a couple—a woman named Clodia and a man with the praenomen Aulus.[23] The ivorist repeated the pattern of joint manumission in his own household. He and his concubine Curiatia Ammia shared a freedman—P. Clodius P. et Curiatiae l. Rufio, whose name records their patronage. Further, Bromus and Ammia each manumitted a slave: the ivorist's ex-slave, P. Clodius P. l. Heraclida, bore his nomen, and Ammia's ex-slave, Suavis Curiatiae l., would have taken her nomen.

Half of the couples under discussion here, like Memphis and Iucundus, had the same nomen, so their freedmen will not have been distinguished by nomen. Where couples had different nomina, like Bromus and Ammia, and where patronage in certain cases was not shared, the freedmen in their households will have had different nomina, and the shape of the household will have been clear. The jeweler M. Lollius Alexander (9433, *gemmarius*) and his wife Flavia Sabina dedicated a tomb that included their freedmen and women (*libertis libertabusque*); the latter will have been named Lollius/a or Flavius/a, depending on whether they had been manumitted by Alexander or Sabina. A couple like them, perhaps, were the patrons of the Babbii and Plotii *gemmarii*—the half of a family business that is missing in the epitaph of the *colliberti*.

Some of the couples with their own freedmen began their relationship in slavery, and they should be associated with artisans who had relations with both *colliberti* and freedmen. Of the twelve couples with the same nomen, eight were *colliberti* or bore the same nomen where neither had status indication. In another case, the artisan's wife was his freedwomen (9975). In the others, the wife's precise non-familial relationship with her artisan-husband is unclear—*colliberta, liberta* of the artisan's *collibertus*, or ex-slave of those related to the artisan's patron.[24] For the purposes of analysis, *colliberti* with their own freedmen have been placed in a separate category on the basis of their relations with their fellow ex-slaves, but, in fact, their social relations are analogous to those of the artisan couples with their own freedmen.

Consideration of the artisan-*colliberti* in light of these couples outlines more fully a movement from one social and productive configuration to another, which perpetuated relations formed in the past. Some artisans began work in their patron's shop or with a group of *colliberti*. Later, they had their own freedmen; in some cases, patronage was shared with *colliberti*, one of whom may have been a spouse. Other freed artisans apparently remained in their patron's shops or with a group of fellow ex-slaves. In some instances, an epitaph discloses multiple and overlapping relationships. In others, an epitaph seems to capture only one moment in a continuing process, and the presentation of an individual will depend on what period in his or her biography is commemorated. Or, as pointed out below, these epitaphs may reflect individual links in networks of artisans joined by ties originating in slavery.

Roman epitaphs depict women as active workers,[25] and some female artisans participated in the relations I have outlined. Several belonged to groups of *colliberti* all of whom have the same occupational title, like the Babbii and Plotii *gemmarii* (9435), the Avillii *vestiarii* (33920), and the Titii and Fannii *ferrarii* (9398). Others appear as one partner of a couple, both of whom have occupational title: Fulvia Melema *brattiaria* (goldbeater) with C. Fulcinius C. l. Hermeros *brattiarius* (9211) and Septicia A. l. Rufa *brattiaria* with

A. Septicius A. l. Apollonius *brattiarius* (6939). Like Susan Treggiari, I suspect that the pairs were married, but, in fact, the bond expressed in their epitaphs was not marriage but that of shared work.[26] Rufa and Apollonius, who were probably *colliberti*, resemble on a smaller scale the groups of *colliberti* that include female artisans.

The circumstances of women entitled "artisan" serve as a background for Cameria Iarine and especially Pompeia Memphis. Neither woman bears an occupational title, yet each had a freedman in a husband's or patron's trade. Treggiari has suggested that Iarine and women like her may have been "involved in the trade, at least as links, if not as active workers."[27] The situation of Pompeia Memphis as the probable *colliberta* of her husband compares with that of Septicia Rufa, the goldbeater, and Avillia Philusa, the tailor; Memphis, too, may have been an artisan or may have belonged to a group of *colliberti* like the Avillii. Her goldsmith freedman certainly marks her own involvement in her husband's livelihood. Other *colliberti* had their own freedmen, and it is tempting to see Memphis and her husband Iucundus, with what seems to be their shared servile past, as a couple who emerged from a group of *colliberti* like the Avillii or who had been the freed half of their own patron's family business. Revealing the complexities of relations based in manumission and slavery, these women figured in a continuing process in which occupation passed from patron to freedman and in which *colliberti* worked together and in turn used their own freedmen in their trade.

At death, women like Memphis, Iarine, Philusa, and Rufa occupied positions analogous to those of the men of their class. Since Memphis and Iarine dedicated the epitaphs, they were not only the links between male artisans—they themselves articulated the connections between the men. Philusa and Rufa shared work, a common legal condition, and a servile past with men. In a sense foreign to the higher ranks of Roman society, where women were not publicly associated with men in their magisterial or military roles, these women, at least in death, were linked with their male counterparts more than they were links between them.

Where freed and uncertain freeborn artisans practiced the same trade and bore the same nomen but appear in different epitaphs, the relations originating in slavery and

manumission seem to have connected artisans in some sort
of networks. The multiple relations that we have observed
in the epitaphs of freed artisans prepared the ground for such
associations. Here, more than in any other situation, the
evidence of death shapes our vision of this level of society.
By dividing artisans by place and circumstances of burial,
the epitaphs construct as discrete units what well may have
formed a cohesive whole.

Although Loane has discussed many of the relevant epitaphs, a comprehensive study would enlarge our understanding of these networks and the organization of trade and labor
in the city.[28] Looking at the recurrence of particular nomina
in the same or related trades, we should consider the names
of spouses, marriage patterns, and the configurations of social relations evident in the inscriptions.

The epitaphs and dedications of the cloak makers (*sagarii*) provide a simple illustration. While seven nomina are
found among the fifteen *sagarii*, nine men have either the
nomen Cornelius (one Aulus and three Quinti) or the name
Lucius Sallvius.[29] The five Sallvii appear in three different
epitaphs:

(1) L. Sall[v]ius L. l. Nasta (7971)
(2–4) L. Sallvius L. l. Theuda,
L. Sallvius L. l. Ascla,
L. Sallvius L. l. Gatta (9870 = 37378)
(5) L. Sal[l]vius L. l. Suneros (9871)

Suneros (5) was interred with a woman who well may have
been his wife, and Nasta (1) had his own burial plot of twelve
by twenty-one Roman feet. The other three, Theuda, Ascla,
and Gatta (2–4), apparently *colliberti* (although, as in other
epitaphs, this relationship is not explicitly stated), form a
group sharing a burial space of eleven by twenty Roman
feet. The evidence of death separates Suneros, Nasta, and
the *colliberti* in 9870, but name, status, and occupation
connect them. As Loane has suggested for the Cornelii *sagarii*, the freedmen may have worked in a chain of different
shops owned by their patron, although only Suneros noted a
specific location. Perhaps they acted as "branch offices" of
a family business, a situation that has been suggested for
some of the *unguentarii* (perfumers) and *thurarii* (incense
dealers). Or they may have been *colliberti* who, by the

time of their deaths, worked in separate establishments, or the freedmen of patrons who were themselves connected by family ties or the relations generated by slavery and manumission.[30]

Artisans' epitaphs pose a problem of interpretation. The frequent use of occupational title where associations with patrons, *colliberti*, and freedmen were so often intertwined sets work relations firmly within a freed slave's social context. Artisans with the same nomen and occupation who are separated by burial only reinforce the impression that productive activities depended on connections made in slavery and by manumission. At points, the epitaphs convey a world closed off to those who did not participate in these relationships. Like Juvenal's freeborn narrator, we could assert that freedmen dominated artisanry. However, what is visible allows another reading. If the productive organization of these artisans depended on manumission and the relations of patrons and freedmen, these bonds not only kept others out, they kept freedmen in. Where freedmen have their own freedmen, the process has not ended but extended to another generation. Finally, it should be clear that where we find freed artisans, we often do not really have free labor.

The dynamics of status and work, however, should not obscure how freedmen's use of occupational title affects their representation of themselves and their situation. As suggested in chapter 2, title altered the marginal position implicit in the conditions of freed status by placing the ex-slave in the center of a world defined by productive activities. Among artisans, occupational title appears to refine or recast conditions that were externally imposed on the freed slave. In the first place, title joined fellow ex-slaves: at death, *colliberti* expressed their relations in terms of work, leaving implicit their experience in a common servile past. They chose neither their trades nor their relations with one another; these were given. How they presented themselves, as fellow jewelers, tailors, and tradesmen, took what was given and reshaped it into an identity based on shared activity.

Second, freedmen with their patron's occupational title made the same *active* connection with the world as their patrons. Although they often may have occupied the position of employee, bound by *obsequium, officium,* and *ope-*

rae to their ex-masters, they portrayed themselves as what their patrons were, artisans and often freedmen. They may have identified the activity valued by the artisan-patron and, like the domestic servants to be considered next, expressed their own importance in relation to the patron. Yet, unlike domestic servants, they were not instrumental in upholding a social position to which they could never aspire. The presentation of self by these artisans associates patron and freedman through work; the freed slave's use of occupational title displays the possibility of acceding to the patron's place.

Finally, where freed artisans presented themselves (or were presented by spouses) as patrons, occupational title appears to have named their role as the head of an establishment composed primarily of freedmen. Where freed patrons were associated with *colliberti*, especially where a *collibertus/a* was a spouse, they may well have emerged from a situation where their identity as artisans tied them to familial relations and where artisan, freedman, or both had been the identity of their own patrons. Unlike Trimalchio, these freed artisans, in their own world, had "arrived."[31]

THE DOMESTIC SERVANT: REFRAMING THE TERMS OF POWER AND DEPENDENCE

The typical slave with a job title worked in a large domestic household; most often, he or she claimed to administer the property of the upper classes (32.6%, $N = 112$) or to maintain their persons and households (31.1%, $N = 107$). While most domestic servants were slaves (67.3%), many of the freedmen in elite households (43.1%, $N = 47$) named this type of work, although freed claims to domestic service depend on the large proportion of freedwomen in child care (42.6%, 20/47). Because gender and status differentiate those in child care from domestic servants as such, the former are omitted from this discussion of domestic servants.[32] Other freed servants are considered, because they reveal what happened to the slave who gained his or her freedom yet remained in the same work environment.

The maintenance of the household defined the work of the men and women in domestic service (see Table 5.5). Bodyguards (*germani*) are found outside of the *familia Caesaris* (the emperor's slaves and freedmen) only in the house-

Table 5.5 Occupations and Legal Status of
Domestic Servants in Large Households

	Legal Status			
Occupation	Slave	Freedman	Uncertain Freeborn	Total
Bodyguards	10 (100)	—	—	10 (100)
Personal and room servants	53 (89.8)	6 (10.2)	—	59 (100)
Cooks	5 (55.6)	4 (44.4)	—	9 (100)
Provisioners	9 (81.8)	2 (18.2)	—	11 (100)
Caretakers (house and objects)	21 (77.8)	6 (22.2)	—	27 (100)
Social organization	4 (44.4)	4 (44.4)	1 (11.1)	9 (100)
Total	102 (81.6)	22 (17.6)	1 (.8)	125 (100)

Note: Figures in parentheses are row percentages.

hold of the Statilii (6221, 6229–37). Personal and room
servants whose labor was oriented directly toward the slaveholder include personal attendants, bedchamber servants,
waiters, and carvers. Other servants were assigned to the
household infirmary.[33] In addition, there were cooks (coqui,
coci) and those who provisioned the household or were in
charge of its stores (cellarius, a cella?, fartor, a frumento).
The term "caretakers" refers to those who tended areas of
the house or specific objects. The former were doorkeepers
(ostiarii), the majordomo and those whose tasks involved
cleaning and maintenance (atrienses), and gardeners whose
work, of course, took place outside the physical confines of
the house. Although not as elaborate as the imperial household, the staff assigned to specific objects in private households show a woman in charge of mirrors or a mirror holder
(? a speculum [sic], 7297), a pearl keeper (ad margarita,
7884), clothes keepers and wardrobe guardians (a veste
[6372, 6374], vestispica [33393, 33395], cistarius [7601]),
and clothes folders and pressers (vestiplicus/a, 7301, 9901).[34]
In some of these jobs, the maintenance of things will have
overlapped with personal service, and these servants should
be associated with hairdressers serving as maids (ornatrices)
and the masseur and masseuse (unctor, unctrix) who min-
istered to the physical needs of the served. The men in social

organization dealt with outsiders and kept order within the household. Announcers (*nomenclatores*) accompanied their masters, telling them the names of individuals they encountered. An attendant for the household's slave children was also in charge of his master's guests (7290, *ab hospitiis et paedagogus puerorum*). The *silentiarius* (6217) was supposed to maintain order among the staff.

These domestic servants lived in the world of the served, and if Roman authors do not perfectly represent that world, their words assume its conditions and structures. They inevitably characterize servants' work and locate servants in particular relations with the served. Roman authors describe the world that was given for servants: some of the conditions of their work, the attitudes they faced, the master's vision of them, and his social and material requirements.

In his famous discussion of the relations of masters and slaves (*Ep.* 47.2–8), Seneca catalogs the duties of domestic servants as the fulfillment of physical appetites and demands. Some cater to the most basic, and base, physical conditions—mopping up vomited food, cleaning up the leftovers of the banquet, carving poultry and meats in an elaborate fashion, serving the master his wine at the table, and satisfying his sexual desires in the bedroom. The existence of all servants is focused on the master. A good example of domestics, Seneca's provisioner pleases by satisfying eyes, mouths, and stomachs. He can succeed only by careful study of the served, by an attentive orientation toward another.

> Think also of the poor purveyors of food, who note their masters' tastes with delicate skill, who know what special flavours will sharpen their appetite, what will please their eyes, what new combinations will rouse their cloyed stomachs, what food will excite their loathing through sheer satiety, and what will stir them to hunger on that particular day.

> Adice obsonatores, quibus dominici palati notitia subtilis est, qui sciunt, cuius illum rei sapor excitet, cuius delectet aspectus, cuius novitate nauseabundus erigi possit, quid iam ipsa satietate fastidiat, quid illo die esuriat.

> (*Ep.* 47.8, trans. Loeb)

In Seneca's portrait of the night owl Sextus Papinius (*Ep.* 122.15–16), the master's demands, reasonable or unreasonable, take precedence over any other activity or schedule.

Papinius begins his day around 8:00 P.M. by punishing slaves: when his neighbor inquires what is going on, he is told Papinius is going over his accounts. At midnight, he exercises his voice. At 2:00 A.M., he goes out for a drive. At dawn, the *pueri*, presumably waiters and attendants, are called; cooks and provisioners are thrown into commotion by their master's desires: Papinius has left his bath and wants something to eat and drink.

Informed by an assumption of the servant's proximity to his master, such descriptions attribute an indefinite quality to domestic service. Seneca names specific jobs but makes it clear that set tasks, schedules, and locations were subsumed under the master's demands, which could breach defined functions and more generally the very definition of a job. For Seneca, waiter, carver, cook, and provisioner were all doing the same thing, catering to their master's physical needs however and whenever they were expressed.

Here, as in the works of other authors, the servant is used to construct a criticism of the served whose behavior is at issue. Seneca's provisioner and his fellows frame the portrait of a man who disdains to eat with the slaves who wait on him; he is cruel, inhuman, proud, and ignorant of both his slaves' humanity and the arbitrary turns of fortune that could place him in their position. Papinius's scrambling domestics form the scenery of an irregular life, disapproved of by Seneca. Where the master is lowborn, he is ridiculed for relying on servants for a sense of self-importance and a display of usurped standing.[35]

For Seneca, the irregularity of Papinius's life lies in his nocturnal schedule, not in the frantic efforts of his servants. Seneca criticizes cruelty, maltreatment, and the base object of the labor that slaves perform, but he does not question the pattern of pleasing. The structure of the situation persists even where the master is humane and rational. Pliny, a kind and liberal master who did not indulge in the kind of physical excess described by Seneca, nonetheless assessed domestics by their obedience, attention to masters and guests, and ability to please (*Ep.* 1.4). More than a display of wealth, servants, unlike estates and precious objects, constantly acted out their owner's importance; giving primacy to the slaveholder's desires, they were a living demonstration of his centrality.

In the slaveholder's view, the master's ability to incul-
cate fear was instrumental in his gaining satisfaction. When
Seneca (*Ep.* 47.17–19) advocated instilling respect rather
than fear in slaves, he had to counter what appears to have
been a commonly held perspective: constant fear keeps the
servant in line. Complaining about the service of his own
domestic staff, Pliny (*Ep.* 1.4) comments that fear loses its
effect among the slaves of indulgent masters (mitium domi-
norum apud servos ipsa consuetudine metus exolescit). They
have no apprehension about the consequences of not pleasing. Papinius begins his day punishing his slaves for their
failures of the preceding day (night?); Juvenal's grande dame
(6.489–95) whips her maid for a curl that will not fall into
place; Martial (8.23) beats his cook for an unsatisfactory
meal.[36]

For house servants especially, work is depicted as, and no
doubt in reality often became, an extension of the relations
of domination. The slave was always vulnerable to the exercise of power within the master's right as owner. Seneca's
emphasis (*De Ira* 3.32.1) on the master's *self*-control makes
clear how the master's irritation about unrelated matters
might be visited on the slave. Behind every order lay the
threat of punishment for failure, real or imagined. Living under their master's roof, domestic servants were always available to command and within reach of a moody owner; avoid-
ance of a flogging as well as the hope of reward made
obedience, responsive service, and pleasing necessary. Isaac
Throgmorton's words provide an instructive comparison: he
felt free as a barber in the marketplace among freemen and
a slave when he worked "close round" his master. Throgmorton cites the change from shop to household as one of
the reasons he ran away. The master's corporal power and
proximity meant that work seemed inextricably intertwined
with the slave's subjection to his or her master.[37]

The ability to command good service and evoke fear offered the slaveholder not only a sense of importance but an
experience of power that Seneca describes as kingly.

> We don the temper of kings. For they, too, forgetful alike of
> their own strength and of other men's weakness, grow white-
> hot with rage, as if they had received an injury, when they are
> entirely protected from danger of such injury by their exalted
> station. They are not unaware that this is true, but finding fault

they seize upon opportunities to do harm; they insist that they have received injuries, in order that they may inflict them.

Regum nobis induimus animos. Nam illi quoque obliti et suarum virium et inbecillitatis alienae sic excandescunt, sic saeviunt, quasi iniuriam acceperint, a cuius rei periculo illos fortunae suae magnitudo tutissimos praestat. Nec hoc ignorant, sed occasionem nocendi captant querendo: acceperunt iniuriam ut facerent.

(*Ep.* 47.20, trans. Loeb)

Seneca's metaphor associates the slaveholder's power with position in a larger social order. The slaveholders under consideration here were members of the elite, not kings. Under the republic, none could be king; under the principate, only one. Yet, potentially, every household made its master a ruler.

Structurally, slaves, especially those, like domestic servants, most visible to others, served an important function in the sensibilities of power, because the experience of dominance was circumscribed in imperial Rome even, and perhaps particularly, for senators whose history and class values associated command and standing. The freeborn, defined by their physical integrity, could not be exploited by a direct exercise of power in order to make the elite feel like an elite; however, nothing inhibited such a use of the slave, who lacked physical integrity. "Slavery permitted the ostentatious display of wealth in the palaces of the rich without involving the direct degradation of the free poor."[38] As in other slave societies, standing could be achieved by a demonstration of absolute control over natally alienated outsiders: according to Patterson, "power over slaves, then, was both the direct exercise and enjoyment of power and an investment in the means of reproducing and accumulating power over others."[39]

In other ways, however, imperial senators were cut off from experiences of power available to their republican predecessors, for the principate limited the magistrate's and general's exercise of authority. The senatorial loss of real political power need not be repeated here, but the display of wealth that remained has a particular structural significance. When wealth included slaves, what remained, in the absence of other forms of power, was a visceral experience of command. Although the state regulated the abuse of slaves over the course of the principate, it never disturbed slaveholders' total control over their human property or the enjoyment of power available in the ownership of slaves.

Ironically, the master's control of the slave and his enjoyment of dominance was thrown into high relief by a characterization of the relations of senator and princeps that emphasized physical vulnerability and fear. The senatorial class faced a princeps with the capacity to reward those who supported him and to punish enemies or the recalcitrant. Control of the army made this capacity a physical one. Tacitus eloquently describes the compulsion experienced in the face of such power, the necessity to please, and fear, raising the dynamics of slave and master to another social level. The restructuring of power and the need to find a pattern of behavior appropriate to class standing, yet at the same time safe, placed the senator in the position of the slave—or, more important, this was how he understood it.[40]

In this context, the consular's ridicule of the wealthy freedman has an unspoken urgency. Petronius's Trimalchio commands his domestic servants; they enable him to exercise a power that he lacks because his freed status bars him from public office. By threatening to punish a cook or waiter for a lapse of service (49, 52), he can feel and act like a member of an elite. Further, his domestic servants allow for a public demonstration of a power that distinguishes Trimalchio as a "big man" and sets him above his fellows.

The power over slaves enjoyed by Trimalchio is not wrong in itself; its exercise in the hands of a freedman disturbs Petronius. He makes Trimalchio look ridiculous by exaggerating the ex-slave's need to display his power. In the absence of birth and office, Trimalchio has wealth, and the only wealth that gives him an arena for the exercise of power lies in his human property. Trimalchio's display merely highlights his former dishonor as an object of another's exertion of power. Yet the consular had, and perhaps needed for his own sense of place, his creature's command over slaves, or perhaps the emperor's senator could too easily change places with Trimalchio's servant. Petronius's ridicule undermines the satisfaction of freedman and emperor in the demonstration of command; it also distances the consular from the structural similarity to his own situation.

Roman authors, many of whom had house servants, denigrated domestic labor, at least theoretically, or espoused philosophical positions that robbed it of importance. While Cicero (*Pis.* 67) criticizes Piso's lack of proper servants, he also expresses great disdain for those who actually labored to meet another's physical pleasures and needs (*Off.* 1.150). Juvenal tends to reduce all sorts of work to pleasing and then mercilessly satirizes those who try to please. Seneca (*Ep.* 47.6) pities the carver (*infelix*) whom necessity has forced to perform such base and meaningless labor, yet it is his own philosophical position that defines such labor as insignificant. According to Seneca, physical needs enslave us all, but, he advises Lucilius, we must try to free ourselves from them and from the tyranny of possessions (*Ep.* 14.1–2, 104.34, 110.14ff., 115); so much the more worthless is work devoted to the care of physical needs.

The man guilty of *luxus*, whose every whim and appetite are satisfied by a slave, does not simply ignore Seneca's good advice; he discloses the implications of living nobly that are masked in the denigration of the servant's labor and the philosophical positions that perceive it as unimportant. In effect, living nobly, so necessary for class position, meant not doing, relying on servants to do what the man of standing could not. However, this could give the appearance of powerlessness, softness, or impotence. The man who revels in luxury acts out the master's inactivity and upper-class reliance on slaves. His lack of bodily self-control puts him into the hands of those he should command and makes him appear as the cared for, not the caretaker. Dependence, however, is displaced by portraying the served as decadent and by constructing a moral practice that makes the servant's labor unnecessary. The master in control of himself cannot be seen to depend on the slave for services that are not essential.

The master's lack of dependence on his slave is reinforced by removing the slave's work from the category of *beneficia*, acts that elicit a reciprocal response. According to the common perception as articulated by Seneca, tasks performed by someone other than a man's slave are considered favors (*beneficia*), but the same tasks performed by a slave are merely the services of a servant (*ministeria*). The distinction lies in the element of coercion.

For a benefit is something which someone has given when he was allowed not to give. However, the slave does not have the power to refuse, so he does not offer a favor, he only obeys. Nor can he claim that he has done something when he was unable not to do it.

> Beneficium enim id est, quod quis dedit, cum illi liceret et non dare; servus autem non habet negandi potestatem; ita non praestat, sed paret, nec id se fecisse iactat, quod non facere non potuit.
>
> (*Ben.* 3.19.1)[41]

Similar assumptions inform Juvenal's ridicule of the work he reduces to pleasing. Pleasing requires base flattery and duplicity; it is servile, because no one acts this way unless compelled, and those who act under compulsion are slaves.

Further, Roman senators envisioned the slave, not the master, as dependent. For Seneca (*Tranq.* 8.8), slaves must be fed, clothed, and cared for. They are a burden, and they impose obligations that cannot be denied. One *must* use their services. Pliny's account of his slaves' privilege of making a will (*Ep.* 8.16) depicts him as the caretaker and his slaves as the cared for. He appears as the permissive master; his complaints (*Ep.* 1.4) that his slaves deal with him without fear and almost indifferently are lighthearted, even boastful. Indeed, Pliny (*Ep.* 5.19.1) sees himself as something of an indulgent father, a role he values and seems to enjoy.

Paternal care implied control, but it covered the enjoyment of power with an aura of responsibility and kindness. The removal of the slave's service from the category of *beneficia* heightened the effect of any humane gesture of the master. The master's behavior toward the slave resulted, not from appropriate reciprocation for a service rendered, but from his kind, indulgent nature or his deeply felt sense of duty.[42] The master's reliance on the slave for his physical maintenance and the demonstration of his standing finds no place in the ethos of Roman paternalism. Indeed, Roman masters were inhibited from acknowledging their dependence, because such a recognition would undermine the implied centrality of their needs and the experience of power available in the violation of slaves' physical integrity as well as in the supposed provision of care.

The large proportion of men and women who claimed

jobs in domestic service seems particularly striking in light of their portrayal by Roman authors: seemingly, their titles would express the immediacy of their subjection to their masters and define them as those who satisfied another's needs. Such a reading, of course, adopts the perspective of the slaveholder: it tends to collapse all domestic work into a form of pleasing and imagines that the servant accepts his or her own subjection. Servants themselves, who occupied a different position in the power relationship, could be expected to have viewed their masters and their work differently. If the epitaphs of domestics are read in terms of their position in the relations of server and served, the identities framed by servants and their peers in the household who would have had parallel experiences seem to encode two messages. One refers to the master: it responds to the slaveholder's perspective on the servant's work and counters the image of the servant created in literature. The other speaks about servants' relations with fellow slaves and ex-slaves working in the same household.

The very use of job titles claims a specific type of work, not the general function of pleasing. Although we cannot recover some of the precise variations of duties, the titles denoted distinct functions for their audience. Moreover, both slaves and ex-slaves in identifiable households often claimed a distinct job but omitted reference to the relations of power in which they labored (i.e., they lack status indication). In other words, servants' identities at death distinguish work from the property relationship that defined their submission to an owner or ex-master.

The actions of ex-slaves after emancipation in the American South at the moment when they spoke publicly about their labor provide a revealing comparison. In negotiations with former masters, freed slaves attempted to separate labor from the relationship of domination. Not only did they seek wages for their labor from former slaveholders; they also sought to limit whites' regulation of their lives. According to Leon Litwack, "they sought to achieve a sense of personal autonomy while widening the area of maneuverability." Their attempts "involved a different perception of themselves and their relationship to whites." This is nowhere clearer than in the position taken by a freed slave of the Reverend John Hamilton Cornish of Aiken, South Carolina. Scolding her for the use of profane language, he asked, "Whose servant are you?" "My own servant," she insisted, although she was willing to remain in his home and work as a domestic servant for wages. Separating her labor from the property relationship that made her his servant, she envisioned a social relationship that made her instead her own person and a domestic worker.[43]

The use of occupational title also can be read as a claim to physicality. Work involves movement and action in the material and social worlds. For the slave defined by physical vulnerability and for the ex-slave whose integrity ceased in relations with his or her former master, job title took what was given in assigned tasks and reapplied it, claiming a physicality denied by legal condition.

By omitting status indication, the sign marking the loss of physical integrity, half the slaves in domestic service in large households instead claimed their work and disregarded the relations that subjected slave to master (51%, $N = 52$). Slaves in transportation and professional and skilled service in the same setting follow a similar pattern.[44] However, ten slave domestics merit special attention, for my categorization of them has obscured part of the picture. Like the freedmen discussed below, these slaves placed emphasis on the person served: for example, Apthonus *cub(icularius)* Tauri *pat(ris)* (bedchamber servant of Taurus the father, 6256) and Clarus *cubicular(ius)* Tauri *adulescentis* (bedchamber servant of Taurus the younger/the young man, 6257).[45] Unlike the freedmen, they have been included among slaves with status indication although, technically, they lack it. In fact, the order of name, job title, and genitive alters the presentation of identity. Apthonus and Clarus both stressed their position as bedroom attendant rather than the relationship of master-slave. Work placed these men in close proximity to their masters and in positions that constantly subjected them to the demands and moods of father and son and, potentially, to the daily loss of physical integrity. Their epitaphs, however, do not refer directly to the property relationship that articulated this loss. Their titles reframe the relationship as one of "doing for." Interestingly, the stress on the person served may lie behind the use of status indication in general. Slaves with status indication tended to name those jobs in which service often would have been limited to a specific person: twenty-three (46%) were *cubicularii* or *a cubiculo* (four of whom emphasized employer).[46]

Freed servants' representations at death, too, give primacy to work rather than legal condition, and this differentiates them from other ex-slaves. Although freedmen with occupational title used status indication more often than slaves, freedmen in domestic service were less likely to claim their legal status than those in any other field.[47] Also, unlike other freedmen in large households, freed domestics more often omitted status indication altogether, identifying themselves as servants rather than as ex-slaves.[48] Strikingly, three of the eight freedmen with status indication buried in single-family *columbaria* lack a nomen, the distinctive mark of the Roman citizen: cognomen and job title frame their presentation; only the abbreviation *l.* or *lib.* distinguishes them from the household's slaves.[49] In other words, freedmen who remained in the household continued to construct their identities in the same terms as their slave counterparts.

Like the slave *cubicularii* discussed above, six freedmen or their commemorators highlighted the relations of work by noting a specific employer. Their terms stress "who does what for whom" rather than "who manumitted whom."

(1) T. Statilius Dasius Tauri l. *ad vestem avi* (freedman of Taurus, wardrobe attendant of (his) grandfather, 6372)

(2) C. Genicilius C. l. Domesticus Sex(ti) Lartidi *cocus* (freedman of Gaius Genicilius, cook of Sextus Lartidius, 9271)

(3) Statilius Phileros Corneliaes *cubicularius* (bedchamber servant of Cornelia, 6264)

(4) L. Volusius Heracla *capsarius idem a cubiculo L(ucii) N(ostri)* (wardrobe attendant and also servant in charge of the bedroom of our Lucius, 7368)

(5) L. Volusius Paris *a cubiculo et procurator L(ucii) N(ostri)* (servant in charge of the bedroom and manager of our Lucius, 7370)

(6) Primus Q(uinti) Hateri *cellarius* (provisioner of Quintus Haterius, 9251)

Dasius (1) and Domesticus (2) have status indication, and occupational title distinguishes employer from patron. Dasius remained in the household of the man whom he had served, receiving his freedom from a grandson. His epitaph portrays him not simply as the freedman of Taurus but as the attendant of his grandfather, the title emphasizing perhaps the personal nature of his duties. In her portrayal of her patron-husband Primus's wife, Dorchas chose to name his work and employer in the space where she could have given his nomen.[50] Phileros (3), Heracla (4), and Paris (5), like Primus, lack status indication per se. No doubt manumitted by the men for whom they worked, they or those close to them stressed the relationship of work rather than that of freedman and patron. And the job titles of Heracla and Paris place multiple responsibilities in the freedman's hands. The *a cubiculo* Heracla also took care of his patron's clothes while he was at the baths or perhaps at all times. Paris's roles as *a cubiculo* and *procurator* covered many aspects of his patron's existence.[51]

Compared with the thirty different households in the occupational epitaphs, the pattern in one *familia* offers a more defined picture of the men and women presented as domestic workers. Of the house servants with job title, 43.2% (N = 54) belonged to the *familia* of the Statilii, and they held the full range of domestic jobs (see Table 5.6). Besides understanding the functions performed by slaves in the household,[52] we can also observe how staff members who did the same work, albeit at different times, presented themselves.

Table 5.6 Occupations and Legal Status of
Domestic Servants in the Household of the Statilii

| | Legal Status | | |
Occupation	Slave	Freedmen	Total
Bodyguards	10 (100)	—	10 (100)
Personal and room			
servants	20 (90.9)	2 (9.1)	22 (100)
Cooks	3 (75.0)	1 (25.0)	4 (100)
Provisioners	2 (100)	—	2 (100)
Caretakers			
(house and objects)	12 (80.0)	3 (20.0)	15 (100)
Social			
organization	—	1 (100)	1 (100)
Total	47 (87.0)	7 (13.0)	54 (100)

Note: Figures in parentheses are row percentages.

In the Statilian household, slave domestics who noted their occupations identified themselves as men and women who performed a particular job, not as slaves. Only 21.3% $(N = 10)$ stated their legal condition, and for seven of them special circumstances account for its use. Three used the form that emphasized the person served rather than the owner: the two *cubicularii* (6256, 6257) mentioned above and an armor-bearer (*armiger*, 6229). Four were *vicarii*, the slaves of other slaves or freedmen (6246, 6261, 6262, 6326). Their status indication names a master within the *familia* itself, distinguishing them as members of a particular group within the household, although they probably worked for the Statilii rather than their owners.[53]

The proportion of Statilian freedmen with status indication is larger than among freed domestic workers as a whole, but certain aspects of their epitaphs also indicate an emphasis on work. Three (6217, 6227, 6248) lack nomina and were identified basically by cognomen and job. Two men noted their employers: Dasius, the *ad vestem* (6372), and Phileros, the *cubicularius* (6264), listed above.[54] Again, in presenting himself at death, Dasius or his commemorator considered it as important to note the man whose clothes he had cared for as the man who had freed him. The work he did traced a particular history; his notation of service to Taurus may reflect his own claim to a debt owed by the consul of 37 and 26 B.C.

In their job titles, domestic servants document their maintenance of the master. Without these servants, the house and its objects would not have been cleaned and kept up, nor would the slaveholder and his family have been fed, dressed, guarded, and cared for. Domestics produced for their masters a life commensurate with their social standing. In effect, social status made the master dependent on others for physical care.

Speaking of a wide range of slave societies, Patterson observes that "the slaveholder camouflaged his dependence, his parasitism, by various ideological strategies. Paradoxically, he defined the slave as dependent. This is consistent with the distinctively human technique of camouflaging a relation by defining it as the opposite of what is really is."[55] Slave testimony from the American South makes it clear that slaves themselves saw through the ideological camouflage that defined them as dependent, helpless, and indulged; they understood the dependence of those who had power over them even while they endured the indignity of their own lack of power. To the charge of former masters that manumitted slaves were lazy, a freedman from South Carolina responded with anger: "They take all our labor for their own use and get rich on it and then say we are lazy and can't take care of ourselves." House servants in the antebellum South derived some satisfaction from their masters' passivity. For those who suffered their own powerlessness and physical vulnerability, the master's dependency brought a sense of their own dignity: "I knew I was doing for him what he could not do for himself, and showing my superiority to others, and acquiring their respect in some degree, at the same time."[56]

We have no such testimony from Roman slaves, but occupational title may indicate a similar awareness. Domestic servants form a substantial group among slaves with occupational title. Of the latter, 27.5% ($N = 129$) have a domestic job (including nurses), and they named this work more often than any other except administration and secretarial service (38.8%, $N = 182$). In private households, they claimed this labor (31.1%, $N = 107$) nearly as often as administrators and secretaries (32.6%, $N = 112$). This significant proportion of slaves who claimed their work had jobs whose conditions gave them an intense experience of the relations between master and slave and put them in a unique position to observe their contradictions. Proximity exposed them directly to the master's power and made clear their own potential and constant loss of physical integrity. Yet the intimate quality of their work will have shown the master's "not doing" and his dependence. The public display of their tasks demonstrated his centrality, but it also marked their importance in *his* relations with free outsiders.

Job titles used by slaves, then, implicitly identified a dual dependency: masters of the upper classes needed slaves to live and behave like members of the social elite, and they relied on these slaves for their daily physical existence. Where the master saw the attendance of his *cubicularius* and *ad vestem* or the preparations of his cook as an expression of his own power and position, the slave or freed *cubicularius, ad vestem,* and cook could see that the master did not put on his own clothes or prepare his own food. At least, their occupational titles express their own activity and his passivity in these areas. If, as Treggiari and Flory believe, these titles were noted for their prestige value, prestige not only stemmed from work, as argued in chapter 2; for a substantial proportion of slaves, it also arose from "doing for [the master] what he could not do for himself."

Yet the slave's activity had a context only in terms of a master or his property. Even where a job title does not mention an employer, it pertains to the household, master, and master's class position, because the duties to which it refers generally had no context but the large domestic household. Any slaves' presentation of themselves and their work would have had this reference point. As Eugene Genovese has observed of Southern planters and their house servants, "neither could easily make any statement about the human condition and their own place within it without some reference to the life of the other."[57] If master and servant lived in the same world, the question must be the way the servant read its terms and conditions.

These titles have another reference point besides the slaveholder; they express the deceased's or commemorator's relations within the community of fellow slaves and ex-slaves who were the epitaph's primary audience. As Tables 2.5 and 3.3 indicate, domestic servants identified themselves as such to maids, bearers, artisans, secretaries, and administrators. Viewed in the context of community, the large proportion of slaves without status indication, especially where we consider a single household, means that slaves were presented to their fellows by name and job. Whatever the realities of their work life, domestic servants portrayed themselves in the community as individuals with defined tasks and functions. Ironically, since the master reduced domestic work to pleasing and saw in it his own centrality, the use of work to frame an identity would not have been viewed by the slaveholder as dangerous or rebellious. A message about his dependence, however, could have been read by fellow slaves and ex-slaves who shared the tomb, celebrated rituals there, and had similar lived experiences in the household.

Title gave slave and freedman a specific place within the *familia* and perhaps should be read in terms of its constitu-

tive relations. As noted earlier, job titles expressed links
with others in the community. Here, *cubicularius* was associated with *cubicularius* and *a veste* in a direct working
relationship where the person served was the same. When
servants attended to different masters, parallel tasks may
have served as a common ground that cut across the bonds
of discrete master-slave relationships. Although service itself must make reference to household, master, and his
class, work expressed place and relations to others within
the community.

If title functioned in the way I have suggested, some
slaves expressed an association with others outside of their
owners' scale of values. Upper-class masters could not or
would not give value to this labor, however much they valued and cared for their servants, as Pliny says he did. They
could not, therefore, observe the links among slaves and ex-
slaves created by work. "The real feelings and opinions of
the slaves were not much known or respected by their masters," observes Frederick Douglass of the antebellum American South. "The distance between the two was too great to
admit of such knowledge."[58] Pliny (*Ep.* 8.16.2) believed that
for slaves the household was a state (*res publica*) that gave
its members a sort of citizenship (*civitas*). Those who used
job title in households like Pliny's, however, made a claim
to community in terms of the shared experience of work,
not to the *res publica* of the senatorial master.

CONCLUSIONS

THE MEN AND WOMEN whose occupations are recorded on epitaphs and dedications from the city of Rome from the late first century B.C. to the late second century A.D. are one source for the study of Roman society. But however well these inscriptions illustrate certain aspects of Roman society, they themselves do not necessarily reflect Rome's population or the city's work force. The large proportion of slaves and freed slaves and small number of freeborn citizens in these inscriptions contradict what has been assumed about the city's population and contrast with the status pattern in the extant epitaphs where no occupation is mentioned. It seems unlikely, too, that the occupational structure formed by the men and women with occupational title accurately reflects the "distribution of the workforce between different kinds of employments"[1] outside the imperial household and bureaucracy: over 40% of the work force would have been engaged in providing services used primarily by the upper classes. Indeed, as pointed out in chapter 4, nearly a third of those with job title can be connected with the households of the wealthy and socially prominent. The needs of these classes, and especially the control of labor that they had in their slaves, are better represented than the interests of any other class.

162

But the men and women in the occupational inscriptions used their work to record who they were in death and in life, and I have tried to read the stories of identity that might be inscribed in the minutiae of commemoration and dedication. Since the people who most frequently claimed a specific kind of work are slaves and freed slaves, attention has been focused on them. Their sizable presence complicates the process of reading, because their experiences and points of view are excluded from the literary and legal sources from which we so frequently draw the assumptions that inform our discussions of Roman society. Reading the terms of the excluded requires critical examination of the terms of the included in order to make room for "other meanings." In an attempt to make audible the particular silence of epitaph and dedication, I have used suggestive insights in the work of sociologists and historians of other slave societies and looked for vocal analogies in the testimony of slaves and freedmen from the American South. I do not assume that the antebellum South or any other slaveholding society precisely parallels Rome, although the aristocratic culture and values of planters in the South provide an enlightening comparison to those of upper-class masters at Rome. The testimony of slaves is at least indicative of a viewpoint other than that of the Roman slaveholder and invites us to reassess the latter's vision of his slaves and freed slaves. Yet, for the reasons noted in chapter 1, the story set out in the preceding chapters must be seen as one reading, partial and incomplete. It is "a dialogue with the dead who are reconstructed through their 'textualized' remainders" and with historians.[2]

Roman law and legitimate society defined the slave as an outsider without rights, kin, or place in the social order. What Patterson has called the slave's natal alienation resulted at Rome in a loss of physical integrity, the condition that defined the freeborn citizen as an insider. The slave's loss was the master's gain: he took control of the slave's person, body, and labor, a control formalized in the definition of the slave as property. Although the slave was thus cut off from the components of identity that defined the individual by family relationships, slave epitaphs include family relations, especially those with spouses. In these terms, the claim to labor assumes an importance lacking for the freeborn. Slaves, of course, neither chose their work nor controlled its products. Yet it was more difficult to divide men and women from their labor than to separate them from their kin; it accompanied the body and person who was sold, given, or lent to another. Despite the absence of legitimate title, slaves or those close to them, often slaves themselves, claimed their labor. Very importantly, the claim asserts that which was lost—physicality and an active connection with the world. Work in various ways put the slave in motion in the world, inside a household or outside: job title makes its bearer a "doer," not a passive extension of another's existence.

Most of the slaves with occupational title called themselves masseurs, barbers, hairdressers and maids, attendants, caretakers, financial agents, secretaries, and administrators of property. Moreover, most of them belonged to the households of the wealthy, and the labor that they identify enabled the served to display social standing. Viewed as an orientation toward another, this work merited only disdain for the perceived powerlessness of the person who performed a service. While the slave was acknowledged as a worker, the activities of many slaves were socially devalued, and, as pointed out in chapter 5, those who used these services could not admit their importance without undermining the experience of power to be gained in the ownership of slaves.

The slave occupied a position that offered a different point of view than the master's. Certain conditions in the urban household may have sharpened the slave's perspective. The requirements of social standing and proximity to the master put the staff in a unique position to observe the slaveholder's dependence, which he covered over by defining his slaves as property, making them extensions of himself, dependent and "socially dead." Further, the material situation of these slaves may have encouraged their acknowledgment of these relations and opened the way for the naming of their employments. What we can gather from other sources indicates that slaves in the *familia urbana* did not suffer the physical deprivation endured by slaves who worked in chains on country estates, in mills, or in the mines.[3] According to Frederick Douglass, the absence of physical misery leaves room for other needs. "When entombed at Covey's [a man to whom slaveowners sent recalcitrant slaves to be "broken in"] and shrouded in darkness and physical wretchedness, temporal well-being was the grand desideratum, but, temporal wants supplied, the spirit put in its claims."[4]

The claim of these slaves to their own labor appears to me to be part of a resistance to depersonalization and desocialization. Looking across cultures, Patterson has observed that

> The slave resisted his desocialization and forced service in countless ways, only one of which, rebellion, was not subtle. Against all odds he strove for some measure of regularity and predictability in his social life. Because his kin relations were illegitimate, they were all the more cherished. Because he was considered degraded, he was all the more infused with the yearning for dignity. Because of his formal isolation and liminality, he was acutely sensitive to the realities of community.[5]

Slaves in the urban household did not recover physical integrity; as noted in chapter 5, proximity made them subject to the direct exercise of the master's power. Also, these slaves stood at a much greater social distance from their masters than artisans working with their masters in the same shop: there, manumission could equalize the positions of ex-slave and ex-master as far as those outside the relationship were concerned. However, against the master's power, slaves in the *familia urbana* could claim what the master did not do for himself and which had to be done in order to maintain the master's social life as well as his physical existence. Job title asserts the slave's physicality and activity against a master's passivity and dependence and quietly resists the depersonalization defined by the loss of physical integrity. The subtlety of this resistance lies in part in the master's devaluation of the slave's labor, which robs the activity of dignity by reducing it to a form of pleasing and by ignoring the neediness of the pleased. He could read the desire to please in the job titles of his slaves; the slaves could read his need.

The subtlety and context for an assertion of dignity, too, lay in a different direction than the master's needs: the reference point is the *familia* without *paterfamilias*. Titles were given by members of the *familia* or used where the slave, at death, appears among his or her fellow slaves and freedmen. Title names a role within the household, and it forms a link between the slave and others with the same or a related job, a link that did not depend on kin relations. Occupational title itself may have been a term expressing degrees of superiority and equality with others. In this sense, banishment to the *familia rustica*, mentioned as a punishment for slaves in the urban establishment, was not only a demotion but, like the sale of a child, parent, sibling, or wife, a disruption of close ties and bonds.[6]

Freedmen had claims that slaves lacked, namely, family and citizenship. Nonetheless, they occupied a marginal position in society, and the stain of a servile past left them continually vulnerable to denigration and to insiders' disdain for any accomplishment in the free present. The loss of origin was permanent and, with it, full physical integrity at least in relation to the former master. For some, the claim to one's own labor continued to be a resistance to that loss. By altering the standard of assessment from birth to economic activity, the claim gives the freedman a central rather than marginal position.

Slaves manumitted by upper-class owners carried the servile past with them into freedom, and manumission in adulthood, when work began at an early age, will have meant a deeply ingrained orientation toward work and master. For a fourth of the freedmen with occupational title who evidence some attachment to a large domestic household, especially those in skilled, domestic, and administrative services, the present will have reinforced the experience of the past. At the least, we can observe that for these freedmen, the setting of work did not change. In the naming of their jobs, they parallel their slave counterparts.

Unlike the slaves in this study, most of the freedmen did not belong to the households of the upper classes, and their work did not maintain the person, property, and standing of those whose social position they could never fill. A fourth of those with occupational title clearly located themselves outside the large domestic household, primarily identifying themselves as shopkeepers. My criteria limit categorization of 48.7% of the freedmen with occupational title, but the type of work that they name and their social relations make it highly unlikely that most in fact were attached to elite households.[7]

Where work is divorced from the maintenance of social

status, the implications of occupational title differ. For some freed slaves, occupation was the source of a prosperity commemorated in a family tomb that included the freedman's own freedmen and women. The tomb presents an image of independence—a man with his family, his slaves, and his ex-slaves. Occupational title names the freedman's means of establishing a normal order in his family and social life. Professional or commercial success enabled the freedman to reduce the disabling aspects of his past and to provide a basis for his children's integration into the society as insiders, although they, too, were vulnerable, as Horace (*Sat.* 1.6.27–37, 45–48) makes clear.

The epitaphs of freed artisans suggest a range of identities outside the large domestic household. As with slaves in the domestic setting, occupational title serves as a term of relationship delineating a place among one's peers in situations in which, as the social relations of artisans indicate, labor was controlled and participation, at least originally, imposed. Occupational title transforms what was given. *Colliberti* who identified themselves as a group by naming their employment make work the framework of what was shared; common tasks and activities appear as the basis of social ties commemorated in burial. The identification of patrons as freedmen, and in some cases as artisans themselves, re-forms the relationship of patron and freedman so as to depict the position of patron as attainable. The comparison with the son in paternal power and his *paterfamilias* is an apt one; it does not deny the relations of authority but admits the possibility of succession. Moreover, where freedman and patron have the same occupational title, it does not seem that the ex-slave names an employment that would have been devalued by his or her ex-master. Here, there is no subtlety in the claims of the freedman (perhaps there was no need of it). Whatever importance is asserted, it does not lie outside the patron's values or at least his social identity as that identity is depicted at death.

Freeborn citizens have not received much attention: few declared their free birth in these inscriptions. The group who appear (the *incerti*) indicate a legitimate place in Roman society through their nomina, omitting filiation or libertination. Most were probably freeborn citizens, not freedmen ashamed of their servile origin (see app. 3). Some may have been the sons or grandsons of freedmen, but descent from a freed father or grandfather, while a source of vulnerability for those who aspired to position, must be carefully separated from the condition of the freed slave. At any rate, what is important is their presentation of themselves. If they were freedmen, they or those who commemorated them chose not to include this information, perhaps for reasons other than shame. Huttunen has suggested that freed artisans and tradesmen used status indication in precisely those situations where it reflected an economic tie with the patron; the artisans discussed in chapter 5 reveal that this was considerably more complex.[8] If the *incerti* were freeborn, free birth was equally unnecessary to record—certainly less meaningful than occupation, which does identify them.

Title may have been connected with a particular position that was more distinctive than free birth. There is a tendency for distributors to appear as the heads of establishments that included their own freedmen. That role, which makes them appear as those who have control over others, may have counted for more than free birth in the empire. Perhaps occupational title expressed the role in certain circumstances, where filiation alone did not necessarily convey an exercise of authority. Further study of the uncertain freeborn in different occupations is needed; ideally, such a study would pay close attention to the recurrence of nomina, indications of property, and presence of family as well as freedmen.

Equally suggestive are the uncertain freeborn in *collegia*. Only 18.9% of the uncertain freeborn note an office or membership in the city's occupational *collegia*, but they are nearly five times more likely than freedmen to give their occupational titles this way, and they follow the pattern of the men clearly identified as freeborn (38.1% noted membership or an office). Affiliation with a *collegium*, a special form of title, makes reference to occupation because this was the only way to represent one's participation in an organization or a community, albeit one composed of fellow tradesmen. I suggested in chapter 4 that membership, and particularly office, was especially important at a time when citizenship no longer determined privilege or signified a role in the state even in the limited fashion of the republic. Also, with the extension of citizenship in the empire, the distinction between conqueror and conquered no longer rested on a citizenship attained by birth (i.e., as Roman or Italian). Nomen by itself suffices to indicate citizenship and free, as opposed to slave, status. By contrast, office in a *collegium* signals elevation for those who were not members of the privileged orders; membership marks a belonging. The free may have found in this form of occupational title a means of distinction not available in their legal condition, and in this way they are not unlike slaves in the large domestic household whose job titles seem to assert their importance in relation to the master and to express a role within their own community—the *familia*.

We must wonder whether a similar dynamic was at work for individuals of uncertain free origin who lack this affiliation with a *collegium*. In their presentation of themselves, they omitted free birth or freed status but characterized themselves by their work. Did occupation condense a life history or ask for some respect that these free citizens might have otherwise lacked? Implicitly, in the latter case, the claim to work would have resulted, at least in part, from social poverty and an absence of other claims.

Generally, the proportions of freeborn citizens, free men and women, freedmen, and slaves with occupational title reflect what each group possessed in what was given by legal condition. Freeborn citizens lacked the distinctions available to their social betters, but they had the claims of family and of belonging without the stain of a servile past. Freedmen had family rights and citizenship, but their assertion of a role in family and community was more limited, and their servile past made them vulnerable in the free present. Slaves lacked rights, kin, and a legitimate place in society. Those men and women who identified themselves by their work articulated some sort of dignity or place. The free who had other means of framing an identity needed this one less often than the slave or ex-slave. Ironically, the men and women with occupational title—freeborn, freed, and slave—made a claim that, given the structure of Roman society and the economy, was neither socially valued nor empowering, at least in the regard of those with the largest claims on wealth, power, and privilege.

APPENDIX I

SOME USEFUL TERMS

LATIN TERMS are translated at their first use for readers unfamiliar with the language and Roman society. For occupational titles, see appendix 2. The following terms appear several times without translation.

beneficium	favor, kindness
collegium	guild, club, society, self-help organization
occupational collegium	society of those with the same trade
domestic collegium	society of slaves and freedmen in the same household
collibertus, -a	fellow freedman (-woman), i.e., freed by the same ex-master
columbarium	"large tomb, either partly or wholly underground, whose walls contain hundreds of niches, . . . set closely together . . . and intended to contain the ashes of the dead in urns or chests" (Toynbee 1971, 113)
conservus, -a	fellow slave, i.e., owned by the same master
contubernalis	slave spouse
decurio	member of a governing committee of a *collegium* or supervisor of a group of slaves

familia	here, slaves (and freedmen) of household
familia urbana	urban staff of a slaveholder
familia rustica	slaves on a rural estate
familia Caesaris	slaves and freedmen of the emperor
incerti	uncertains, the term Taylor (1961) applies to persons with Roman family names (nomina) but without status indication: they were either freedmen or freeborn citizens. Here, they are called uncertain freeborn
ingenuus, -a	freeborn Roman citizen
libertinus, -a	freedman (-woman), in reference to legal status
libertus, -a	freedman (-woman), in reference to his or her ex-master
libertis libertabusque	formula used in epitaphs often with *posterisque eorum:* to (the commemorator's) freedmen and freedwomen
magister	here, chief officer of a *collegium*
mercennarius	hired worker
natio	nationality, origin
obsequium	compliance, deference, the behavior required of an ex-slave toward his or her former master
officium	duty
operae	work services
paterfamilias	male head of the family and household
patria potestas	paternal power (here, several times as simply *potestas*)
patronus, -a	former master in relation to his or her freed slave
peculium	property or funds managed by person incapable of legal ownership, like a slave or son in paternal power
posterisque eorum	formula used in epitaphs: to their descendants
servus, -a	slave
sepulcrales	epitaphs lacking any individual with occupational title
suis	formula used in epitaphs: to (the commemorator's) family (relatives)

APPENDIX II

OCCUPATIONAL CATEGORIES AND GLOSSARY

I HAVE CATEGORIZED the occupations named in Roman inscriptions according to functional similarity rather than place in a social ranking based on wealth or prestige. A functional, or what Michael Katz calls a structural, system looks at "the distribution of the workforce between different kinds of employments;" a "principle of hierarchy . . . is irrelevant" to it.[1] Constructing a hierarchy of the occupations noted in inscriptions involves methodological difficulties, especially where the issue is the identities of workers and tradesmen. The standards for a social ranking, which cannot be drawn from the inscriptions themselves, must rely on the literary sources and thus import the perspective of those who did not work (see chap. 3). A system of occupational ranking based on role in the productive process, scale of economic activity, relationship to property, or control of labor cannot rest on occupational title alone. In most cases, classification depends on other evidence drawn from the text of an inscription—the presence of freedmen, tomb size, *collegium* office, age, shop address (see chaps. 3 and 4). For many individuals with occupational title, the relevant information is not given.

A functional classification relies on the occupational title itself. Even where title is obscure or susceptible to several interpretations, a general functional category can be ascertained. When other evidence suggests a combination of activities, as with artisans whose involvement in distribution is signaled by a shop address, the functional categorization can be qualified without abandoning reliance on the one piece of information available for every individual. When workman, manager, and owner end up in the same category, they can be distinguished by separate analysis of the factors named above.[2]

Despite the overlapping of some occupational roles, I have attempted to "classify by dominant function"—building and manufacture, distribution, and service.[3] Certain distinctions made by Roman authors are preserved without hierarchical rank and with some obvious alterations. I divide the building trades, which were generally concerned with immovable objects, from artisanal work (here labeled manufacture), which produced movable objects or constituted some stage in their production. Artisans are grouped on the basis of the material in which they worked or the type of goods they made. Distribution includes all those whose titles denote sales activity. Bankers, money changers, and collectors, who facilitated exchange, occupy a separate category.

I classify other service occupations by the type of service, attending to the kind of skills involved. The grouping of architects with doctors and teachers parallels Cicero's (*Off.* 1.151) category; here, the basis is the professional character of these occupations and the intellectual element that ideally characterized their practitioners' training.[4] Certain aspects of these employments, however, connect them with the building trades or other service work. The architect's technical knowledge, possibly his training, and his role as a supervisor of construction associate him with builders.[5] The medical profession involved physical care or at least the supervision of assistants who performed the requisite procedures. The activities of some teachers link them with those in child care.[6]

Entertainers and those involved in grooming, like hairdressers, barbers, and masseurs, were ideally highly skilled, but their training lacked an intellectual element. Although many belonged to large households, I separate them from "domestic servants" on the basis of their particular skills and because their work, unlike that of *cubicularii, atrienses,* and others in the category of domestic service, was not confined to the domestic setting. The latter also applies to those in transportation, although, in comparison with the other groups, many were fairly unskilled. Related capacities and duties associate administrators, financial agents, clerks, and secretaries, who must be distinguished from personal and house servants, although most worked in large households.

These considerations produce the following "distribution of the workforce between different kinds of employments."

CONSTRUCTION (112)
    Carpenters and builders (71)
    Stoneworkers (13)

Stucco workers, mosaic workers, painters (23)
Contractors (5)
MANUFACTURE (331)
Jewelers (26)
Metalsmiths (89)
Workers in ivory and glass (12)
Producers of cloth (55; inc. spinners, wool weighers, weavers, dyers, fullers)
Makers of clothing (83)
Shoemakers (8)
Artisans in leather (4)
Butchers and bakers (30)
Artisans of other products (24; inc. artisans of tools, pipes, furniture)
SALES (108)
Dealers in food products (46; inc. dealers in meats, fish, produce, oil, wine)
Dealers in unguents and perfumes (35)
Dealers in leather, cloth, and clothing (7)
Dealers in books and paper, etc. (7)
Dealers in metal and marble (4)
Dealers in slaves (1)
Dealers, product unspecified (8)
BANKING (42)
EDUCATED SERVICE (120)
Architects and surveyors (15)
Doctors and midwives (83)
Teachers (22)
SKILLED SERVICE (75)
Barbers, hairdressers, masseurs/euses (57)
Entertainers (18)
DOMESTIC SERVICE (321)
Child attendants and nurses (90)
Bodyguards (11)
Personal, room, and table servants (100)
Cooks (19)
Provisioners (22)
Caretakers (41)
Gardeners (16)
Social organizers (22)
TRANSPORTATION (55)
Animal tenders and baggage handlers (13)
Runners and bearers (40)
Drivers and boatmen (2)
ADMINISTRATION, FINANCE, SECRETARIAL SERVICE (306)
Financial agents (99)

Administrators (153)
Secretaries, clerks, copyists (54)

OCCUPATIONAL TITLES IN ROMAN INSCRIPTIONS

There are hundreds of discrete occupational titles in the epitaphs and dedications from the city of Rome. The following list is representative of the titles covered in this study: it includes only the titles borne by named individuals (see also Treggiari 1980). Inscription numbers can be found by consulting the *index vocabulorum* of E. J. Jory and D. G. More (*CIL* 6.vii).

abietarius	joiner (*OLD:* timber merchant?)
actarius	scribe, record keeper, bookkeeper
actor	agent, administrator
ad aedificia, supra aedificia, curator aedificiorum	superintendent of urban property
aedituus	keeper of a temple
aerarius	coppersmith
aerarius statuarius	maker of copper statues
aerarius vascularius	maker of copper vessels
albarius	worker in stucco
alipilus	plucker of body hair
aluminarius	dealer in alum
anagnostes	reader
anatiarius	dealer in ducks
arcarius	treasurer, cashier
architectus	architect
argentarius	banker
argentarius	silversmith
argentarius vascularius	maker of silver vessels
armiger	armor-bearer
aquarius	workman for a household's water supply
asturconarius	breeder and/or driver of *asturcones* (horses from Asturia in Spain)
atriensis	majordomo and servants who cleaned and maintained the house
aurarius	goldsmith
auri acceptor	goldsmith or dealer in gold?
aurifex	goldsmith
auri vestrix	tailor of clothes of gold cloth?
aviarius	dealer in birds
aviarius altiliarius	dealer in fattened birds (bird fattener?)
axearius	axle maker

balneator	bath attendant
bybliopola	bookseller
brattiarius, -a	goldbeater, maker of gold leaf
brattiarius inaurator	goldbeater, gilder
cabator (cavator)	engraver, gem cutter (Gummerus 1915), excavator (Treggiari 1980)
caelator	engraver
calcariensis	limeburner
caligarius	bootmaker
candelabrarius	maker of candelabra, lampstands
cantor, -trix	singer
capsarius	servant who carried a child's book-case, wardrobe custodian
cassidarius	helmet maker
cellarius	provisioner, storeskeeper
centonarius	patchwork maker, ragman
chartarius	dealer in paper
cistarius	guardian of a chest or wardrobe
citharoedus	lyre player and singer
clostrarius	locksmith
coactor	collector
colorator	painter of houses?
comoedus	comic actor
cocus, coquus	cook
coriarius subactarius	preparer of hides for tanning
corinthiarius	worker in Corinthian bronze, an alloy of gold, silver, copper
a corinthis	caretaker of Corinthian ware
coronarius	garland maker
crepidarius	maker of sandals
cubicularius	bedchamber servant
a cubiculo	servant in charge of bedroom
cullearius	maker of *cullei* (leather bags)?
cunaria	infant attendant
custos	guard, keeper
custodiarius	jailer
dispensator	steward
eborarius	worker in ivory
ep(h)ippiarius	maker of horsecloths, saddler?
equiso	groom, stableman
exactor	collector or overseer
exactor ad insulas	rent collector
exonerator calcariarius	lime unloader
faber	worker in some material; if unnamed, usually builder or carpenter

faber argentarius	silversmith
faber automatarius	maker of *automata* ("machines")
faber balneator	provider of services in the baths?
faber eborarius	worker in ivory
faber ferrarius	ironsmith
faber intestinarius	joiner, inlayer (carved fine interior woodwork)
faber lectarius	maker of beds
faber oculariarius	maker of eyes for statues
faber soliarius baxiarius	maker of woven footwear
faber tignuarius	carpenter
ferrarius, -a	ironsmith
flaturarius	caster
frumentarius	grain dealer
a frumento	custodian of (household) grain
fullo	fuller
gaunacarius	furrier
gemmarius, -a	jeweler
gemmarius sculptor	gem engraver, gem carver
geometres	geometrician
germanus	bodyguard
gerulus	bearer
gladiarius	swordmaker
glutinarius	maker of glue or paste
grammaticus	grammar teacher, teacher of language
harundinarius	seller of reeds (for hunting or fishing) or writing pens?
ad hereditates	financial administrator or account keeper of inheritances
holitor	kitchen gardener, vegetable grower
horrearius	superintendent or manager of a warehouse
ab hospitiis et paedagogus puerorum	servant in charge of guests and attendant/teacher of slave children
hymnologus	singer of hymns
iatralipte	"doctor" who cured by ointments and massage
iatromea	midwife
infector	dyer
ad inpedimenta	caretaker of baggage
inpiliarius	maker of felt footwear
institor unguentarius	perfume seller
insularius	rent collector or supervisor of an *insula*

supra iumenta	person in charge of pack and draft animals
iumentarius	driver or supplier of coaches and carts (and draft animals?)
lanarius	maker of woollen cloth
lanarius coactiliarius	maker of felt
landipendus, -a	wool weigher, spinning supervisor
lanius	butcher
lapicida	stonecutter
lapidarius	stoneworker
lecticarius	litter bearer
lector, -trix	reader
librarius	bookseller?
librarius, -a	scribe, copyist, secretary
librarius (-a) a manu	scribe, secretary
lyntrarius	boatman
ad locationes	administrator or account keeper of contracts or leases?
loc(u)larius	maker of *loculi* (niches)?
lorarius	harness maker
macellarius	provisions dealer
machinator	engineer
a manu, amanuensis	secretary
ad margarita	caretaker of pearls
margaritarius, -a	pearl setter
marmorarius	marble mason
materiarius	carpenter (*OLD:* timber merchant?)
mediastinus	servant, medical assistant
medicus, -a	doctor
medicus chirurgus	surgeon
medicus equarius et venator	horse doctor and huntsman
medicus iumentarius	doctor of draft animals
medicus ocularius	eye doctor
mellarius	dealer in honey
mensor	surveyor
mensor aedificiorum	surveyor/measurer of buildings
mensor machinarius	grain measurer
mercator	dealer, trader, merchant
mercator bovarius	dealer in cattle
mercator olei hispani ex provincia Baetica	dealer in Spanish oil from the province of Baetica
mercator sagarius	dealer in cloaks
mercator venalicius	slave dealer
minister, -tra	servant

ministrator	waiter
mulio	mule driver
musicarius	person in charge of music?
musicus	musician
negotiator	slave manager of master's business
negotiator, negotians	tradesman, dealer
negotiator aerarius et ferrarius	dealer in copper and iron
negotia(n)s coriariorum	dealer in tanned hides
negotiator fabarius	dealer in beans
negotiator, negotians ferrarius	dealer in iron
negotiator frumentarius	dealer in grain
negotiatrix frumentaria et legumenaria	dealer in grain and pulse
negotians lagonaris	dealer in wine bottles
negotiator lanarius	dealer in woollens
negotiator lintiarius	dealer in linens
negotiator marmorarius	dealer in marble
negotiator olearius ex Baetica	dealer in oil from Baetica
negotiator penoris et vinorum	dealer in food and wine
negotians perticarius	dealer in poles or rods
negotians pigmentarius	dealer in paints and cosmetics
negotiator sagarius	dealer in cloaks
negotians salsamentarius et vinariarius maurarius	dealer in salted fish and Moroccan wine
negotians salsarius et malacitanus	dealer in salted fish and fish sauce from Malaga
negotians siricarius	dealer in silk
negotiator suariae et pecuariae	dealer in pigs and cattle
negotiator vestiarius	dealer in clothing
negotiator, negotians vinarius	dealer in wines
negotians vinarius, navicularius	dealer in wines, shipper
nomenclator	name teller
notarius, -a	shorthand writer, stenographer
numida	messenger or outrider
nummularius	money changer
nutrix	child nurse
obstetrix, opstetrix	midwife
officinator, -trix	manager of a workshop
olearius	oil dealer

ornatrix	hairdresser
ostiarius, -a	porter, doorkeeper
paedagogus, -a	child attendant
pedisequus, -a	attendant, foot servant
philosophus	philosopher
philosophus Stoicus	Stoic philosopher
philosophus Epicureus	Epicurean philosopher
pictor	painter
pigmentarius	dealer in paints and cosmetics
pilicrepus	ballplayer
piscator, -trix	fisherman (-woman)
pistor	baker
plumarius	embroiderer, brocader with feathers
plumbarius	maker of (lead) pipes, plumber
plutiarius	maker of balustrades
poeta	poet
politor	polisher
politor eborarius	ivory polisher
pomarius	fruit seller
popa (popinaria?)	keeper of a cookshop
praebitor vinarius	supplier of wine
praeceptor	teacher, instructor
procurator	manager
promus	distributor of provisions
pugillariarius	maker of writing tablets
purpurarius, -a	dyer
quasillaria	spinner
redemptor	contractor
resinaria	dealer in resin
sagarius	maker of cloaks
salarius	dealer in salted fish
salsamentarius	dealer in salted fish
sarcinatrix, -tor	mender, seamstress
scalptor	stone carver
scriniarius	maker of *scrinia* (cases)
scutarius	shieldmaker
sericarius, -a	silkworker
segmentarius	maker of *segmenta* (decorative strips for clothes)
sigillarius	maker of *sigilla* (statuettes)
silentiarius	silence maintainer
solatarius	maker of women's shoes
spec(u)larius, spec(u)lariarius	worker in mica or isinglass, mirror maker?
a speculum	caretaker of mirrors
staminaria	weaver

strator	groom
structor	carver
structor	builder or mason
structor parietarius	builder of walls
subaedianus	worker on interiors
sumptuarius	agent in charge of household expenditures, cashier
supellectilarius, ad supellectilem	caretaker of furniture
sutor	shoemaker
symphoniacus	musician
tabellarius	courier
tabularius	accountant, bookkeeper
tector	plasterer, stucco worker
textor, -trix	weaver
thurarius, -a	incense dealer
tibiarius	maker of reed pipes
tonsor, -trix	barber
tractator, -trix	masseur, masseuse
tritor argentarius	silver polisher
topiarius	ornamental gardener
unctor, -trix	masseur, masseuse
unguentarius, -a	perfumer
ad valetudinarium	infirmary staff
supra valetudinarium	person in charge of an infirmary
vascularius	maker of metal vessels
velarius	curtain closer, curtain or awning maintenance man
a veste, ad vestem	caretaker of clothing
vestiarius, -a	tailor
vestiarius tenuiarius	tailor of fine clothing
vestificus, -a	tailor
vestiplicus, -a	clothes folder, presser
vestispica	caretaker of clothing
vilicus	overseer, manager
vinarius	wine dealer

APPENDIX III

THE ROMAN POPULATION WITH OCCUPATIONAL TITLES

THE MEN AND WOMEN in the occupational inscriptions probably do not well represent the population of the city of Rome. Table A.1, which considers deceased and commemorator separately in the epitaph material alone, offers a picture of the legal statuses of the population distinguished by occupational title. The proportion of slaves among this population is larger than the proportion of slaves estimated for the actual population of the city. Over 30% of the deceased as well as dedicators have servile status indication or can be categorized as slaves on the basis of the other criteria, and many of the uncertain slaves would in actuality have been slaves.[1]

Similarly, the proportion of freedmen among those with occupational title is comparatively large, and it is their representation in relation to other status groups that is problematic. Freedmen whose nomenclature includes libertination and those who can be categorized as freed slaves on the basis of the other criteria compose slightly more than 30% of the deceased with occupational title. They are far better represented than *ingenui* and those whose free birth remains uncertain, and proportionally their presence nearly equals that of slaves. Despite the belief of some ancient authors and modern historians that freedmen were a predominant group in Rome, this seems unlikely for the population as a whole. Freedmen were a decreasing group within the population. They did not reproduce themselves, since their children were *ingenui* (pro-

183

Table A.1   Legal Status of Deceased and Commemorators
in the Occupational Epitaphs

Legal Status	Role in Epitaph		
	Deceased	Commemo-rator	Total
Slave	340 (32.4)	77 (31.8)	417 (32.3)
Uncertain slave	142 (13.5)	37 (15.3)	179 (13.8)
Freedman	333 (31.7)	65 (26.9)	398 (30.8)
Freeborn	31 (2.9)	4 (1.7)	35 (2.7)
Uncertain freeborn	205 (19.5)	59 (24.4)	264 (20.4)
Total	1,051 (81.3)	242 (18.7)	1,293 (100)

Note: Figures in parentheses are percentages.

vided the mother was not a slave). Their numbers, in fact, could only be maintained by new manumissions.[2]

By contrast, slaves and the freeborn were increasing groups at least in relation to freedmen. The freeborn population grew from two sources, the children of *ingenui* and the children of freedmen. Even if the slave population did not reproduce itself, birth contributed to the number of slaves where it did not for freedmen, because the children of slaves were, in most cases, slaves. Moreover, the slave population was augmented from other sources: from captives taken in war, from brigandage on land and piracy, from foundlings, and from children sold into slavery by their parents. Manumission, of course, decreased the number of slaves, but the pattern of leaving children behind in slavery as replacements would have offset this decrease.[3]

In order for the proportion of freedmen to equal or exceed those slaves or *ingenui*, the birthrate of slaves and the rate of increase from other sources, on the one hand, and the birthrate of *ingenui* and freedmen themselves, on the other, would have had to have been considerably lower than the rate of manumission since slave and freeborn were originally the larger groups and since manumission itself potentially increased the freeborn population. The representation of freedmen among those identified by their occupations, like that of slaves, probably does not correspond to their actual proportion in the city's population.

The proportion of *ingenui* among those with occupational title is comparatively small. Only a few of the individuals with nomina and without status indication (3.3%, $N = 14$) can be categorized as freeborn on the basis of any criteria at all, so the population of *ingenui* among the deceased with occupational title, identified by filiation or family relations, is 2.9% ($N = 31$). The precise status of the men and women in the uncertain freeborn category becomes a critical issue in the actual representation of different status groups, especially the freeborn.

By Lily Ross Taylor's estimation, there were, in fact, many freedmen among these individuals. Taylor argues that freedmen more than the freeborn desired commemoration, because they had something special to record—the *tria nomina*, the mark of the Roman citizen. Yet, at the same time, according to Taylor, they wanted to hide their servile origin and hence avoided the use of status indication. Thus, their special desire for commemoration and their attempts to cover up a servile past result in a large number of freedmen who are hidden among the uncertain freeborn.[4] The use of status indication decreased in the first century A.D., and Taylor assumes that the use of libertination decreased more than the use of filiation.

Beyond its circularity, Taylor's argument makes a questionable assumption about the behavior of freedmen. Ex-slaves seeking to hide their origin approximate the freedman of satire who always tries to cover the stain of slavery, whether by beauty patches or the accoutrements of wealth. Such an assumption, as Amy Richlin points out, takes the stereotypes of satire as "exaggerated but basically realistic versions of their prototypes" rather than as reflections of the feelings of the poet and his audience.[5] Moreover, Taylor's claim does not account for the documented use of status indication by freedmen. According to Huttunen, the large proportion of freedmen who used libertination in their epitaphs makes it highly unlikely that freedmen in particular avoided status indication.[6]

His point is confirmed by the men and women with occupational title who, although they lack libertination, were probably freed slaves. Eighty-one individuals can be categorized as freedmen on the basis of criteria other than status indication. For most of them (75.3%, $N = 61$), status is conveyed by a term of relationship, burial location, domestic *collegium, natio,* agnomen, or notation of employer instead of patron. The omission of formal status indication in contexts that would have been associated with slavery does not point to a desire to hide one's background: the statement made by libertination is missing, but servile origin is concealed neither by burial location nor by the information given on the epitaph.

According to Huttunen, the large proportion of freedmen and the small proportion of freeborn with status indication make a decreased use of filiation more likely.[7] Why this is so is more difficult to determine. Satirists' emphasis on the freeborn citizen's legitimate origin and mockery of the rich freed slave's vain pretension suggest that freeborn author and audience looked to heritage for a sense of power over those who lacked free birth but possessed the advantage of wealth. Yet, in fact, the power and privileges associated with freeborn Roman citizenship declined in the empire. Perhaps the omission of filiation, the badge of the freeborn voter, should be connected with the decline of the legislative and electoral assemblies at Rome and thus of the individual citizen's formal political role.[8] In addition, with the extension of citizenship, freeborn citizen status no longer distinguished conqueror and conquered, nor, by the second century A.D., did it guarantee its holder a preferential position in terms of treatments and punishments. Social status, not citizenship, determined legal privilege.

Whatever the cause of the decreased use of filiation in epitaphs, Huttunen's analysis points to a large number of *ingenui* among those with nomina and no formal status indication. Nonetheless, even if all the individuals in the uncertain freeborn category were, in fact, *ingenui*, their representation is weak compared to that of slaves and freed slaves. As pointed out in chapter 2, the latter did not dominate Rome's economic life: they simply found their work a more compelling source of identity at death than freeborn citizens.

NOTES

1. Except where otherwise indicated, all translations are by the author.

CHAPTER I · Listening to Silence:
Problems in the Epistemology of Muted Groups

1. On satirists' stereotypes, see Richlin 1984, 67; and see chap. 3, 63–65. For analysis of Willis, see Marcus 1986.

2. On the problem of class in a conceptual framework of Roman society, see Finley 1973, 35–61, and Fredericksen's (1975) review; De Ste. Croix 1981, esp. 31–204, and Ernst Badian's review (*New York Review of Books* 2 [December 1982]: 47–51). The English terms "freeborn citizen" and "slave" present no difficulties where gender is concerned; "freedman" (or "freedmen") for freed slave(s), although accepted usage, is hardly neutral. I follow the common practice and use "freedman" and "freedmen" to indicate freed slaves of both genders; however, I distinguish between male and female freed slaves where the general term does not convey important differences.

3. "Legitimate social order," used throughout to mean the community of free citizens, is borrowed from Patterson 1982, 5, passim.

4. Thompson 1989, 86–88, esp. 86, and Bradley 1987, 26–39, esp. 29.

5. Carby 1987, 22.

6. Ibid. See also Blassingame 1979; Bhabha 1986.

7. Bradley 1987, 32; Genovese 1976, 285–309.

8. No one modern term (occupation, job, work, livelihood, labor) adequately covers the economic activities and productive roles indicated in the inscriptions. Although the terms are often used interchangeably, I try to

distinguish those who worked for others from those who were "self-employed" or had their own businesses.

9. Hopkins 1983, 217, 233–34; Toynbee 1971, 61–64. For epitaphs that address the passerby, see 9204, 9437, 9545, 9659. All inscription numbers refer to *CIL* 6, unless otherwise indicated. On the social processes of death and burial, tombs, and sepulchral law, see Hopkins 1983, 205–56; Toynbee 1971; De Visscher 1963.

10. For sepulchral and burial costs, see Duncan-Jones 1974, 79–80, 99–101 (Africa), and 127–31, 166–71 (Italy), primarily of the more "economically privileged classes"; see 131 for expenses of the unprivileged. For burial by friends, see 6220, 6326, 9109, 9394, 9450, 9821, 9916; by fellow slaves and freedmen, 1892, 4355, 6595, 7008, 7285, 9820, 9868, 9980; and the examples of Flory 1978, 80–87.

11. Provision of burial by *collegia* or their officers: 6215–19, 7281–82, 9148, 10260–64 (domestic); 9144, 9405, 33875 (occupational).

12. Cixous and Clément 1986, 6.

13. LaCapra 1985, 18; Gordon 1986, 22.

14. Gordon 1986, 21–22.

15. Ibid., 22; see also LaCapra 1985, 21.

16. Gordon 1986, 20, 28–29.

17. Cixous and Clément 1986, 6.

18. Most notably Le Roy Ladurie 1979; Ginzburg 1982, 1985; Davis 1975, 1983. On recent ethnographic history, see Davis 1981; Cohn 1980, 1981. On Le Roy Ladurie's *Montaillou* and the pitfalls of historical ethnography, see Rosaldo 1986.

19. Crapanzano 1986, 51.

20. LaCapra 1985, 36; see Rosaldo (1986, 78–81), who shows how Le Roy Ladurie's use of the inquisitor's records places the historian in the inquisitor's position vis-à-vis the peasants who are the subjects of his study.

21. Crapanzano 1986, 51–52.

22. Clifford 1986, 6–7, 10.

23. Ibid., 7; see also LaCapra (1985, 25–26) on the dream of a "total history."

24. See chap. 5, 147–53.

25. Clifford 1986, 22–23.

26. Smith-Rosenberg 1986, 32.

27. Cic. *Pis.* 67.

28. For exceptions, see chap. 4, nn. 2, 5, 6.

29. Weaver 1972; Chantraine 1967; Boulvert 1970, 1974.

30. For dating by means of paleography, type of stone, and archaeological setting, see Gordon and Gordon 1958–65, 1957; Gordon 1936; Thylander 1951–52, 1952.

31. Huttunen (1974, 48) finds occupational title for only 10% of the people in his samples (every fifth epitaph of *CIL* 6), and this figure includes senators and equestrians.

32. Huttunen (1974, 67–68) argues that the *sepulcrales* (epitaphs in which no individual has occupational title) and the occupational epitaphs (in which at least one individual has occupational title) cannot be clearly divided, contrary to the assumptions of Taylor (1961, 113) and Frank (1916, 690) that the *sepulcrales* represent the "lower population" (Taylor). The

distributions of status groups in them, however, do differ; see chap. 2, 47–48.

33. Huttunen (1974, 16–17) rightly insists that the "sources of the data must . . . be fairly coherent," and for his purposes this means "undamaged Latin inscriptions in prose form." Since my concern is the circumstances in which occupational title was used, I include dedications and epitaphs of all types. Where a question requires that all individuals appear in comparable circumstances, epitaphs are separated from dedications, deceased from commemorators.

34. Hopkins 1966, 247; see also n. 10 above.

35. See chap. 3, n. 37.

36. Hopkins 1966, 247; cf. Huttunen 1974, 44–45, and Saller and Shaw 1984, 127–28.

37. For the potter's field on the Esquiline excavated by Lanciani, see Hopkins 1983, 208–11, and Huttunen 1974, 43–45. On the amphorae at Isola Sacra, see Calza 1940, 44–46, 54, 80, figs. 9–10. For commemoration on perishable material, see Hopkins 1966, n. 6.

38. On the exaggeration of the propertied status of those in Latin epitaphs, see Rawson 1986b, 55 n. 116.

39. The total sample is relatively large and especially meaningful compared to the method of drawing conclusions from a few references in the literary sources. Statistical inference from these inscriptions is less meaningful and inhibited by the nature of the sample. Examination of discrete groups within the entire sample reduces the number of cases so as to make some statistics unstable. In addition, in some tables there are sampling and structural zeros that cannot be avoided. Finally, this group of inscriptions cannot be considered a random sample. Individuals are specially chosen, and certain groups within the population are specially excluded, so that all those who lived in Rome do not have an equal probability of appearing in this sample.

40. See chap. 2, n. 36.

41. General: H. Gummerus, "Industrie und Handel," *RE* 9.1439–1535; Loane 1938; see also Maxey 1938. Occupations of particular groups: Le Gall 1969; Kampen 1981; Duff 1928; for imperial slaves and freedmen, see n. 29 above. Specific occupations: Kühn 1910; Gummerus 1956, 1913, 1915, 1918; Burford 1972; Calabi Limentani 1958; Panciera 1980; Bradley 1986; Joshel 1986. For the work of Susan Treggiari, see n. 44 below.

42. Treggiari 1980, 55.

43. Maier 1953–54.

44. Treggiari 1979a, 1976, see also 1979b, 1973, 1975b, 1980. See also Treggiari 1969, 1975a, 1981a, 1981b.

45. Treggiari 1976, 77.

46. Huttunen 1974, 14–15. Some differences in collection, categorization, and coding limit comparisons with Huttunen. He samples every fifth epitaph of *CIL* 6, excluding metrical epitaphs (17), where I include inscriptions of all types (see n. 33 above). His "basic unit" of study is the social relationship (20); here, it is the individual with occupational title. Consequently, Huttunen's figures for the occupational epitaphs include every individual, regardless of title (138); I count only those whose occupation is specifically named. Thus, Huttunen discusses deceased and commemorator

in the occupational epitaphs, while I discuss individuals with occupational title, distinguishing their roles in the epitaphs where necessary. Huttunen's commemorators set epitaphs for his deceased; in my study, the deceased with occupational title often had commemorators without title, and, similarly, the commemorators with occupational title usually set epitaphs for those without title. Finally, Huttunen's definition of occupation is much broader: in addition to members of the imperial households with administrative and domestic jobs and those connected with the theater, circus, and amphitheater, it includes senators, equestrians, *apparitores*, soldiers, and the military support staff (70−71). See also chap. 2, n. 67.

47. Huttunen 1974, 22−23.

48. Ibid., 71; see also n. 46 above. On the limitations of Huttunen's study, see Treggiari 1980, 55−56.

49. For example, Huttunen 1974, 34, 107, 112, 186, 189.

50. For example, ibid., 52, 115, 116, 125, 150−51, 189, 191. Some assumptions seem questionable or overgeneral (e.g., his notion of social divisions, 35 n. 47). At times, Huttunen observes a pattern in the epitaphs and then finds a social situation to fit the pattern without close consideration of point of view. For instance, he observes a tendency for freedmen to indicate both occupation and status (186); a close relationship with the patron, pride in the trade learned in slavery (186), working with or for the patron (189), and dependence (189, 151) are cited as explanations. However, interpretation must consider whether the freedman with status indication expresses dependence or whether the patron (if he is the commemorator) claims it: what other claims are possible in specific circumstances? In addition, the occupational categories, servants in private households and private *officiales*, seem too broad. More generally, Huttunen categorizes "employments" according to a ranking determined by wealth and prestige rather than by functional similarity; his groupings too easily reinscribe the upper-class perspective embodied in law and literature.

51. Whose point of view, e.g., is represented in Treggiari's assumptions about servants: "morale of each servant is safeguarded" (1975*b*, 61), "humane concern . . . would . . . make the servants more loyal" (63), "considerable satisfaction in being employed by the wife and mother of a *princeps* and the daughter of a god" (64)? Huttunen is careless in his use of the literature and, at points, inconsistent: he discounts the prejudice against work and trade in ancient authors (123) but assumes that Lucian's perspective on public service represents a common attitude (70).

52. Patterson 1982, 7, 38−51.

CHAPTER II • Slavery, Freedom, and the Construction of Identity

1. Carroll [1865] 1987, 45.

2. Bradley 1987, 13−14.

3. On the limits of *patria potestas* in recorded examples from the republic, see Crook 1967*c*. For the liabilities and economic limitations of those in paternal power, see Gaius 2.87, 4.75−80. On son and slave, see Watson 1987, 75−77; n. 24 below.

4. General definition: *Dig.* 47.10.1, 15.25 and 27. Specific offenses: Gaius 3.220; *Dig.* 47.10.5.pr., 5.9−10, 7.5, 13.7, 15.2−10, 15.15−22, 15.33.

Iniuria and a man's wife, children, and slaves: Gaius 3.221; *Dig.* 47.10.1.3, 2, 17.11–18.2. See Kaser 1956; Greenidge 1894; Daube 1951.

5. Gaius 3.225; *Dig.* 47.10.7.8, 9.1. See Patterson 1982, 10–11, 77–101) on honor and power.

6. On inequalities of wealth and prestige, see MacMullen 1974, 88–120; Thompson 1989, 142–56.

7. Garnsey 1970; see also Jones 1960, 51–65; Garnsey 1966.

8. See Buckland [1908] 1970, 3–5, 10ff. On the importance of the slave as property, cf. Finley 1980, 73–83, with Patterson 1982, 21–34. For the Roman law on slavery, see Buckland 1970; Robleda 1976; Watson 1987.

9. Slave as outsider: Pliny *HN* 33.26; Tac. *Ann.* 14.44. Symptomatic of the Roman view of the slave as the outsider was a tendency to give slaves, regardless of origin, Greek names; see Gordon 1924. On sources of slaves, see Harris 1980; Westermann 1955, 60–63, 84–90.

10. De Zulueta 1969, 233; cf. Patterson 1982, 38–51. Florentinus (*Dig.* 1.5.4.2–3) claims slaves were called *servi* because, captured in war (*captivos*), they were saved (*servare*) and sold rather than killed, and *mancipia* because they were seized from the enemy by force (*manu capiuntur*): see Buckland [1908] 1970, 1; Westermann 1955, 58–59; Patterson 1982, 5.

11. Finley 1980, 75.

12. *Dig.* 21.1.31.21; Juv. 3.73–75.

13. Finley 1980, 75. For the disposition of slave mothers, see Buckland [1908] 1970, 21–29. On the separation of slave families, see Rawson 1966; Bradley 1978, 246–49; Bradley 1979, 260–61. See below, pp. 42–46.

14. Patterson 1982, 7; Finley 1980, 75.

15. Gaius 1.52, 2.87; see Watson 1987, 102–14.

16. Punishment of cooks: Mart. 8.23 (cf. Plut. *Cat. Mai.* 21.3), 3.94; Pet. 49.4–6. Of hairdressers: Mart. 2.66; Juv. 6.489–95; cf. Ov. *Am.* 1.14.16–18, *Ars Am.* 3.239–40. Of waiters: Sen. *Ep.* 47.3. For master's irritation and arbitrary punishment, see Juv. 6.219–23, 476–84, 14.15–24; Pet. 52.4–6; Sen. *De Ira* 3.24.2, 32.1. Other punishments for specific offenses: Pet. 53.3 (crucifixion), 45.8 (*ad bestias*); Mart. 2.82 (cutting out tongue). On the corporal punishment of slaves, see Bradley 1987, 118–23. The moral disapproval of excessive cruelty and legal restrictions on treatment affirm the constant threat of the use of force (see below). Thus, on the one hand, punishment was frowned on, and, on the other, it remained a source of laughter from Plautus to Juvenal. For slaves' punishment in Plautus, see Parker 1989.

17. Finley 1980, 95. Sexual vulnerability and use: Sen. *Ep.* 47.7, 95.24; Mart. 1.58, 1.84, 2.34, 3.82, 4.42, 6.39, 9.21, 9.25, 10.98, 11.70, 11.73; Hor. *Sat.* 1.2.116–19; Sen. *Controv.* 4.praef.10; *Cod. Iust.* 9.9.25; Pet. 74.9. Hair: Mart. 1.31, 9.16, 12.84. Castration: Mart. 9.6; Juv. 6.366–79. Maintenance of youth: Sen. *Ep.* 47.7, 123.7. Attitudes toward the sexual use of slaves divide on gender lines (cf. Watson 1987, 15). Women's relations with their slaves are regarded critically; men's relations with male and female slaves are noteworthy only if the master takes the pathic role or becomes obsessed with "boys." Law makes explicit the sexual vulnerability of the female slave: unlike the freeborn woman, she could not be said to commit adultery, since her fidelity was not there (*Dig.* 48.5.6.pr; *Cod. Iust.* 9.9.23).

18. On affronts to proper Roman women, see *Dig.* 47.10.15.15–23 (no insult if dressed as a slave, 15). On the Lex Scantinia and the rape of *ingenui*

(male): Juv. 2.36–37, 43–44; Cic. *Fam.* 8.12.3 and 14.4; Livy 8.28; Suet. *Dom.* 8.3; Quint. *Inst.* 4.2.69 and 71.

19. Richlin 1981*a*, 1981*b*, 1983.

20. See Buckland [1908] 1970, 36–38, 70–71, 603–4, and Watson 1987, 115–33.

21. For the possibilities of punishing cruel masters, the difficulties of slaves' legal recourse, and the limits of the relief offered by legislation, see Watson 1987, 127–29; Bradley 1987, 123–29. On bias, see Garnsey 1968.

22. Gaius 3.222. With slaves, the act had to be considered especially heinous (*atrox*) and an affront to the master (*Dig.* 47.10.15.34, 43, 44); see Ulpian's requirement (47.10.15.38) "against good morals" that excluded a slap for the purpose of correction. On *iniuria* and a slave's chastity, see *Dig.* 47.10.9.4 and 15.15. Sexual assault on a virgin slave girl might constitute damage to property (*Dig.* 47.10.25), but the castration of a slave boy (9.2.27.28) would give his master grounds for injury, not damage, because it increased his value. On cases of insult directed at slaves, see Buckland [1908] 1970, 79–82. The *actio iniuriarum servi nomine*, unknown to Gaius (3.222), is explicitly mentioned only by Ulpian (47.10.15.44); see Watson 1987, 62–63. On killing or wounding a slave as damage to property, see *Dig.* 9.2. passim.

23. On torture, treatments, and punishments, see Mommsen 1899, 405ff.; Garnsey 1970, 103–52, 213–16; Finley 1980, 94–95.

24. On the *peculium*, see Buckland [1908] 1970, 187–238, and Watson 1987, 95–101. On noxal actions, see Gaius 4.75–80; Buckland [1908] 1970, 99–130 (slaves); Kaser 1971–75, 1:163; De Visscher 1947; Watson 1987, 67–77. For slaves' judicial capacity, see Biscardi 1975; for slaves and contracts in law, see Watson 1987, 90–95.

25. Freedmen's sons and descendants held Roman and municipal offices (see Duff 1928, 66–67; Treggiari 1969, 52–64; Gordon 1931; Garnsey 1975; D'Arms 1981, 134–40), although they might, like Horace, the son of a freed father, feel the stigma of such origin (*Sat.* 1.6.27–37, 45–48; cf. Pliny *Ep.* 3.14.1).

26. On the dynamics of power in Roman satire, see Richlin 1983, esp. chaps. 2 and 3. On the stigma of foreign origin, see Juv. 1.26–30, 101–9, 3. Petronius ridicules Hermeros's (57–58) and Trimalchio's (39.3–4) attempts to live as "a man among men" by adopting their patrons' values and lifestyles. On Trimalchio's career and aspirations, cf. Veyne 1961, with D'Arms 1981, 97–120.

27. Weaver 1972, 184, 188–93. Weaver (185–86) finds a pattern of early manumission for women, probably *matrimonii causa*.

28. On the effects of the SC Claudianum and the status of children of "mixed marriages," see Weaver 1972, 162–69, and 1986; Crook 1967*a*. For children left in slavery, see Weaver 1986, 157, and 1972, 178; Hopkins 1978, 165. For patrons' interference, see *Dig.* 37.14.6.pr. and 3, 38.1.13.5, 40.9.31.

29. *Beneficium* and the display of *obsequium: Dig.* 37.14.19, 38.2.1; see the complaints of Tacitus's senators (*Ann.* 13.26–27; Cosentini 1948–50, 1:96–99). For the implications of reciprocity in *beneficium* and related terms, see Saller 1982, 17–39. For the restrictions imposed by *obsequium*, see *Dig.* 37.14.1, 37.15.2, 37.15.7.2 and 4, 47.10.7.2 (only when the offense was *atrox*), 47.10.11.7. For the technical meaning of *obsequium*, see Lambert 1934, 8–33; Cosentini 1948–50, 1:69–103; Duff 1928, 37–43; Fabre

1981, 148–50, 225–26; Treggiari 1969, 69–75 (with analysis of Duff, Cosentini, and Lambert).

30. For freedmen's vulnerability with respect to patrons, see *Dig.* 1.16.9.3, 37.14.1, 37.14.7.1; Suet. *Claud.* 25. A similar vulnerability characterized freedmen's relations with the state, especially in cases involving patrons. See the treatment of the freedmen of the murdered Pedanius Secundus (Tac. *Ann.* 14.42–45) and Afranius Dexter (Pliny *Ep.* 8.14.12–26). For the SC Claudianum that dealt with slaves manumitted by a murdered master and Trajan's ruling that extended to freedmen, see *Dig.* 29.5.3.16, 10.1; Tac. *Ann.* 13.32.1.

31. Pliny *Ep.* 9.21 and 24; Tac. *Ann.* 13.26.3.

32. *Dig.* 38.2.1, 44.5.1.5–6; cf. Tac. *Ann.* 13.26.5: "at criminum manifestos merito ad servitutem retrahi, ut metu coerceantur quos beneficia non mutavissent."

33. Other services included guardianship of the patron's children, management of his property, and support for the patron, his children, and parents (*Dig.* 25.3.5.19–20 and 26; 37.14.19). Support in times of illness and indigence was reciprocal (*Dig.* 25.3.5.18, 38.2.33). On *operae,* see Lambert 1938; Cosentini 1948–50, 1:105–85; Fabre 1981, 318ff.; Duff 1928, 44–49; Treggiari 1969, 74–81. Negotiations and oath: *Dig.* 38.1.7.pr. and 2, 44.5.2.2, 40.12.44.pr. Excessive claims: see above, n. 32, and *Dig.* 38.1.2.pr. Patron's profits from freedmen's services to third parties and inheritance of *operae* by patrons' heirs: *Dig.* 38.1.9.1, 23.pr., 25, 27, 37.4; 38.1.6.

34. *Dig.* 37.14.20, 38.2.1.2. On patron's claims, see Gaius 3.41ff.

35. Van Gennep 1960, 62; Cassirer 1953, 49–52 (see also Patterson 1982, 55).

36. The bibliography on Roman nomenclature is extensive; only a few works are mentioned here. For a survey of the topic, see E. Fraenkel, "Namenwesen. Die Lateinischen Personennamen," *RE* 16.1648–70, and Thylander 1952, 54–133. For a summary of the principles of nomenclature, see Calabi Limentani 1968. For slave names, see Baumgart 1936. On cognomina, see Kajanto 1965, 1968; Solin 1971, 1982; Taylor 1961; Frank 1916. See also Wilkinson 1961; Kajanto 1963; Shackleton Bailey 1976, 1988, esp. 3–8. On the nomenclature of imperial freedmen and slaves, see Weaver 1972, 24–92; Chantraine 1967. For a recent bibliography, see Rawson 1986c, 252.

37. "Libertination" is used by Solin and Huttunen as analogous to the term "filiation."

38. Kajanto 1965. Since some slaves had their parents' names (e.g., 365, 7284, 9326), we must wonder about their role in naming their children.

39. *FIRA* 3.88–89, 132.

40. Patterson 1982, 54–58, esp. 55.

41. Huttunen 1974, 129, 138 (on different proportions of deceased and commemorators).

42. Terms name inferiors (*libertus, servus, verna, vicarius*), superiors (*dominus, patronus*), or peers (*conservus, collibertus, contubernalis*). *Contubernalis* (partner in a slave marriage) poses interpretive problems where one or both partners have nomina. See Rawson 1974; Treggiari 1981a, 1981b.

43. Huttunen (1974, 140) finds a marked difference in the use of status indication in the *sepulcrales* and the occupational epitaphs: the deceased

(68.8%) and commemorators (39.2%) with occupational title were more likely to have accurate status indication than in the *sepulcrales* (21.8% and 18.5%).

44. Taylor 1961, 117.

45. Solin 1971, 45–47; Huttunen 1974, 159, 165–66.

46. *PIR* S. 622. The editors of *CIL* 6 think the epitaph may have originally come from the tomb.

47. Only *columbaria* that include individuals predominantly from one *familia* are considered: e.g., Monumentum libertorum et familiae L. Arrunti (5931–60), Monumentum Statiliorum (6213–6640), Monumentum Volusiorum (7281–7394a, 33250–54), Monumentum C. Anni Pollionis (7395–7429), Monumentum Iuniorum Silanorum (7600–7643). On inscriptions from the Monumenta Liviae, Volusiorum, and Statiliorum, see Treggiari 1975a, 1975b. On domestic *collegia*, see Waltzing 1895–1900, 4: 167–76.

48. Treggiari 1975a, 394.

49. Fifteen individuals in domestic *collegia* appear in single-family *columbaria*: eleven in the Monumentum Statiliorum (6215, 6216, 6217, 6218, 6219, 6221) and four in the Monumentum Volusiorum (7281–81a).

50. *PIR* S. 622 and 595; see also 6323–24 (*nutrices*), 6325 (*obstetrix*), 6256–57, 6264 (*cubicularii*). The situation is more complex: see chap. 5, 155–57.

51. See, e.g., T. Statilius Dasius Tauri l. *ad vestem avi* (6372: T. Statilius Dasius, freedman of Taurus, clothes caretaker of (his) grandfather, *PIR* S. 615 and 617) and Iasullus Philerotis lib. Sisennae *paedagogus* (6328: Iasullus, freedman of Phileros, child attendant of Sisenna, *PIR* S. 613). Status indication often identifies an individual, like Iasullus, as the slave or freedman of another member of the *familia*: see, e.g., the slaves of T. Statilius Posidippus, a freedman in the same *familia* (6261–62, 6274, 6277–79).

52. Of the fifteen individuals with notation of *natio*, ten lack status indication. The foreign *nationes* include: Dardanus/a (6343), Sura (6340), Cilix (9675), Paphlago (9675), Eudaemon (7614), Sidensis (9580), Bessus (9709), *de familia rege* Mitredatis (*sic*, 5639). On *natio*, see Bang 1910, 1912; Gordon 1924; Westermann 1955, 96–98; Harris 1980, 117. For the association of slave and foreign origin, see, e.g., Mart. 6.39, 7.80, 10.76; Pet. 57.4–10; Juv. 1.102–5, 3.60–84, 5.50–55. An Italian location used by someone without status identification is not taken as an indication of servile origin: Pollentinus (9587), Blera (9629), Aquensis (9717), *domo* Cortona (9785), Reatinus (37776), *ordindus civitate* Miseni (33887).

53. All but one of the twenty-one individuals with agnomina lack status indication. Thirteen have single names and were probably slaves; indeed, burial location reveals that ten were actually members of large *familiae*. Most of the work on agnomina concerns their use in the *familia Caesaris*: Chaintraine 1967, 293ff.; Boulvert 1964, 2:464ff.; Weaver 1972, 90–92, 212–23, and 1964. For agnomina in the nomenclature of adopted *ingenui*, see Thylander 1952, 128ff.

54. For Cornelia, see *PIR*[2] C. 1455, 1477, and *PIR* S. 613.

55. See the groups indicated by agnomina in the *familia Caesaris*, Weaver 1972, 90–91, 212–18. Six individuals without status indication have a nomen and an agnomen: Q. Glitius Felix Vergilianus *poeta* (638), L. Arruntius Sempronianus Asclepiades imp. Domitiani *medicus* (8895, cf. Huttu-

nen 1974, 105 n. 209), Ti. Claudius Priscus Secundianus *coactor* (9187), C. Iulius Felix Demetrianus *marmorarius* (9553), T. Statilius Eros Caninianus *pistor* (9808), Spurinnia Nice Torqu[atiana] *nutrix* (7290, cf. Treggiari 1976, 88–89). In each case, the association of agnomen and nomen or the particular agnomen suggests freed status.

56. The presence of family members in the occupational epitaphs has little effect on the use of status indication: it occurs for 51.3% (*N* = 154) of those with a spouse (only), for 51.4% (*N* = 19) of those with siblings, and for 46.5% (*N* = 416) of those with no relations. However, when an individual appears with parents or children, he or she is less likely to have status indication (34.4%, *N* = 33). Generally, there is a tendency for both relative and individual with job title to have status indication or for both to lack it.

57. Arescusa and her daughter may have the same nomen because both were slaves manumitted by the same patron (see Huttunen 1974, 134). A Q. Haterius Valens and a Q. Haterius Felix also appear, but it is not clear whether they were Evagogus's *liberti, colliberti,* or sons (in which case, given Euraesis's nomen, they would have been born after Evagogus's manumission). On a possible background for Arescusa and Evagogus, see chap. 4, 119.

58. For spouses whose statuses were not intertwined to the same degree, we can only observe whether they tended to come from different status groups and assess the comparative strength of certain marriage patterns. As Weaver (1972, 179–95) and Huttunen (1974, 145–55) found in larger samples of couples, men and women from the same status group tended to marry each other (the tendency is especially strong for women with occupational title). This pattern has limited predictive value (see Huttunen, 146). The legal condition of some couples was quite different: twenty-three slaves had married those who were at least free (uncertain freeborn), and twelve uncertain slaves had uncertain freeborn spouses. Other circumstances, chiefly the extrafamilial relationship between husband and wife (*patronus idem coniunx* or *liberta et uxor*), affect the status pattern of spouses. For example, we find fifteen uncertain freeborn males married to freedwomen, six of whom were described as the freedwomen of their husbands (9567, 9569, 9590, 9609, 9975, 33880). Although we cannot be sure (see Weaver 1972, 190–91), the husband may have been a freedman, even a former *contubernalis* (see Treggiari 1975a, 396–97). The intention to marry a freed slave was one of the grounds for early manumission in the Lex Aelia Sentia (Gaius 1.19). A *libertina* could manumit a former *conservus matrimonii causa* (*Dig.* 40.2.14.1), but women, especially *ingenuae*, marrying their *liberti* was not acceptable (Mart. 2.34), and the unions were banned by Septimius Severus (*Cod. Iust.* 5.4.3); see Weaver 1986, 153–54.

59. See n. 45 above.

60. In the analysis of the uncertain categories, cases in which a name pattern strongly suggests a particular legal status are compared with others in which at least some of the parties have status indication; the use of a cognomen without a nomen is evaluated in light of factors like the age of the bearer and the relationship of commemorator and deceased.

61. Of the uncertain freeborn, 19% (*N* = 81) were probably freedmen; they could establish a family of creation but claim a family of origin only with difficulty. This may explain why 10.9% of the uncertain freeborn

(32.5%, $N = 13$, were probably freed slaves) noted children, whereas only 1.6% and 1.4% (all of whom were probably freeborn or show no signs of servile origin) acknowledged a mother or father, respectively.

62. Factors other than status—different chronologies of death in the family, space on the epitaph, and financial resources—are less important than they may seem. First, there is no reason to assume different chronologies of death for freeborn, freed, and slave families. Second, 310 individuals (23.2%) are found in *columbaria* (32.2%, $N = 88$, of the slaves; 41.2%, $N = 142$, of the uncertain slaves) where the typical epitaph is small, usually naming a single person. However, when family relations were indicated, the relative was generally a spouse.

63. Compare Plut. *Cat. Mai.* 21.2. See Bradley 1987, 47–80. On other quasi-familial relations within the *familia*, with *alumni*, and with *vernae*, see Rawson 1986a.

64. On the passage, cf. Flory 1978, 78.

65. See Varro's warning (*Rust.* 1.17.5) about too many slaves from the same *natio:* "ex eo enim potissimum solere offensiones domesticas fieri." Implicitly, too, this could create a separate group within the *familia* based on a common ethnic background, cultural heritage, and language, experiences that were not shared by other slaves and the master.

66. Treggiari 1975a, 396. On slave marriages, see above, n. 42.

67. On Huttunen's (1974) categorization, see chap. 1, n. 46. In contrast to this study, Huttunen relies exclusively on name form at the first stage of categorization, which increases his figures for uncertain freedmen. Here, only individuals with nomina and without status indication who were buried in household *columbaria*, members of domestic *collegia*, or noted the name of their employer are considered uncertain freedmen. Huttunen categorizes only those involved in certain name patterns as uncertain freedmen. I do not consider name patterns where common imperial nomina are involved and omit certain name patterns used by Huttunen (1974, 132–37, cf. 187).

68. Compare Huttunen's findings (1974, 192); but he includes senators, equestrians, and soldiers, "occupations" implying free birth.

69. Huttunen 1974, 41–45 (cf. Maier 1953–54, 343–44); Taylor 1961, 130–31.

70. Huttunen 1974, 195, 41–42; Maier 1953–54. Huttunen's index of representation considers those covered by formulas—*sibi, suis, libertis libertabusque eorum, posteris.*

71. Huttunen 1974, 67–68. For older assumptions of commercial predominance, see Frank 1916, 694–95, and 1933–40, 5:235; Duff 1928, 103–25; Taylor 1961, 131.

72. For labor and the history of slavery in literature, see, e.g., App. *BCiv.* 1.1.7–8; Plut. *Ti. Gracch.* 8; and accounts of slave revolts that consider slaves' labor, Diod. 34.2.1–4, 27–29. For examples in Seneca, see *Ep.* 27.5–8, 47, 110.17, 122.15–16, 123.7; *De Ira* 3.29.1; *Ben.* 3.22.1. On behavior and jobs, see Pet. passim, esp. Habinnas's favorite (68.6–8) who imitates trades; Juv. 5.56–69, 9.102–23; Sen. *Ep.* 47.

73. Compare Patterson 1982, 99.

74. On slaves in the census, see *Dig.* 50.15.4.5 (*officia et artificia*). Work and the use of the slave: *Dig.* 7.1.15.1. In wills: *Dig.* 32.99.4–5, 40.4.24. See Finley (1980, 74–75) on control of labor as a facet of the master's total con-

trol of the slave. The slave's labor and acquisitions were a major concern in law: see Buckland [1908] 1970, 131ff.

75. The discussion focuses on those who named the deceased (including those who dedicated their own tombs) in order to examine men and women in the same circumstances. The category "other or unclear" covers those whose epitaphs are commemorated by individuals whose relation to the deceased is not specified or is obscured by breakage, "inferiors" (primarily *servi* and *liberti* of the deceased), teachers, and nurses.

76. 7946 (*musicus*), 8012 (*paedagogus*), 9222 (*caelator*), 9437 (*gemmarius*), 9447 (*grammaticus* and *lector*), 9449 (*grammaticus* and *procurator*), 9545 (*margaritarius*), 9659 (*negotiator*), 9797 (*pilicrepus*).

77. On the treatment and conditions of slaves on rural estates, see Varro *Rust.* 1.17.1–7, 2.10.1–11; Columella *Rust.* 1.8–9; Cato *Agr.* 5.1–5; and the discussion of White 1970, 332–76.

78. "D(is) M(anibus). quincunque es, puero lacrimas effunde, viator. bis tulit his senos primaevi germini[s] annos deliciumque fuit domini, spes grata parentum, quos male deseruit longo post fata dolori. noverat his docta fabricare monilia dextra et molle in varias aurum disponere gemmas. nomen erat puer Pagus. at nun[c] funus acerbum et cinis in tumulis iacet et sine nomine corpus. qui vixit annis XII . . .'"

79. Treggiari 1975b, 57; Flory 1978, 80.

80. Huttunen 1974, 48, 71.

81. Patterson 1982, 11.

82. Hegel [1807] 1977, 115–17; see Patterson 1982, 97–101, esp. 98–99. This discussion owes much to conversations with Paul Breines, Avery Gordon, Andrew Herman, and Charles Sarno.

83. Patterson 1982, 97–98.

84. Hegel [1807] 1977, 118; cf. Patterson 1982, 98–99.

85. Patterson 1982, 99.

86. Ibid., 38, 40, 46. Cf. *Dig.* 50.17.209: "servitutem mortalitati fere comparamus."

87. Patterson (1982, 200) observes that "the slave as an active agent was recognized only when he behaved in a criminal manner." The occupational inscriptions represent a different assessment by the slave.

88. See chap. 3, 82–83.

89. Physical maintenance: *Dig.* 38.1.17–18, 22.2, 34, 38. Earning a living and family: *Dig.* 38.1.19, 33, 50. Freedwomen as wives: *Dig.* 38.1.14, 48. Children's and patron's claims: *Dig.* 38.1.37.pr.; Gaius 3.41–42.

90. See Lambert 1934, 97ff.; Cosentini 1948–50, 1:8off.; Treggiari 1969, 69ff.; Fabre 1981, 318ff. For excessive demands, see *Dig.* 38.1 and 2 passim; cf. 38.1.22. pr. (*operarum editio nihil aliud sit, quam officii praestatio*). For a summary of the patron's limitations, see Duff 1928, 43ff.

91. The emphasis on his honesty is interesting in light of the usual expectation of slaves' and freedmen's dishonesty: e.g., Pliny *HN* 33.26; Sen. *Tranq.* 8.8; Pet. 38.12–14; Pliny *Ep.* 1.21.

92. See also the description of the *actor* as *fidelissimus* (9119, 9128).

93. On the age of manumission of female slaves, see n. 27 above. According to Weaver (1972), the normal age of manumission of male private slaves appears to be thirty (184); for imperial male slaves, between thirty and forty (97–104). Compare Alföldy (1972), who finds that three-fifths of the private freedmen in the western half of the empire whose age at death

is recorded died before reaching thirty, but note Hopkins's warning (1978, 127 n. 63) on the limits of this figure.

94. *Operae* were demanded of minors (*Dig.* 38.1.7.5). On training young slaves, see Forbes 1955; Mohler 1940. All five individuals who died before age sixteen were slaves or uncertain slaves: 9437 (*gemmarius*), 9649 (*musicarius*), and 9726, 9728, 9731 (*ornatrices*).

95. See chap. 5, 131–36, 144.

96. Patterson 1982, 249.

CHAPTER III • The Meanings of Work

1. On Roman attitudes toward work, see De Robertis 1963, 21–97; Treggiari 1980; D'Arms 1981, 20–47, 149–71.

2. On wealth as a determinant of social priorities, see Mart. 6.8, Juv. 3.126ff., 212ff., 5.132ff., 7.139ff. For the stereotypes of satire, see Juv. 3.58ff. (greasy foreigners), 2.77ff., 8 (decadent nobles), 5 (needy clients and insensitive patrons), 6 (unchaste women).

3. Doctors and teachers: Mart. 1.30, 1.47, 6.53; Juv. 10.222–24; *Anth. Pal.* 113–14, 116, 118–25, 257, 280; Pet. 42.5; Quint. *Inst.* 1.2.4, cf. 2.2.1–5 and 2.3.15. Waiter and *dispensator:* Pet. 30; Juv. 5.59–69, 7.218–19. Businessmen and auctioneers: Juv. 1.26–33, 10.222; Mart. 6.8; Hor. *Epist.* 1.7.55ff.; Trimalchio's vulgar, cash-minded friends, Pet. 45–46, 57–58; cf. n. 4 below. On the presumptions of the rich but lowborn, see Juv. 1.101ff., 3.153ff., Mart. 5.8, 23.

4. Juv. 3, 14.201–7; Mart. 3.16, 7.64; Cic. *Off.* 1.150.

5. Compare MacMullen 1974, 115–16. On pleasing and force, see chap. 5, 149–50.

6. Juv. 3.34–38, 154–59; Mart. 3.16, 5.8, 5.14, 5.23, 6.17, 7.64; see also Trimalchio (Pet. 32), whose napkin with broad purple stripe and gilded ring with iron stars imitate a senator's toga and an equestrian's ring.

7. Goffman 1963, 41ff. For other examples, see Mart. 2.29, 5.13, 10.27, 11.12, 11.37, and Petronius's (57–58) Hermeros, who makes virtues of the characteristics that stigmatize him (Goffman, 11).

8. Cato *Agr.* praef.; Suet. *Aug.* 2.3, 4.2; see also *Vit.* 2.1, *Otho.* 1.1, *Vesp.* 1.2–4. Dio Cass. 46.4–5, 7.4. For political invective and trade, see D'Arms 1981, 3–6.

9. Dirt: Juv. 14.201–7, Cic. *Flac.* 18, Sen. *Ep.* 87.15–18; on the "good" dirt of camp and farm, Sen. *Ep.* 86.12. Skills and objects: Cic. *Off.* 2.12–13; Mart. 12.66.5–7, 14.95, 109; cf. Seneca's (*Ep.* 90) arguments against Posidonius's elevation of skills (esp. 15–16, 19, 25). Philosophical metaphors: Sen. *Ep.* 31.6, 87.12–14; Todorov 1985, 129.

10. This passage has been much discussed: De Robertis 1963, 52–63; Finley 1973, 41ff. (see Fredericksen 1975, criticizing Finley's claim that Cicero's views were representative); Brunt 1973, 26–34 (whose views Cicero presents); D'Arms 1981, 23–24 (n. 18, on representativeness); Treggiari 1980. On Cicero's views, cf. Sen. *Ep.* 88.

11. Hiring the labor of an individual (*locatio conductio operarum*) was distinguished from a contract for a specific task (*locatio conductio operis faciendi*). On *mercenarii* and contracts for labor, see De Robertis 1963, 117–81; Nörr 1965; Treggiari 1980; De Ste. Croix 1981, 197–201; Martini 1958; Thomas 1961. On the equation of labor and laborer, see De Robertis,

143ff., and De Ste. Croix, 198; cf. Patterson 1982, 9. See Petronius's (117.11–12) Corax, who asserts his free birth when he has hired himself out as a porter: "nec minus liber sum quam vos, etiamsi pauperem pater me reliquit" (see De Ste. Croix, 199; Crook 1967b, 195–96).

12. Friedländer [1907] 1965, 2:111, and Balsdon 1969, 279ff. (with references).

13. Cic. Off. 1.92; see D'Arms 1981, 20–22, 152–54 (with references).

14. Gell. 3.1; on avarice, see also Hor. Epist. 1.1.53–54, Cic. Flac. 7, and D'Arms 1981, 153 n. 11. Martial's list also associates negotiator with the delator, calumniator, fraudator, and lanista. On money and dirt, see above, n. 9, and Sen. Contr. 1.2, Gell. 1.12.5. On os impurum, see Richlin 1983, 26–29, 69, 99, 150–51. Money and odor: Juv. 14.201ff., Sen. Ep. 86.12–13, Suet. Vesp. 23.3. On impurity, see Douglas 1984.

15. See Douglas 1970, esp. 70–71, 80–81.

16. A few in administration, finance, and secretarial service worked in public capacities: aeditui (11); men connected with the public horrea, etc. (5); mensores (of grain, 4); custodiarii (2); ministratores with business address (2); a tabularius with a business address; and a procurator sociorum miniariarum.

17. Fabri tignuarii (148, 321, 996, 9405–8); marmorarii (9550); subaediani (33875); sectores serrarii (9888); brattiarii inauratores (95); pausarii et argentarii (348); aerarii (9136, 36771); fabri ferrarii (1892); aurifices (9202); calcar(i)enses (9224, cf. 9223); fullones (268, magistri fontani); centonarii (7861, 7863–64, 9254, 37784a); sagarii (339, 956); fabri soliarii baxiarii (9404); lanii (167–68); pistores (22, 1002); restiones (9856); coronarii (4414); anularii (9144); citrarii (9258).

18. Negotiatores ole(ari) ex Baetica (1625b, 2); negotians vinarius item navicularius, cur(ator) corporis maris hadriatici (9682); negotians salsarius q(uin)q(uennalis) corporis negotiantium Malacitanorum (9677); cf. 1620 (mercatores frumentari et oleari Afrari).

19. Mensor (of grain, 22); mensor machinarius (9626, 33883); custodiarius (327); those connected with the horrea (188, 236, 338). The others include: aedituus aedis Concordiae, patron of a collegium speclariorum (2206), procurator sociorum miniariarum (9634), and aedituus collegi tabernaclarioriorum (sic, 5183b). The collegia that they served or supported belong in other occupational categories; they appear here because individuals are classified by occupation.

20. Huttunen 1974, 127; see D'Arms 1981, 62–71 (esp. n. 62 for commercial involvement of senators).

21. For the proportion of the elite in the population, MacMullen 1974, 88–89 n. 1. On the wealth of senators, see Shatzman 1975; Duncan-Jones 1974, 17–32, 343–44; Rawson 1976.

22. On the importance of display, see MacMullen 1974, 106ff.; on spending in the republic, see Shatzman 1975, 84–98, 108.

23. General criticism: Juv. 1.94–95, 11.90ff., 14.86–95, 304–8; Mart. 2.43, 9.59, 10.80; see also Sen. Ep. 27.5–8, 51, 86, 87.5–11, 110.14–20, 115.9–11 (no evidence, of course, for the Flavian period). Criticism of the spending of parsimonious patrons: Juv. 1.95–96, 5.43ff., 7.178ff.; Mart. 2.43, 2.46, 3.82, 10.49. Use of luxury by the lowborn: Mart. 2.29, 2.57, 3.82, 5.8, 5.23, 10.27, 11.37.

24. Juv. 11.56ff.; Mart. 5.78; Hor. Epist. 1.5.

25. Compare Epict. 4.6.4 (cited by MacMullen 1974, 110–11); see also Tac. *Ann.* 3.53.5, Sen. *Ep.* 110.14–17, Mart. 2.53, 9.22.

26. *PIR* S. 383; *PIR* V. 664; on Caecilia Metella, see 6.1274 (Gordon and Gordon 1958–65, n. 23). Producers of luxury goods are more numerous in the *familia Caesaris* and especially in the *familiae* of members of the emperor's family. In the *familia Caesaris*: *spec(u)liarii* (5203, 8659–60), *aurifices* (3950–51), *barbaricarius* (33766), *corinthiarii* (33768, two). In the *familiae* of imperial family members: *marg(aritarius)* (3981), *argentarii* (4328, 4422–24, 4715, 5184, 8727), *aurifices* and *inaurator* (3927–28, 3943–45a, 3949, 8741), *caelator* (4328), *siricaria* (?9892), *un[g]u[en]ta(rius)* (?4252). Six of the former and all eighteen of the latter can be dated to the Julio-Claudian period. Interestingly, fifteen or sixteen belonged to *familiae* of imperial women related to Augustus, who had imposed sumptuary laws (Suet. *Aug.* 34, and Tac. *Ann.* 3.54) and was supposed to have lived simply (Suet. *Aug.* 72–73): Livia (9), Marcella (5), Octavia, daughter of Claudius (1), and an unidentified Augusta (1).

27. Loane 1938, 35, 50–55. Shopping for luxury goods: Mart. 9.59, 10.80.

28. Treggiari 1975b, 60. On the ridicule of the parvenu, see Mart. 3.82; Juv. 7.129ff., 11.146–61; Pet. passim; see also Sen. *Ep.* 47, 110.14 and 17, *Tranq.* 8.6. On travel with an entourage of servants, see Sen. *Ep.* 123.7; Juv. 1.64–68, 7.141–43; Mart. 6.77, 9.22. On the lack of proper servants, see Cic. *Pis.* 67 and Sen. *Ep.* 87.2–4 (see n. 33 below).

29. Employments of individuals attached to large households: building (6.9%, $N = 32$); manufacture (9.9%, $N = 46$); sales (.4%, $N = 2$); professional service (6%, $N = 28$); skilled service (7.1%, $N = 33$); domestic service (34.2%, $N = 159$); transportation (7.1%, $N = 33$); administration, finance, and secretarial service (28.4%, $N = 132$).

30. Treggiari 1975b, 57.

31. See Syme [1939] 1979, 379–82, 498; Shatzman 1975, 399 (T. Statilius Taurus, cos. 37 B.C.). Assessments of their wealth point to this *columbarium*.

32. On land, plate or cash, and slaves as the formula for property holding, see Pet. 37.8–10, 57.6; Mart. 9.22; Juv. 3.141–44. The constituents of respectable property differ only in degree for the very wealthy Trimalchio (Pet. 48.2–3, 31.9–10, 73.5, 52.1–3, 53.4, 47.11–13, 53.2) and his more humble guest Hermeros (Pet. 57).

33. Juv. 1.64–68, 7.141–43; Mart. 2.81, 6.77; Pet. 27; Sen. *Ep.* 17.3. Westermann (1955, 88–89) cites Sen. *Ep.* 87.2–4 and Augustus's limitation of twenty slaves for exiles (Dio Cass. 56.27.3) as evidence against exaggerating the numbers of slaves kept by the wealthy. However, Seneca's point is that he was traveling unusually simply, and inappropriately, for his rank; nonetheless, he was accompanied by a *vehiculum* of slaves (according to Westermann, four or five slaves). Presumably Augustus's restriction intended to shame men of standing. If twenty servants was punitive, what can we assume about the normal numbers of servants?

34. See Petronius's portrayal of service in Trimalchio's house and the impression it was supposed to make on the guests (31.3ff., 36.7–8, 47.11–13, 53, 70, 71.1–4). See Hopkins 1978, 112.

35. Figures here include nurslings/charges; in most cases the nurse or

child attendant will have been a slave or freedman of the family, if not the charge. Excluded are those titled by spouse-patrons.

36. Juv. 1.101–6, cf. Mart. 2.29, 5.13, 5.35, and Hor. *Epod.* 4.

37. The number of people included in a tomb by name or formula suggests the responsibilities assumed by the commemorators and hence their resources (whether those named were eventually buried in the tomb is another issue). I use the term "tomb size" to indicate the total number of burials specified in an epitaph. I add the number of named deceased to the number of unnamed individuals covered by an epitaph's formulas—*sibi, suis, libertis libertabusque* (usually with *posteris eorum*), and *posteris* and variations. I equate the number covered by *sibi* with the number of commemorators and follow Huttunen's (1974, 30–42) calculations for the closest estimates for *suis* (3) and *posteris* (3) and his minimum figure for *libertis libertabusque* (3), so the calculation of an individual's freedmen will be conservative. In the following discussions, the figures for tomb size usually apply to a group of individuals; the median of the tombs under consideration is given, because the mean is distorted by a few epitaphs that name a large number of people. Tomb size is only a suggestive measure. We cannot be sure precisely how many people were actually intended by the formulas; exact numbers would have varied with family size and number of freedmen. And, of course, some tombs (e.g., the Baker's Tomb, 1958 = 1.1203) whose epitaphs name a small number of deceased were nevertheless large and therefore costly structures. Although tomb sizes do reflect the actual number of burials, the figures are more important here as representations of the funds that individuals could expend in the social rituals of death and commemoration.

38. Median tomb size for tradesmen in luxury goods in 5.3. Ten (50%) claim freedmen by formula; five (25%) name freedmen individually. For a clear example of the commemoration permitted by success, see the burial arrangements of L. Aufidius Aprilis, *corinthiarius de theatro Balbi*, *NSA* 1975, 205ff. On the prosperity of goldsmiths and jewelers, see Gummerus 1918, 259ff.

39. Lugli 1938, 3:493–95; Nash 1968, 2:329–32 (with bibliography); Toynbee 1971, 128; Treggiari 1969, 96.

40. The figure 800,000 is the inference of Bormann (*ILS* 7812). See also *CIL* 11.5399: "P. Decimius P. l. Eros / Merula VI vir / viam a cisterna / ad domum L. Muti / stravit ea pecunia / . . ."

41. Finley 1973, 51.

42. The fears of the advantaged were not groundless if Pliny (*Ep.* 3.14) is correct about the freed lineage of Larcius Macedo. On freedmen's descendants, see chap. 2, n. 25.

43. Pet. 37.8–38.5, 53, 76, assuming his fortune at the time of the dinner party is vested primarily in land and loans, not directly in the commercial ventures that built it. Also, Trimalchio, no doubt like his creator Petronius, originally inherited money. On his career, see chap. 2, n. 26.

44. MacMullen 1974, 61–63. For examples of freedmen's contributions to their communities, see Duthoy 1978, 1267, 1281–83.

45. Pet. 52.10–11.

46. For the literary context of rich freedmen, see, e.g., Juv. 1.101ff.; Mart. 2.29; Tac. *Ann.* 12.53. Duncan-Jones 1974, 343–44. On wealthy

freedmen, De Ste. Croix 1981, 176–79. On *Augustales* and *serviri Augustales*, see A. von Premerstein, "Augustales," *DE* 1.824–77; Taylor 1914; Duthoy 1978, 1974; D'Arms 1981, 126–40.

47. In other cases, the freedmen themselves commemorated the epitaph. Twenty-five of those in manufacture, sales, and banking were buried by their freedmen; seventeen of them were themselves freedmen. Of the 197 freedmen in these fields who figure as the deceased or self-commemorator, 23 appear with a patron (*N* of tombs = 13). For freedmen's representations of themselves as members of families, see Kleiner 1977.

48. ". . . ossa hominis boni misericordis amantis / pauperis . . ." See Gummerus 1915, 170; Treggiari 1969, 98 n. 7. See also L. Licinius M. f. Pol. Nepos (9659), whose claim ("cuius de vita merito pote nemo queri. qui negotiando locupletum se speravit esse futurum; spe deceptus erat . . .") is belied by the long epitaph and his burial of parents, brother, and friends.

49. Pliny *Ep.* 2.4.3 (cf. D'Arms 1981, 155, 169); Pliny *HN* 18.20, Livy 3.26 (Cincinnatus, see Garnsey 1980, 36–37); Livy *Epit.* 48, Sen. *Ep.* 87.9–10, Gell. 13.24 (Cato); see also Gell. 1.14, Sen. *Ep.* 87.41. For the virtue of poverty in philosophical discourse, see Sen. *Ep.* 4.10–11, 17.3–5, 87.38–40. On contempt for poverty in the "real" world, see Juv. 3.144–53 and MacMullen 1974, 116 (esp. n. 91), 139 (with references); cf. Dio Chyrs. *Or.* 7.103, cf. 115, 125.

50. On the training of architects, see Vitr. 1.1; Burford 1972, 101–7. For the qualifications of teachers, see Quint. *Inst.* 2.3; for the background of noted *grammatici* and *rhetores*, see Suet. *Gram.* and *Rhet.* On doctors, see Scarborough 1969, 122–33. On the education of slaves in these fields, see Forbes 1955; Mohler 1940. Criticism of doctors and teachers focuses on the lack of this element in their training and the injuries they inflict on society; see Pliny *HN* 29.12ff.; Scarborough 1969, 94–108 (with references); Quint. *Inst.* 2.2.15. On secretaries, see Mart. 1.101; Suet. *Ner.* 44.1; Nep. *Att.* 13.3; on Cicero's Tiro, see Treggiari 1969, 259–63.

51. Pet. 30; Juv. 1.89–92, 7.218–19; Pliny *HN* 7.129. On the master's vulnerability through his *dispensator*, see Mart. 5.42.5; Pet. 45.8.

52. "Pudens M. Lepidi l. grammaticus / procurator eram Lepidae moresq(ue) regebam / dum vixi mansit Caesaris illa nurus / Philologus discipulus." Pudens's student commemorated his deceased teacher, but the sentiments expressed in the first person make Pudens the speaker. Another example may be 9447: "grammaticus lectorque fui, set lector eorum more incorrupto qui placuere sono." On the importance of teachers' moral character, see Pliny *Ep.* 3.3. See also those described as *fidelissimus* (9119, 9128, 9834) and the praise in 8991 and 9604.

53. Treggiari 1975 b, 57.

54. Flory 1978, 80.

55. On the reading of *lecticarius*, see Baldwin 1978, 92. See also Pet. 31.3–4: the servants lack job title, but Petronius perhaps ridicules Trimalchio's literal understanding of the tasks of *pedisequi*.

56. For the percentages of domestic servants, transport workers, and administrators, financial agents, and secretaries who are slaves or uncertain slaves, see Table 5.1.

57. For Roman practices of recording age at death, see Hopkins 1966. Commemorators include a son (6301), a *vicaria* and two slaves (?) whose relation to the deceased is unstated (6303), four slaves (?) whose relation to

the deceased is unstated (6306, cf. 6217 and 6220), two slaves named in 6303 (6308). In addition, an Agatho appears as the deceased in 6303 and as a commemorator in 6306; see Flory 1978, 80.

58. "Iucundus Tauri / lecticarius quandi/us vixit vir fuit et se et / alios vindicavi [sic] quan/dius vixit honeste vixit / Callista et Philologus dant." The use of *vindicavi(t)* may be charged with its legal meaning of asserting a claim, especially in *vindicare in libertatem*—to claim as free one wrongly held in slavery. Cf. Pet. 43 for ridicule of the claim *honeste vixit*.

CHAPTER IV · Work in Its Social Context: The Question of Community

1. Douglass [1892] 1962, 177, 185, 153, 38.

2. Figures here record those placed in domestic settings on the basis of the factor named. Four others, slaves and uncertain slaves, belonged to staffs charged with the care of buildings, estates, gardens (745, 8684, 9991, 4330). Their titles, *vilicus* (Columella *Rust.* 1.8.1ff.; Cato *Agr.* 5) and *atriensis* (Varro *Ling.* 8.61; Pliny *Ep.* 3.19.3; Pet. 29.9, 72.8), point to a private staff organized as a *familia* (see *DE* 3.31–32); location may associate the *vilici* with the *familia Caesaris* (see Boulvert 1970, 36, 222 n. 113, 184 n. 649).

3. On the *columbaria* considered here, see chap. 2, n. 47. For domestic *collegia*, see Waltzing 1895–1900, 4:167–76.

4. *Supra lec(ticarios)* (6301); *supra cocos* (9261); *supra cubic(u)l(arios)* (9287, 33842).

5. Where 36.9% (173/469) of all slaves with job title named upper-class masters, only 11.6% (49/421) of all freedmen noted upper-class patrons, despite the very large proportion of freedmen with status indication. In the domestic setting, the proportion of slaves with status indication or clearly identified masters (54.9%, $N = 189$) approximates that of freedmen (61.5%, $N = 67$), so the relatively small proportion of freedmen manumitted by members of the upper classes does not result simply from different uses of status indication in large households. Rather, it would appear that most of the freedmen in the occupational inscriptions were not freed by members of the elite; see below, 98, 103–105. Fourteen individuals named an upper-class employer or household but were not his/its slaves or freedmen: five nurses (1354, 16440, 16592, 16587, 8942); six doctors (8646–47, 8671, 9585, 8895 [see chap. 2, n. 55], 8905 [Tac. *Ann.* 12.61, 67; Pliny *HN* 29.7–8; *PIR* S. 666]); an architect (8724); a *procurator* (9021, Mindius Secundus *procurator* Matidia Aug(usti) *f(ilia)*); a cook (9271, C. Genicilius C. l. Domesticus Sex. Lartidi *cocus*).

6. *Aeditui* (122, 675, 2203–7, 2210); *disp(ensator) cellae Nigrinianae* (3739, see *DE* 2.151); *ex horreis Faenianis* (37796, see *DE* 3.988).

7. *Apparitores:* 1923, 1925, 1926, 1935, 1958 = I.1203 ("pistor redemptoris apparet," see Treggiari 1969, 96n). Officials of tribes: 196, 198. *Magistri vici* or *pagi:* 2226, 37169. *Quinquennalis perpetuus collegii dendrophorum matris deum m. I. et Attis:* 30973 = 641 (Hilarus), cf. 1925. *Oriundus civitate Miseni, omnibus muneribus et honoribus patriae suae perfunctus:* 33887. M. Sutorius M. l. *Pamphilus lictor curia[t]. [a] sacris publiciis* (sic) *p. r. Quiritium viator qui cos. et pr. apparet decurio conlegi fabrum ferrarium* (1892) and L. Trebius Fidus *quinquennalis collegi perpetuus fabrum soliarium baxiarium . . . et immunis Romae regionibus XIIII*

(9404) are considered with the officers of occupational *collegia*; M'. Publicius Nicanor *ung(uentarius) de sacra via maximus accensus velatus* (1974) with shopholders. Unlike officers of occupational *collegia*, these men did not have to name their trades to indicate rank; for *apparitores*, it was unusual to do so (Huttunen 1974, 90−91, 127).

8. Frank 1933−40, 5:211, n. 66; Loane 1938, 147. Compare Weaver 1972, 7−8; Treggiari 1975*b*, 55. Households could easily have used the labor of domestic artisans in the occupational inscriptions (46); most were involved in cloth and clothes making (31, including a *sutor*) and baking (11). The extent to which the household would have absorbed the labor of a *specularius, politor, aurifex,* or *argentarius* is more problematic (although cf. Treggiari 1975*b*, 55). The *familiae* of the imperial family show more artisans in these latter trades (see chap. 3, n. 26); even there, however, most artisans ($N = 47$) made cloth or clothing (21) or baked (5).

9. Those with signs of private social contexts: 28.6%, $N = 32$ (building); 13.9%, $N = 46$ (manufacture); 1.9%, $N = 2$ (sales); 23.3%, $N = 28$ (professional service); 44%, $N = 33$ (skilled service); 49.8%, $N = 160$ (domestic service); 33%, $N = 60$ (transportation); 44.1%, $N = 135$ (administration, finance, secretarial service). Those with signs of public social contexts: 34.8%, $N = 39$ (building); 37.2%, $N = 123$ (manufacture); 32.4%, $N = 35$ (sales); 54.8%, $N = 23$ (banking); 3.3%, $N = 4$ (professional service); 10.7%, $N = 8$ (skilled service); 7.3%, $N = 4$ (transportation); 9.2%, $N = 28$ (administration, finance, secretarial service).

10. Two of the twenty-five *vestiarii* (6373, 9963) are attached to households; in one case, however, the title is abbreviated *vest.* Two *vestifici* (9979, 37724) clearly worked in domestic settings; another was commemorated by a *conservus* (9980); a fourth appears in a fragmentary inscription with freedmen, one of whom was a *paedagogus* (9744). Only one *sarcinatrix* clearly worked outside a household (9884); five belonged to identifiable households. Nine (9875−80, 9882−83, 33162, 33907) cannot be categorized, although their epitaphs, with job title and name only, are of a type commonly found in *columbaria.* On *sarcinatrices,* see Treggiari 1976, 85.

11. See below, n. 59. The pattern is only suggestive because, aside from freedmen and their descendants, some provincials bore senatorial and imperial nomina, depending on the date and circumstances of their or their progenitors' enfranchisement; see Weaver 1972, 85−86.

12. See also the *pistores* M. Livius Faustus (9806) and T. Statilius Eros Caninianus (9808). For an alternative progenitor, see M. Iunius Iunci Maioris l. Eros *pistor* (9805). For the expectation of an in-house baker, see Cic. *Pis.* 67. On marriages between slaves and freedmen of different noble families, see Treggiari 1975*a*, 397−98.

13. *Fabri* (6283−85); *fabri tignuarii* (6363−65, 9415); *faber structor parietarius* (6354); *marmorarius* (6318); see Treggiari 1975*b*, 54.

14. There are two other pairs of fathers and sons: L. Cincius L. f. Suc. Martialis *quinquevir* and L. Cincius L. f. Pal. Martialis; Ti. Iulius Taurisus and Ti. Iulius Speratus. See also T. Statilius Vol. Aper *mensor aedificior(um)* and his father T. Statilius Vol. Proculus *accensus velatus* (1975).

15. The titles of a *dispensator* (3739: slave), *aedituus* (2203: uncertain slave), and man attached to one of the city's warehouses (37796: slave) signal work on a public staff. A butcher (168: slave) and *subaedianus* (33875:

uncertain slave) are associated with the city's *collegia;* an *olearius* has a shop address (9719: slave). For 25.4% (*N* = 119) of the slaves and 97.6%, *N* = 200 of the uncertain slaves, we find no indication of context. Most have service jobs, and many bear titles found most typically in large *familiae: nutrix* (10), *paedagogus* (8), *cubicularius* (13), *pedisequus* (17), *coquus* (6), *cellarius* (7), *dispensator* (30), *actor* (27), and *vilicus* (17).

16. A total of 18.3% (*N* = 20) were administrators and secretaries; another 9.2% (*N* = 10) doctors (*medici*) or midwives (*obstetrices*); 22.9% (*N* = 25), over half of those in domestic service, were nurses. Others in domestic service: cooks (4), *cubicularii* (4, including a *supra cubicularios*), a *cubiculo, a cubiculo et procurator, cellarii* (2), *a veste* (2), *cistarius, vestispica, aquarius, ostiarius, nomenclatores* (3), *silentiarius.* One of the freedmen in transportation was a *supra lecticarios* (6301); another a *supra iumenta* (7987). A *numida* (7582) had his own freedmen; given burial space by his patron's son, *ex frugalitate,* he built a tomb for himself, a named freedman, and his other freedmen and their descendants.

17. Freed slaves lacking any sign of social context follow a similar pattern of employment, concentrated in artisanry (35.1%, *N* = 72), sales (16.6%, *N* = 34), and banking (5.4%, *N* = 11). However, we do find larger proportions in construction (7.8%, *N* = 16), professional service (10.7%, *N* = 22), and domestic service (18.8%, *N* = 38); many of the latter, in actuality, would have worked in large households.

18. Artisans with a shop address: 55 freedmen, 2 freeborn, 24 uncertain freeborn. Bankers with a shop address: 16 freedmen, 5 uncertain freeborn. Skilled service workers with a shop address: 5 freedmen, 1 freeborn, 2 uncertain freeborn.

19. L. Volusius Urbanus *nomenclator censorius* (1968) lacks libertination, but his name and job connect him with the censor L. Volusius Saturninus, *cos. suff.* 12 B.C. (Tac. *Ann.* 3.30); *PIR* V. 660. For architects and doctors, see n. 5 above. A total of 19.1% (*N* = 8) of the freeborn and 17.4% (*N* = 56) of the uncertain freeborn lack signs of private contexts but were in fields generally populated by slaves and associated with the domestic setting (domestic service and administration). However, the work of the free administrators and agents tends to be nondomestic. The freeborn include: 327 (*custodiarius*); 2210 (*aedituus Dianae Plancianae*); 9626 (*mensor machinarius*); 9627 (*mensor . . .*); 33883 (*me(n)sor machinarius frumenti publici*). The uncertain freeborn include: 122, 675, 2204–7, 2213, 5183 (*aeditui*); 188, 236, 338 (connected with public or imperial *horrea*); 327 (*custodiarius*); 22, 33883 (*mensores,* of grain); 9921 (*tab(u)larius a porta fontinale*); NSA 1914, 394 (*ministrator a foro Esquilino*). The uncertain freeborn in domestic service are more problematic, for they worked at the most typical household jobs: nurses (13), child attendants (3), announcers (3), personal and room servants (2), cooks (1), provisioners (2). They may have been poor freeborn Romans employed in private households; perhaps some were freedmen. Their epitaphs show practically no evidence of independent resources. Similar circumstances characterize the freedmen without status indication whose legal condition is revealed by other factors; they, too, were more concentrated in domestic service (43.2%, *N* = 35) than in any other field.

20. Employments of freedmen in public contexts: .9%, *N* = 1 (build-

ing); 63.6%, N = 68 (manufacture); 11.2%, N = 12 (sales); 15.9%, N = 17 (banking); .9%, N = 1 (professional service); 4.7%, N = 5 (skilled service); .9%, N = 1 (transportation); 1.9%, N = 2 (administration). Employments of freeborn in public contexts: 36.4%, N = 8 (building); 22.7%, N = 5 (manufacture); 13.6%, N = 3 (sales); 4.5%, N = 1 (skilled service); 4.5%, N = 1 (transportation); 18.2%, N = 4 (administration). Employments of uncertain freeborn in public contexts: 22.5%, N = 29 (building); 38%, N = 49 (manufacture); 14.7%, N = 19 (sales); 4.7%, N = 6 (banking); 2.3%, N = 3 (professional service); 1.6%, N = 2 (skilled service); 1.6%, N = 2 (transportation); 14.7%, N = 19 (administration). The free in administration held different jobs than freed administrators in large households. Freeborn and uncertain freeborn in administration with public orientation: *mensor machinarii* (3), *mensor corporis pistorum* (1), *custodiarii* (2), *aeditui* (11), connected with *horrea* (4), *tabularius* (1), *ministrator* (1). Freedmen in administration with private orientation: *dispensatores* (2), *sumptuarius* (1), *ad hereditates* (1), *procuratores* (6), *ad aedicia* (1), *horrearii* (3), *aedituus* (1), *a tabulario* (1), *tabularius* (1), *a manu* (2).

21. For a definition of *familia*, see Flory 1978, 78–79. See also below, 105–106, 120–22.

22. Flory 1978, 78–95.

23. For this discussion, see Treggiari 1975 *b*, 58–60.

24. Ibid., 59.

25. In Table 4.4, slaves include only those whose status can be determined by formal status indication or a term of relationship; possible slaves, all those with a single name. Disregarding informal indications of status permits a clearer comparison of those without status indication, since the factors that suggest the actual status of most possible slaves point to membership in a large domestic household. The larger proportion of clearly identified slave administrators without indication of context results in part from the general tendency toward the use of formal status indication in this field.

26. *Fabri* (9), *structor* (1), *quasillariae* (9), *mediastini* (2), *balneatores* (3), *capsarius* (1), *ministra/er* (2), *pedisequi/ae* (7), *structor* (waiter) (2), *mulio* (1), *stratores* (2), *equiso* (1), *asturconarius* (1), *medicus equarius et venator* (1), *tabellarii* (2), *lecticarii* (20).

27. *Cubicularii* (35), *a cubiculo* (1), *coqui* (5), *cellarii* (5), *a cella*(?) (1), *fartor* (1), *a frumento* (2), *a speculum* (1), *ad margarita* (1), *vestiplicae/i* (2), *vestispica* (1), *ostiarii* (2), *atrienses* (9).

28. Note Flory 1978, 79–80, and Treggiari 1973, 250.

29. On shops and workshops with living quarters at Ostia, see Girri 1956, 37–43; Packer 1971, 66–70. On urban property holding and the urban investments of the wealthy, see Frier 1980, 21–34; Garnsey 1976.

30. Only sixteen in the service fields left an address: three doctors, six barbers or hairdressers (see Mart. 2.17, 7.61.7; Hor. *Epist.* 1.7.48–51), an *alipilus a Tritone* (9141), an *hymnologus de campo Caelimontano* (9475), a *tabularius* (9921), and two *ministratores* (9645, NSA 1914, 394). The job title of L. Poblicius Montanus [*lecti*]*carius a* [*porta f*]*ontinal(e)* (9514) is uncertain; Tib. Claudius Auctus *tabellarius a ripa* may have been in public service (9918).

31. Conspicuously absent from shopholding artisans are those involved

in the making or treatment of cloth (*N* = 55): only two *lanarii* and five *purpurarii* have shop addresses. However, nine *quasillariae*, two *lanipendi*, and four *textores* clearly belonged to large domestic households. Most fullers appear in the same situation (5) or as officers of *collegia* (6).

32. All but one jeweler and one *vestiarius tenuiarius* have such addresses. Besides the ten *ferrarii* whose address is obscured by breakage, there are six metal artisans with shops on the Via Sacra (9207, 9212, 9221, 9418–19, 37824); all but two (*flaturarii*, 9418–19) dealt in precious metals. On shopping locations in the city, see Loane 1938, 113–21.

33. *Aedes Castoris* (363, 9177); *ab sex areis* (sic, 9178); *forum Esquilinum* (9179–80); *macellum magnum* (9183); *vicus . . . ionum ferrariarum* (9185); *portus vinarius* (9189); *basilica Iulia* (9709, 9711); *theatrum Marcellianum* (sic, 33838*a*); *a Mercurio sobrio* (9714). See also 9186 (*coactor inter aerarios*) for a specific clientele.

34. 1974 (*ung(uentarius) de sacra via*); 9662 (*negotiator de sacra via*); 9671 (*negotiator penoris et vinorum de velabro a llll scaris*); 9795 (*pigment(arius) de sacra via*); 9796 (*pigme[ntarii] vici lorari*); 9993 (*vinarius de velabro*).

35. Note also 9178 (father and son or patron and freedman): "L. Suestilius L. l. Clarus argentarius ab sex areis sibi et L. Suestilio Laeto nummulario ab sex areis vixit ann. XIIX . . ."

36. For distributors with *colliberti*, see the Trebonii *thurarii* (9933). In fact, we are observing a different pattern of productive relations; see chap. 5, 131ff.

37. For perfumers and unguent dealers, see Suet. *Aug.* 4.2; Hor. *Sat.* 2.3.228; Pet. 74.15; Mart. 1.87.2, 3.55.1, 3.82.26, 12.65.4 (Cosmus), and 6.55, 10.38.8, 12.65.4 (Niceros). Only four (*unguentarii*: 1974, 10006; *pigmentarii*: 9795–96) mention a specific location. However, the social relations of *unguentarii* and *thurarii* and the recurrence of four nomina suggest that nineteen of the thirty dealers belonged to one of four enterprises and may have been involved in large-scale distribution. On the activities of the Faenii, see Loane 1938, 143; Fredericksen 1959, 111; D'Arms 1981, 167–68. On the Trebonii *thurari* (9933–34), Popillii *unguentarii* (845, 10001), Cornelii *thurarii* (9930–31), see Loane 1938, 142–43; Treggiari 1969, 97–98; Pavis D'Esurac 1977, 347–49.

38. On *mercator* and *negotiator,* see Hatzfeld 1919, 196–97; Nicolet 1966, 1:358–62; Rougé 1966, 279ff.; D'Arms 1981, 24–31.

39. Title and location suggest four or five wholesale traders (9631, 9660, 9661: uncertain freeborn; 37806: freeborn; and perhaps 37807: freedman). The rest seem to have been retail tradesmen (9662, 9671, 9664, 9683, 33886: freedmen; 9673: uncertain freeborn). See Loane 1938, 29, 120–21, 124–25, 127, 136; cf. 41 on 33886.

40. Of the four whose spouses are named, two or three married a patron or *colliberta* (9683, 37807, cf. 9661). Four men were commemorated by or appear with women identified as *collibertae* (9662, 33886) or *libertae* (9673, 37806), not as wives, although the circumstances of the epitaphs suggest a living together. Five or their families (9660, 9661, 9664, 9683, 33886) included freedmen in their tombs, an indication of property and the control of labor; for two others (9673, 37806), the only freed slave mentioned is a woman who may have been a spouse.

41. Uncertain freeborn: 1625b (two), 1935, 9676, 9677, 9682, 33887; freedmen: 9675 (two). On 9677, see Loane 1938, 31; cf. Waltzing 1895–1900, 2:108. On 1625b and 1935, see Frank 1933–40, 5:271–74; Loane 1938, 20–23; cf. Panciera 1980, 242–45.

42. Material prosperity is indicated for ten others. Seven have their own freedmen: 9630 (two colliberti with at least one freedman), 9632 (at least one), 9670 (formula), 9672 (three), 9679 (three), 9680 (formula). The burial dimensions (in Roman feet) are given in three cases: 9628 (12 × 14), 9629 (19 × 20), 9659 (12 × 12; a long epitaph that claims, "qui negotiando locupletum se speravit esse futurum; spe deceptus erat"). For use of plots as evidence of prosperity, see Cébeillac 1971.

43. Of the ten whose spouses are named, seven (18, 9629, 9665, 9672, 9677, 33889) married free women with nomina different than their husband's (only one clearly identified as a freedwoman); only one married a colliberta or liberta (9675). In 9630, one of the mercatores seems to be the husband of Scantia L. l. Ammia (a liberta or colliberta) and the father of Scantia Sp. f. Putilla and/or L. Scantius L. f. Status. The nomen of T. Iulius Secun[dus negoti]ator lintiarius (9670) and his wife Iulia Martinu[la] recurs too frequently to assume a nonfamilial tie between spouses.

44. A few, like L. Scribonius Ianuarius or P. Clodius Athenio (cited above), noted both an occupational title and a collegium office.

45. Only one officer, P. Sulpicius Felix, decurio of the carpenters' collegium (9405: uncertain freeborn), was commemorated by the collegium or its officials, but he heads a list of twenty-one collegium members and is distinguished from them by his title. It should be noted that seven of the officers (deceased or dedicator) appear with other members, officers, or individuals in the same trade without collegium affiliations: 7861 (three), 7863–64, 9405, 33837. Ti. Cl(audius) Zosimus's role in the collegium iumentariorum qui est in cisiaris Tiburtinis Herculis is not specified (9485), but he seems to have been an important member; his wife commemorated what appears to have been a fairly large, elaborate tomb. The evidence of burial for those in collegia is skewed by a large number of men concentrated effectively in two tombs. In 9405, L. Cincius L. f. Suc. Martialis, quinquevir of the collegium of fabri tignuarii, provided burial space for the tenth decuria of the collegium by the will of L. Mamilius Felix, whose connection with the collegium is not specified, and donated ollae for a decurio, twenty-one members of the collegium, and members of his family. The epitaph accounts for twenty-one of the twenty-six deceased members of collegia. Five centonarii, all L. Octavii (7861, 7863–64), were buried in a columbarium apparently used by members of the same familia. Their epitaphs account for five of the fourteen deceased officers, five of the thirty-four artisans in collegia, and five of the nine ragmen.

46. The men in administration were supervised by or connected with the state: grain measurers (22, 9626, 33883), jailers (custodiarii, 327), and men who worked in public horrea (188, 236, 338). All but one of the merchants in collegia sold food: 1625b (negotiatores ole[ari], see n. 41 above); 9677 (negotians salsarius, q(uin)q(uennalis) corporis malacitanorum); 9682 (negotians vinarius item navicularius, cur(ator) corporis Hadriatici); 36819 (quaestor, collegium thurarior[um et] unguentarior(um)), dedication to salus domus A[ugustae], cf. 845 and D'Arms 1981, 167).

47. See above, n. 45.

48. On the Octavii *centonarii* and this *collegium*, see Waltzing 1895–1900, 1:88 n. 1, 282, 2:112; Loane 1938, 74–75. What connection, if any, the L. Octavii had with M. Octavius M. l. Attalus *centonar(ius) a turre Mamilia* and M. Octavius M. [l.] Marcio *mag(ister) conleg(ii) centon-(ariorum)* (33837) is unknown; cf. Loane 1938, 75 n. 54. Note also the *sagarius* M. Octavius Carpus (339) with the same nomen and praenomen.

49. Of those outside the domestic setting, six of the eight *fullones*, eight of the nine *centonarii*, four of the six *lanii*, and four of the ten *pistores* gave their *collegium* offices. Three other bakers with more specified activities were not associated with *collegia*: 1958 = 1.1203 ("pistoris redemptoris apparet"), 9810 (*pistor magnarius pepsianus*), 9812 = 1.1207 (*pistor simi-[laginarius]*).

50. The fuller's trade was dirty (see chap. 3, 66); butchers and bakers, little more respectable, practiced an *ars vulgaris* in what seems to be the conventional view (Cic. *Off.* 1.150, *Rosc. Am.* 134). The *centonarius* in Petronius (45–46) is the archetypically crude tradesman—wealthy, pompous, and ignorant.

51. Waltzing 1895–1900, 1:383ff.

52. Five of the ten men who were commemorators or commemorated by a family member (the prosperity reflected in the epitaph points to family resources) included freedmen in the tomb: 1892 (six named), 9404, 9408, 9677, 9682 (formula). In general, the number of people included in these tombs is comparatively large: outside the *columbaria*, median tomb size (see chap. 3, n. 37) is 1.3, but for these men and their families, it is 5.5. See also the arrangements made by C. Turius C. f. Lollianus (9626).

53. State and officials (266, 1002, 1620, 1625b); gods (167–68, 236, 268). Note the officials of *collegia* at Ostia; Meiggs 1973, 311–36. On relations between *collegia* and the state, see Waltzing 1895–1900, 1:114–54, 188–95.

54. On fuller's relations with the state and use of water, see 266, 10298. On the role of the state in the grain trade, see Rickman 1980a, 1980b; Casson 1980; Garnsey 1983. On building, see Brunt 1980. On taxes, regulations, policy, see Rostovtzeff 1957, 353ff.; Rougé 1966; Loane 1938, 113ff. For the role of the gods, see 18 ("domino Aesculapio et Hygiae expermissu eorum negotiationis fabariae gratias agentes numini et aratis eorum," sic).

55. Huttunen 1974, 71, Table 11. See n. 7 above.

56. *ILS* 2927; see Duncan-Jones 1974, 29–32. See Saller 1982, 17–39, on *beneficium* and *gratia*.

57. See chap. 2, 42.

58. Tac. *Ann.* 1.13, 2.33, 2.51.1, 3.57, 4.61 (cf. Suet. *Tib.* 29); see Syme 1958, 1:323–24, 2:580, and *PIR*² H. 24–25.

59. See above, 97–98. Among *fabri tignuarii*: T. Statilius (3), C. Petronius (1), C. Vibius (2), Ti. Iulius (2), P. Licinius (1), M. Antonius (1), C. Iulius (1), P. Cornelius (2), Q. Haterius (1), M. Valerius (2), Q. Hortensius (1), T. Flavius (1), Q. Lollius (1). Among fullers: Q. Hortensius (1), M. Antistius (1), C. Iulius (1).

60. *Collegia* like the *conlegiu lanii piscinenses* (167), however, based their formal organization on shared place as well as occupation; see also 9136 (*sodales aerari a pulvinar(e)*).

CHAPTER V · The Re-formation of What Was Given

1. Blassingame 1977, 432–34, 440, 431.

2. H. Gummerus, "Industrie und Handel," *RE* 9.1439ff.; Gummerus 1915, 1918; Kühn 1910; Duff 1928, 9off.; Huttunen 1974, 183–93. See also Treggiari 1969, 91ff., and 1975*b*, 1980, 1979*a*; Calabi Limentani 1958.

3. Frank 1916, 694; Taylor 1961, 131. On stereotyping, see chap. 1, 6–7.

4. Treggiari 1980, 55–56; Garnsey 1981, 359.

5. For specific job titles, see app. 2. Freedmen have the largest presence among metal artisans and tailors of various types, but their representation among jewelers and those in food production only equals that of the uncertain freeborn. Also, they are less well represented than the uncertain freeborn in the treatment and production of cloth (primarily fullers and dyers). The dyers tend to be freedmen (57.1%, $N = 8$); the fullers, uncertain freeborn (75%, $N = 6$), all of whom, like other officers of *collegia*, omit status indication in preference to office. Most of the bakers are uncertain freeborn (53.8%, $N = 7$) and freeborn (7.7%, $N = 1$), and all but one butcher are freedmen (83.3%, $N = 5$). Table 5.3 includes those with no attachment to a household and those with indications of public contexts. A few in the former group, especially in cloth and clothes making, where certain titles are often found in large households, in fact may have worked in domestic settings. Some of their epitaphs suggest this: small plaques with a name and job title as in the epitaphs from *columbaria* (e.g., 9879–80) or the presence of *conservi* or possible *conservi* (e.g., 9495, 9980).

6. Juv. 1.101–9, 3.76ff.; Pet. 42–46, 57–58, 68.6–8, 75.8–9, 77.6.

7. D'Arms 1981, 45. See also Pavis D'Esurac 1977; D'Arms, 167–68.

8. Twenty-one freed artisans (16%) appear alone; thirty-one (23.7%) only with family members; and six (4.6%) with others.

9. "L. Naevius Eleuther et Naevius Narcissus et L. Naevius Thesmus h(eredes) L. Naevio Heleno patro(no) suo ex testamento eius fecerunt sibi et suiis et libertiis libertabusquae et posterisquae eorum (a)erari vasc(u)-l(arii) h(oc) m(onumentum) s(ive) s(epulcrum) e(st) h(eredem) nostrum sequetur [*sic*]."

10. *ILS* 2927 (bequest to Comum to support 100 of Pliny's freedmen during their lifetimes, after which the money was to be used to provide an annual dinner for the people of Comum) and *CIL* 6.10229, 35ff.

11. For example, T. Titius T. l. Philemo, Fannia Ɔ l. Pieris, and T. Titius T. Ɔ l. Nicephor. A Fannia C. l. Callist(e) points to three patrons—T. Titius, Fannia, and C. Fannius.

12. On dyes, dyeing, and workshops at Pompeii, see Moeller 1976, 35–39; Forbes 1956, 4:98ff. There appear to be two different patterns here: (1) the *colliberti* themselves named shared freedmen as in 9138 (by formula), 33923 (one named), 37820 (one named; in the latter two cases, the *colliberti* are married); and (2) a successful freed artisan with his own freedmen (1892, 33906) included one or more fellow ex-slaves in his tomb.

13. 1892, 9528, 9546, 9868 (spouses?), 33923 (spouses?), 37820.

14. *Colliberti*: 1892, 9499, 9528, 33921, 37820. Same nomen and no status indication (probably *colliberti*): 2226, 3592, 9404, 9418, 9547, 37781.

Colliberta or *liberta:* 9494, 9864, 9443. In 37826 and possibly 9824, the artisan was his wife's *libertus.* Generally here, there are few expressions like *libertus idem coniunx* or *patronus idem coniunx* (9975). On the manumission of a *contubernalis,* see chap. 2, n. 58. In the seven cases where neither nomenclature, status, nor relational term indicates a connection begun in slavery, three spouses were freed slaves. Sex. Giganius Sex. Ↄ l. Felix tailor (*vestiarius,* 33921), the freedman of a man and a woman, who was married to Ammia, whom he called *colliberta,* reminds us that freedmen with different nomina could well have been *colliberti* if their patrons were associated (most probably married, see below). The status indication of A. Cornelius A. l. Priscus *sagarius* and his wife Cornelia Dextri *liber(ta)* Erotis (33906) seems to indicate different patrons, who themselves may have been *colliberti* or relatives.

15. *Colliberta:* 33923. Same nomen no status indication (probably *colliberti*): 9808. *Colliberta* or *liberta:* 6939 (see below, 141), 7885, 9202, 9376, 9392, 9429, 9434, *NSA* 1922, 144. Of the six possible spouses with no apparent nonfamilial relation with their partners, three were freed slaves, and the situation of Giganius and Ammia is a possibility (33921; see n. 14 above).

16. Fedra identified her patron as a freed slave like herself. Here, job title is read as *purpuraria Marianeis,* but if, as Barbieri (see *ILLRP* 809) suggests, it should be *purpurari a Marianeis,* Fedra will have identified herself, her patron, *collibertus* and husband, and freedman all as *purpurarii.*

17. See Moeller (1976, 29–56) on wool-processing shops that included living quarters. On the ties among *colliberti,* see Flory 1978, 83–86.

18. 9215, 9283, 9442, 9547 (with spouse), 9971, 37826 (for one freed patron, the commemorator was his freedman's *liberta,* see below).

19. *PIR* S. 595.

20. Iarine married her own freedman, although he may have been a *conservus* whose freedom she had purchased. Her acquisition of a slave or funds for purchasing Onesimus's freedom may stem from her own involvement in the trade; see below, 142.

21. Freedmen named: 9208, 33423. Freedmen included by formula: 9545 ("neque condi licet nisei eos lib(ertos) quibus hoc testamento dedi tribuique"), 1818, 2226, 9404, 9864, 9869, 9954, 37781 (and named).

22. Three freed patrons refer to family members (1818, 9864, 9208 [only by the formula *suis*]). The other commemorations mention no family (9545, 9869, 9954, 33423) or only spouses, all of whom appear to have been the artisans' *collibertae* (2226, 9404, 37781).

23. If Publius is not the praenomen of Clodia's patron or father, there may be three patrons: Clodia, an Aulus, and a Publius. Other artisans whose status indication notes a male and female patron: 1952, 9134, 9212, 9398 (five; see above, n. 11), 9419, 9491, 9867, 33921; cf. 33923 (two men, one woman).

24. *Colliberti:* 1892, 9528, 33923, 37820. Same nomen and no status indication: 2226, 9404, 9547, 37781. In the other three cases, one spouse lacks status indication (9864 [wife], 9865 [husband]), or the spouses have status indications that point to different, albeit related, patrons (33906; see n. 14 above).

25. On the occupations of women, see Treggiari 1979a, 1976; Kampen

1981; Le Gall 1969. Thirty-three artisans without private orientation were women: 9.1% (N = 3) were slaves; 33.3% (N = 11) uncertain slaves; 33.3% (N = 11) freedwomen. Most (78.8%, N = 26) were involved in cloth and clothes making: *sericaria* (9891), *quasillaria* (9495), *lanipendae* (9496–98), *staminaria* (33371), *purpurariae* (9846, 9848, 37820), *vestiaria* (33920), *vestificae* (9744, 9980), *sarcinatrices* (9875–80, 9882–84, 33162, 33907). Others include: *gemmaria* (9435), *margari[taria]* (5972), *brattiariae* (6939, 9211), *auri vestrix* (9214), *ferrariae* (9398), *officinatrix* (9715).

26. Le Gall's (1969, 125–26) assumption that Melema sold rather than made gold leaf (see Treggiari 1979a, 67) seems to be based solely on gender. The appearance given by the epitaph is of shared work, not different functions. We also find a couple who were *thurarii* (9934) and a *popa* married to a *sculptor v(as)c(u)larius* (9824); cf. *CIL* 6.18. Other couples with occupational titles had jobs often found in large households: 5200 (*ministrator, pedisequa*), 9266 (*cocus, pedisequa*), 9345 (*dispensator, ornatrix*), 9901 (*strator, vestip[lica]*), 9495 (*lanipendus, quasillaria*), 37303 (*vestispica, sumptuarius*), 37811 (*to(n)sor, ornatrix*). See also 9754 (*colliberti* and *paedagogus/a*).

27. Treggiari 1979a, 67. See also the Veturii *purpurarii:* 37820 and *NSA* 1922, 144 (cf. L. Plutius Eros *purpurarius* commemorated with a Veturia C. C. l. Attica [14.2433] and a C. Cafurnius C. l. Antiochus *lanarius* married [?] to a Veturia C. l. Deutera [9489]: Loane 1938, 76–77; Treggiari 1979a, 71–72). D. Caecilius D. l. Diadumenus *sagarius* and his wife Caecilia Lucida (9864) and Q. Caecilius Spendo *sagarius* and his wife Caecilia Cosmiae l. Cognata (9865) may be cases where women were links between artisans.

28. Loane 1938, 76–77, 98, 132–33, 142–43. See also Treggiari 1969, 96–98, and 1979a, 70–72; D'Arms 1981, 167–68; Fredericksen 1959, 111; Pavis D'Esurac 1977, 347ff.

29. Sex. Aufidius (339); M. Octavius (339); Caecilius (D. in 9864 and Q. with a wife Caecilia Cosmiae l. in 9865); Q. Conelius (9867, cf. p. 3895); Cornelius (Q. in 9866, 9868–69 and A. in 33906); C. Terentius (9872). Cf. n. 27 above.

30. On the Cornelii, see Loane 1938, 133; she assumes the economic activities of the Sallvii from their cognomina (36, 132). For the other possibilities, see n. 28 above. The L. Octavii *centonarii* (7861, 7863–64, see chap. 4, nn. 45, 48) seem to be a similar group, not divided by the evidence of burial (cf. the M. Octavii *centonarii*, 33837).

31. Veyne 1961, 244–45; Finley 1973, 51.

32. On nurses, see Treggiari 1976, 87–89; Kampen 1981, 109–10 (for images of nurses, 33–44, 96, 146–49); Bradley 1986; Joshel 1986. On domestic servants, see Treggiari 1975b, 1973.

33. For specific job titles, see app. 2. According to Mohler (1940, 268–69), some young slaves served as waiters or "ornamental domestics"; since this was not the primary job that they eventually held, there are few job titles for waiters per se (Treggiari 1975b, 51). In the *familia Caesaris*, we find: *ministratores* (4351, 5200, 5351, 5751, 5858, 5873, 8914–23, 33781, 33795, 37760); *a cyato* (8815–16); *structores* (8795, 9045–48, 33235, 33795); *praegustatores* (602, 5355, 9003 [*procurator*], 9004); *tricliniarchus* (9083); *diaetarchae* (5187, 5196, 8643–45, 8666, 8818); also, a *glaber ab cyato* of Antonia Minor (8817) and two *structores* of Livia (4034, 8911; cf. Treggiari 1975b, n. 85).

34. On the history of the *atriensis* and his role, see Treggiari 1975b, 49, 51. On Phoebe *a speculum* (*sic*, 7297), see Treggiari 1975a, 396. On the functions of *capsarii*, see Boulvert 1970, 29–30; Treggiari 1975b, 53.

35. See chap. 3, n. 28.

36. For instances of corporal punishment, see chap. 2, n. 16.

37. On the effects of proximity in the antebellum South, see Genovese 1976, 331–34.

38. Hopkins 1978, 112.

39. Patterson 1982, 33.

40. Tac. *Ann.* 3.65; *Agr.* 2.3. Cf. Sall. *Cat.* 20.6–17 where Catiline uses the metaphor of slavery and liberation to stir his disadvantaged followers.

41. See also 3.19.2–20.2. On the term *beneficium*, see Saller 1982, 17–21.

42. Compare the attitudes of planters in the American South: "duty" and "burden" punctuate their comments on their positions as slaveholders and "were central to the self-image and self-respect of the master class." See Genovese 1976, 75–86; Litwack 1980, 192, 359–63.

43. Litwack 1980, 338–39, 432ff.

44. Thirteen (46.4%) of the slaves in transportation in large households lack status indication; four (44.4%) in professional service; thirteen (46.4%) in skilled service.

45. 4455 (*nom(enclator)* Cullionis), 6229 (*armiger Tauri* f.), 7301 (*vestipli[cus* L.? Vol]usi Saturnini), 7602 (*coc[us]* Torqua[ti]), 9298 (*cubicul(arius)* Pulchri), 9300 (*cubiclarius* Lusci Ocreaes), 9700 (*nomenclat(or)* Potiti Messallae), and perhaps 34272 (*cubucul(arius)* D[ecimi] n[ostri]?). For the masters of the *cubicularii*, see *PIR* S. 617, 618.

46. Others whose occupations suggest a close working relationship or special position: *armiger* (6229), *ab hospitiis et paedagogus puerorum* (7290), *nomenclatores* (4455, 9694, 9696, 9699, 9700).

47. Freedmen without status indication: 26.7%, $N = 8$ (building); 9.5%, $N = 14$ (manufacture); 15.2%, $N = 7$ (sales); 17.9%, $N = 5$ (banking); 34.3%, $N = 12$ (professional service); 15.4%, $N = 2$ (skilled service); 47.1%, $N = 40$ (domestic service); 25%, $N = 2$ (transportation); 34.5%, $N = 10$ (administration, finance, secretarial service).

48. Freedmen in the large household without status indication: 38.5%, $N = 5$ (building); 14.3%, $N = 1$ (manufacture); 33.3%, $N = 4$ (professional service); 40%, $N = 2$ (skilled service); 55.3%, $N = 26$ (domestic service); 20%, $N = 1$ (transportation); 40%, $N = 8$ (administration, finance, secretarial service).

49. 6217, 6227, 7601; Faustus l. *cubicular(ius)* (5942) and Phileros l. *cocus* (6248) also lack status indication, but they appear in the identification of a wife and slave, respectively.

50. "Hateria Dorchas sibi et Primo Q. Hateri cellario viro suo et patrono emit d(e) s(uo)."

51. On Heracla's duties, see Boulvert and Treggiari (n. 34 above). Perhaps the combination of jobs means that Heracla had been Volusius's servant since childhood, and his role had expanded from *capsarius* (also an attendant who carried a schoolchild's case) to *a cubiculo*. Three other freedmen had special responsibilities: Chius l. Sisennae *silentiarius* (6217), T. Statilius Tauri l. Synistor *supra cubic(u)l(arios)* (9287), [Se]x. Lartidius Ur-

banus *nomenclator, trib(unus!), mag(ister), q(uaestor) in familia patroni su[i]* (37461).

52. Treggiari 1975*b*, 57.

53. Pa(n)sa (?) (6326; cf. 6220, 6393) and Posidippus (6261–62, 6246) were the masters. Posidippus had many slaves and freedmen: 6246 (slave, *cocus*), 6261–62 (slaves, *cubicularii*), 6274, 6277–79 (slaves, *dispensatores*), 6410, 6415, 6426, 6493, 6498, 6590 (slaves), 6476, 6479 (freedmen?), 6525, 6535, 6574 (freedmen). His occupation is not named, but four of his slaves were *dispensatores*. The jobs of the *vicarii* suggest service for the Statilii themselves (Treggiari 1975*b*, 51). However important Posidippus was in the household, it is difficult to believe the cook, both bedchamber servants, and four *dispensatores* worked for him, unless he should be compared with Musicus Scurranus *dispensator ad fiscum Gallicum provinciae Lugdunesis* (5197).

54. On Phileros l. *cocus* (6248), see n. 49 above; Chius l. Sisennae *silentiarius* (6217) and Menander l. *ostiarius ab amphitheatr(o)* (6227) appear as the deceased. The other freedmen include: T. Statilius Malchio *ad vestem* (6374, without status indication) and T. Statilius Tauri l. Synistor *supra cubic(u)l(arios)* (9287).

55. Patterson 1982, 337. On mutual dependency, see Genovese 1976, 89–91, 344.

56. Litwack 1980, 388; Genovese 1976, 344. For slaves' understanding of their masters' dependence, see Genovese 1976, 344–47; Litwack 1980, 334, 387ff.; Douglass [1892] 1962, 99, 146–47, 185ff.

57. Genovese 1976, 351.

58. Douglass [1892] 1962, 63.

CONCLUSIONS

1. Katz 1972, 64.

2. LaCapra 1985, 36.

3. Chaining: Pliny *Ep.* 3.19.7; Pliny *HN* 18.21; Columella *Rust.* 1.8.17–18, 1.9.4. Mills: Apul. *Met.* 9.12. Mines: Dio Cass. 5.38.1.

4. Douglass [1892] 1962, 150.

5. Patterson 1982, 337.

6. Hor. *Sat.* 2.7.117–18.

7. The pattern of employments for freedmen not associated with a large household: 5.4% ($N = 17$) in building; 44.9% ($N = 140$) in manufacture; 14.7% ($N = 46$) in sales; 9% ($N = 28$) in banking; 7.4% ($N = 23$) in professional service; 2.6% ($N = 8$) in skilled service; 12.2% ($N = 38$) in domestic service; 1% ($N = 3$) in transportation; 2.9% ($N = 9$) in administration. Of the freedmen with no indication of social context, 25.9% ($N = 53$) appear with *colliberti*, patrons, or both; 14.6% ($N = 30$) with their own freedmen; and 21.5% ($N = 44$) with family members.

8. Huttunen 1974, 186ff.

APPENDIX II • Occupational Categories and Glossary

1. Katz 1972, 64–65; on occupational classification, see also Armstrong 1972.

2. Cf. Katz 1972, 67.

3. Ibid., 81–82.

4. On the training of architects, doctors, and teachers, see chap. 3, n. 50.

5. On architects and builders, see Vitr. 1.1.1 and Burford 1972, 102. See P. Cornelius Thallus, son of P. Cornelius Architectus and a *magister quinquennalis* of a *collegium* of *fabri tignuarii*, and his son P. Cornelius Architectianus, a *decurio* in the same *collegium* (148): the cognomina of Thallus's father and son indicate the family's involvement with architecture and a career pattern (see Burford 1972, 86–87). *Mensores* are included in this category, although their education and activities were less "intellectual" (see Dilke 1971, 47–65).

6. On doctors, see Scarborough 1969, 120–21, 127, and Forbes 1955, 346–47. Included here are *obstetrices* and *medicae* whose activities involved actual physical care: see Treggiari 1976, 86. On teachers, see Pliny *Ep.* 3.3 and the career of Q. Remmius Palaemon (Suet. *Gram.* 23).

APPENDIX III • The Roman Population with Occupational Titles

1. The size and shape of Rome's population has been a subject of controversy: Beloch 1886, 392–414; Maier 1953–54; Oates 1934; Brunt 1971, 376–88; Hopkins 1978, 96–98. Assumptions of an exceptionally large slave population have been criticized by Maier (336ff.); cf. Hopkins 1978, 68–69. The estimate of Hopkins (with Beloch) would make slaves around 30% of Rome's population under Augustus (1978, 69 j., n., cf. 97); cf. Huttunen 1974, 183. Brunt (383) estimates a slave population of 100,000–200,000 and a free population of 640,000 or 500,000 in the mid-first century B.C., but he assumes a very high rate of manumission. Beloch (418, 436) believes there were fewer than 2 million slaves in Italy as a whole in the late first century B.C. out of total population of 5.5 million; Brunt (124) thinks there were closer to 3 million slaves in Italy out of a total population of 7.5 million.

2. On the freed population, see Frank 1916; Taylor 1961; Treggiari 1969, 31–36; Brunt 1971, 377ff. Frank and Taylor (see also Thylander 1952, 134–85) rely on the Greek cognomen as evidence of servile origin: Weaver (1972, 83–86) has pointed out the problems of this approach (cf. the findings of Kajanto 1965). Even if the Greek cognomen signals servile origin, we cannot pinpoint the generation of manumission. Estimates based on the epitaph material often fail to consider how it represents the total population; see below, esp. references to Huttenen's analyses.

3. On the ability of the slave population to reproduce itself and the importance of birth as a source of slaves, see Westermann 1955, 72, 85–90; Finley 1980, 130, and 1973, 86; Hopkins 1978, 141; Harris 1980, 118–21; cf. Patterson 1982, 132–34. Harris argues that the ratio of male to female slaves, the manumission of nubile female slaves for the purpose of marriage, the exposure of children, which tended to decrease the female population, as well as nutrition, childbirth, and child rearing militate against the possibility that slaves reproduced themselves. Several factors he cites need closer evaluation. Although the epigraphical sources show that female slaves were manumitted more frequently and earlier than male slaves (Weaver 1972, 184–86; Alföldy 1972, 109–14; Hopkins 1978, 139–40), the manumitter and cause of manumission need to be considered. If manumissions resulted from ex-slaves' buying the freedom of a former *conserva* and perhaps *contubernalis*, the women probably had already borne children who

remained slaves (Weaver 1972, 100, 109–10, 186). The assumption that infant exposure had a greater effect on the female population has been questioned by Engels (1980, 1984).

4. Taylor 1961, 122–23, 129–30.

5. Mart. 2.29, 6.17, 11.37; Pet. 32; cf. Juv. 1.104–5. Richlin 1984, 67.

6. Huttunen 1974, 139, 141, 187–88.

7. Ibid., 137, 142, 187.

8. Compare Huttunen's analysis of the freeborn in his samples (1974, 137, 191–93). On the changes in electoral procedure and transfer of the elections to the Senate, see Frei-Stolba 1967; Tibiletti 1953; Levick 1967. On the decline of the legislative power of the popular assemblies, see Jolowicz 1972, 326, 355–56.

BIBLIOGRAPHY

Alföldy, G. 1972. Die Freilassung von Sklaven und die Struktur Sklaverei in der römischen Kaiserzeit. *RSA* 2:97–129.

Armstrong, W. A. 1972. The use of information about occupation. In *Nineteenth century society: Essays in the use of quantitative methods for the study of social data,* ed. E. A. Wrigley, 191–310. Cambridge: Cambridge University Press.

Baldwin, B. 1978. Trimalchio's domestic staff. *AClass* 21:87–97.

Balsdon, J. P. V. D. 1969. *Life and leisure in ancient Rome.* New York: McGraw-Hill.

Bang, M. 1910. Die Herkunft der römischen Sklaven. *MDAI(R)* 25:223–51.

———. 1912. Die Herkunft der römischen Sklaven. *MDAI(R)* 27:189–221.

Baumgart, J. 1936. *Die römischen Sklavennamen.* Breslau: R. Nischkowsky.

Beloch, J. 1886. *Die Bevölkerund der griechisch-römischen Welt.* Leipzig: Duncker & Humbolt.

Bhabha, H. K. 1986. The other question: difference, discrimination, and the discourse of colonialism. In *Literature, politics and theory,* ed. F. Barker, P. Hulme, M. Iverson, and D. Loxley, 148–72. London: Methuen.

Biscardi, A. 1975. La capacità processuale dello schiavo. *Labeo* 21:143–71.

Blassingame, J. W., ed. 1977. *Slave testimony.* Baton Rouge: Louisiana State University Press.

———. 1979. *The slave community.* New York: Oxford University Press.

Boulvert, G. 1964. Les esclaves et les affranchis impériaux sous le haut-empire romain. 2 vols. diss. Université d'Aix. Marseilles.

———. 1970. *Esclaves et affranchis impériaux sous le haut-empire romain: rôle politique et administratif.* Naples: Jovene.

———. 1974. *Domestique et fonctionnaire sous le haut-empire romain: La condition de l'affranchi et de l'esclave du prince.* Annales Littéraires de l'Université de Besançon 151. Paris: Belles Lettres.

217

Bradley, K. R. 1978. The age at time of sale of female slaves. *Arethusa* 11 (Spring, Fall): 243–52.

———. 1979. Response. *Arethusa* 12 (Fall): 259–63.

———. 1986. Wet-nursing at Rome: A study in social relations. In *The family in ancient Rome*, ed. B. Rawson, 201–29. Ithaca, NY: Cornell University Press.

———. 1987. *Slaves and masters in the Roman Empire*. Oxford: Oxford University Press.

Brunt, P. A. 1971. *Italian manpower 225 B.C.–A.D. 14*. Oxford: Clarendon.

———. 1973. Aspects of the social thought of Dio Chrysostum and of the Stoics. *PCPhS* 19:9–34.

———. 1980. Free labour and public works. *JRS* 70:81–100.

Buckland, W. W. [1908] 1970. *The Roman law of slavery*. Cambridge: Cambridge University Press.

Burford, A. 1972. *Craftsmen in Greek and Roman society*. London: Thames & Hudson.

Calabi Limentani, I. 1958. *Studi sulla società romana: Il lavoro artistico*. Milan: Istituto Editoriale Cisalpino.

———. 1968. *Epigrafia latina*. Milan: Istituto Editoriale Cisalpino.

Calza, G. 1940. *La necropoli del Porto de Roma nell'Isola Sacra*. Rome: Libreria dello Stato.

Carby, H. V. 1987. *Reconstructing womanhood*. New York: Oxford University Press.

Carroll, L. 1987. *Alice in wonderland* [1865] and *Through the looking glass* [1872]. New York: Grosset & Dunlap.

Cassirer, E. 1953. *Language and myth*. Trans. S. K. Langer. New York: Dover.

Casson, L. 1980. The role of the state in Rome's grain trade. In *The seaborne commerce of ancient Rome*, ed. J. H. D'Arms and E. C. Kopff, 21–33. MAAR 36. Rome: American Academy in Rome.

Cébeillac, M. 1971. Quelques inscriptions inédites d'Ostie de la république à l'empire. *MEFR* 83:39–125.

Chantraine, H. 1967. *Freigelassene und Sklaven im Dienst der römischen Kaiser: Studien zu ihrer Nomenklatur*. Wiesbaden: Steiner.

Cixous, Helene, and C. Clément. 1986. *The newly born woman*. Trans. B. Wing. Minneapolis: University of Minnesota Press.

Clifford, J. 1986. Introduction: Partial truths. In *Writing culture*, ed. J. Clifford and G. E. Marcus, 1–26. Berkeley: University of California Press.

Cohn, B. 1980. History and anthropology: The state of play. *CSSH* 22: 198–221.

———. 1981. History and anthropology: Toward a rapprochement. *Journal of Interdisciplinary History* 12 (2): 227–52.

Cosentini, C. 1948–50. *Studi sui liberti*. 2 vols. Catania: Presso La Facoltà Guiridica.

Crapanzano, V. 1986. Hermes' dilemma: The masking of subversion in ethnographic description. In *Writing culture*, ed. J. Clifford and G. E. Marcus, 51–76. Berkeley: University of California Press.

Crook, J. A. 1967a. Gaius, *Institutes*, 1.84–86. *CR* 17:7–8.

———. 1967b. *Law and life of Rome*. London: Thames & Hudson.

———. 1967c. Patria potestas. *CQ* 17:113–22.

D'Arms, J. H. 1981. *Commerce and social standing in ancient Rome*. Cambridge: Harvard University Press.

Daube, D. 1951. "Ne quid infamandi causa fiat": The Roman law of defamation. *Atti del congresso internazionale di diritto romano e di storia del diritto* 3.413–56.

Davis, N. Z. 1975. *Society and culture in early modern France*. Stanford: Stanford University Press.

———. 1981. The possibilities of the past. *Journal of Interdisciplinary History* 12 (2): 267–75.

———. 1983. *The return of Martin Guerre*. Cambridge: Harvard University Press.

De Robertis, F. M. 1963. *Lavoro e lavoratori nel mondo romano*. Bari: Adriatica Editrice.

De Ste. Croix, G. E. M. 1981. *The class struggle in the ancient Greek world*. Ithaca, NY: Cornell University Press.

De Visscher, F. 1947. *Le régime romain de la noxalité*. Brussels: A. De Visscher.

———. 1963. *Le droit des tombeaux romains*. Milan: Giuffrè.

De Zulueta, F. 1969. *The Institutes of Gaius*. 2 vols. Oxford: Clarendon.

Dilke, O. A. W. 1971. *The Roman land surveyors*. New York: Barnes & Noble.

Douglas, M. 1970. *Natural symbols*. London: Barrie & Rockliff, Cresset Press.

———. 1984. *Purity and danger*. London: ARK Paperbacks.

Douglass, F. [1892] 1962. *Life and times of Frederick Douglass*. New York: Collier.

Duff, A. M. 1928. *Freedmen in the Roman Empire*. Oxford: Clarendon.

Duncan-Jones, R. 1974. *The economy of the Roman Empire: Quantitative studies*. Cambridge: Cambridge University Press.

Duthoy, R. 1974. La fonction sociale de l'Augustalité. *Epigrafica* 36: 134–54.

———. 1978. Les *Augustales*. *ANRW* II (Principat) 16 (2): 1256–1309.

Engels, D. 1980. The problem of female infanticide in the Graeco-Roman world. *CPh* 75 (April): 112–20.

———. 1984. The use of historical demography in ancient history. *CQ* 34 (2): 386–93.

Fabre, G. 1981. *Libertus. Recherches sur les rapports patron-affranchi à la fin de la république romain*. Rome: Collections de l'Ecole Française de Rome, vol. 50.

Finley, M. I. 1973. *The ancient economy*. Berkeley: University of California Press.

———. 1980. *Ancient slavery and modern ideology*. New York: Viking.

Flory, M. B. 1978. Family in *familia*: Kinship and community in slavery. *AJAH* 3 (1): 78–95.

Forbes, C. A. 1955. The education and training of slaves in antiquity. *TAPhA* 86:321–60.

Forbes, R. J. 1956. *Studies in ancient technology*. 4 vols. Leiden: Brill.

Frank, T. 1916. Race mixture in the Roman Empire. *AHR* 21:689–708.

———. 1933–40. *Economic survey of ancient Rome*. 6 vols. Baltimore: Johns Hopkins University Press.

Fredericksen, M. W. 1959. Republican Capua: A social and economic study. *PBSR* 14:80–130.

———. 1975. Theory, evidence, and the ancient economy. *JRS* 65:164–71.

Frei-Stolba, R. 1967. *Untersuchungen zu den Wahlen in der römischen Kaiserzeit.* Zurich: Juris.

Friedländer, L. [1907] 1965. *Roman life and manners under the early Empire.* 4 vols. Trans. and rev. L. A. Magnus. London: Routledge & Kegan Paul.

Frier, B. W. 1980. *Landlords and tenants in imperial Rome.* Princeton: Princeton University Press.

Garnsey, P. 1966. The Lex Julia and appeal under the Empire. *JRS* 56: 167–89.

———. 1968. Legal privilege in the Roman Empire. *Past and Present* 41: 3–24.

———. 1970. *Social status and legal privilege in the Roman Empire.* Oxford: Clarendon.

———. 1975. Descendents of freedmen in local politics: Some criteria. In *The ancient historian and his material: Essays in honor of C. E. Stevens,* ed. B. Levick, 167–80. Farnsborough: Gregg.

———. 1976. Urban property investment. In *Studies in Roman property,* ed. M. I. Finley, 123–32. Cambridge: Cambridge University Press.

———. 1980. Non-slave labour in the Roman world. In *Non-slave labour in Graeco-Roman antiquity,* ed. P. Garnsey, 34–47. *PCPhS,* suppl. vol. 6. Cambridge.

———. 1981. Independent freedmen and the economy of Roman Italy under the Principate. *Klio* 63:359–71.

———. 1983. Grain for Rome. In *Trade in the ancient economy,* ed. P. Garnsey, K. Hopkins, and C. R. Whittaker, 118–30. Berkeley: University of California Press.

Genovese, E. D. 1976. *Roll, Jordon, roll.* New York: Vintage.

Ginzburg, C. 1982. *The cheese and the worms.* Trans. J. and A. Tedeschi. New York: Penguin.

———. 1985. *The night battles.* Trans. J. and A. Tedeschi. New York: Penguin.

Girri, G. 1956. *La taberna nel quadro urbanistico e sociale di Ostia.* Rome: L'Erma di Bretschneider.

Goffman, E. 1963. *Stigma.* Englewood Cliffs, NJ: Prentice Hall.

Gordon, A. E. 1935. *Epigraphica II: On marble as a criterion for dating republican Latin inscriptions.* Berkeley: University of California Press.

Gordon, A. E., and J. S. Gordon. 1957. *Contributions to the paleography of Latin inscriptions.* Berkeley: University of California Press.

———. 1958–65. *Album of dated Latin inscriptions.* 4 vols. Berkeley: University of California Press.

Gordon, L. 1986. What's new in women's history. In *Feminist studies/Critical studies,* ed. T. de Lauretis, 20–30. Theories of Contemporary Culture. Center for Twentieth Century Studies, University of Wisconsin–Milwaukee. Bloomington: Indiana University Press.

Gordon, M. L. 1924. The nationality of slaves under the early Roman Empire. *JRS* 14:93–111.

———. 1931. The freedman's son in municipal life. *JRS* 21:65–77.

Greenidge, A. H. J. 1894. *Infamia: Its place in Roman public and private law*. Oxford: Clarendon.

Gummerus, H. 1906. *Der römische Gutsbetrieb*. Leipzig: Dieterich.

———. 1913. Dartellungen aus dem Handwerk auf römischen Grab und Votivsteinen in Italien. *JDAI* 28:63–126.

———. 1915. Die römische Industrie I, II. *Klio* 14:129–89.

———. 1918. Die römische Industrie III. *Klio* 15:256–302.

———. 1956. *Der Arztestand im römischen Reiche nach der Inscriften*. Societas Scientiarum Fennica; Commentationes Humanorum Litterarum, 3.6. Helsingfors: Akademische Buchhandlung.

Harris, W. V. 1980. A study of the Roman slave trade. In *The seaborne commerce of ancient Rome*, ed. J. H. D'Arms and E. C. Kopff, 117–40. MAAR 36. Rome: American Academy in Rome.

Hatzfeld, J. 1919. *Les trafiquants italiens dans l'orient hellénique*. Paris: E. de Boccard.

Hegel, G. W. F. [1807] 1977. *Phenomenology of spirit*. Trans. A. V. Miller. Oxford: Oxford University Press.

Hopkins, K. 1966. On the probable age structure of the Roman population. *Population Studies* 20:245–64.

———. 1978. *Conquerors and slaves*. Cambridge: Cambridge University Press.

———. 1983. *Death and renewal*. Cambridge: Cambridge University Press.

Huttunen, P. 1974. *The social strata of the imperial city of Rome*. Acta Universitatis Ouluensis, ser. B. Oulu.

Jolowicz, H. F. 1972. *Historical introduction to the study of Roman law*. Ed. B. Nicholas. Cambridge: Cambridge University Press.

Jones, A. H. M. 1960. *Studies in Roman government and law*. Oxford: Basil Blackwell.

Joshel, S. R. 1986. Nursing the master's child: Slavery and the Roman child-nurse. *Signs* 12 (1): 3–22.

Kajanto, I. 1963. *Onomastic studies in early Christian inscriptions of Rome and Carthage*. Acta Instituti Romani Finlandiae, 2.1. Helsinki.

———. 1965. *The Latin cognomina*. Societas Scientiarum Fennica; Commentationes Humanorum Litterarum, 26.2. Helsinki.

———. 1968. The significance of the non-Latin cognomina. *Latomus* 27:517–34.

Kampen, N. 1981. *Image and status: Roman working women in Ostia*. Berlin: Mann.

Kaser, M. 1956. *Infamia* und *Ignominia* in den römischen Rechtsquellen. *ZRG* 73:220–78.

———. 1971–75. *Das römische Privatrecht*. 2 vols. Munich: C. H. Beck.

Katz, M. B. 1972. Occupational classification in history. *Journal of Interdisciplinary History* 3 (1): 63–88.

Kleiner, D. E. E. 1977. *Roman group portraiture: The funerary reliefs of the late Republic and early Empire*. New York: Garland.

Kühn, G. 1910. *De opificum romanorum condicione privata quaestiones*. diss. Halle-Wittenberg.

LaCapra, D. 1985. *History and criticism*. Ithaca, NY: Cornell University Press.

Lambert, J. 1934. *Les operae liberti*. Paris: Dalloz.

Le Gall, J. 1969. Métiers des femmes au *Corpus Inscriptionum Latinarum*. *REL* 47:123–30.

Le Roy Ladurie, E. 1979. *Montaillou: The promised land of error*. New York: Vintage.

Levick, B. M. 1967. Imperial control of the elections in the early Principate. *Historia* 16:207–30.

Litwack, L. F. 1980. *Been in the storm so long*. New York: Vintage.

Loane, H. J. 1938. *Industry and commerce of the city of Rome (50 B.C.–200 A.D.)*. Baltimore: Johns Hopkins University Press.

Lugli, G. 1930–38. *I monumenti antichi di Roma e suburbio*. 3 vols. Rome: G. Bardi.

MacMullen, R. 1974. *Roman social relations*. New Haven: Yale University Press.

Maier, F. G. 1953–54. Römische Bevölkerungsgeschichte und Inscriftenstatistik. *Historia* 2:318–51.

Marcus, G. E. 1986. Contemporary problems of ethnography in the modern world system. In *Writing culture*, ed. J. Clifford and G. E. Marcus, 165–93. Berkeley: University of California Press.

Martini, R. 1958. "*Mercennarius.*" *Contributo allo studio dei rapporti de lavoro in diritto romano*. Milan: Giuffrè.

Maxey, M. 1938. *Occupations of the lower classes in Roman society*. Chicago: University of Chicago Press.

Meiggs, R. 1973. *Roman Ostia*. Oxford: Clarendon.

Moeller, W. 1976. *The wool trade in ancient Pompeii*. Leiden: Brill.

Mohler, S. L. 1940. Slave education in the Roman Empire. *TAPhA* 71:262–80.

Mommsen, T. 1899. *Das römisches Strafrecht*. Leipzig: Duncker & Humbolt.

Nash, E. 1968. *Pictorial dictionary of ancient Rome*. 2 vols. New York: Praeger.

Nicolet, C. 1966. *L'ordre équestre à l'époque républicaine*. Vol. 1. Paris: E. de Boccard.

Nörr, D. 1965. Zur sozialen und rechtlichen Bewertung der freien Arbeit in Rom. *ZRG* 82:67–105.

Oates, W. J. 1934. The population of Rome. *CPh* 29:101–16.

Packer, J. E. 1971. *The insulae of imperial Ostia*. MAAR 31. Rome: American Academy in Rome.

Panciera, S. 1980. *Olearii*. In *The seaborne commerce of ancient Rome*, ed. J. H. D'Arms and E. C. Kopff, 235–50. MAAR 36. Rome: American Academy in Rome.

Parker, H. 1989. Crucially funny or Tranio on the couch: The *servus callidus* and jokes about torture. *TAPhA* 119:233–46.

Patterson, O. 1982. *Slavery and social death*. Cambridge: Harvard University Press.

Pavis D'Esurac, H. 1977. Aristocratie senatoriale et profits commerciaux. *Ktema* 2:339–55.

Rawson, B. 1966. Family life among the lower classes at Rome in the first two centuries of the empire. *CPh* 61:71–83.

———. 1974. Roman concubinage and other *de facto* marriages. *TAPhA* 104:279–305.

————. 1986a. Children in the Roman *familia*. In *The family in ancient Rome*, ed. B. Rawson, 170–200. Ithaca, NY: Cornell University Press.

————. 1986b. The Roman family. In *The family in ancient Rome*, ed. B. Rawson, 1–57. Ithaca, NY: Cornell University Press.

————, ed. 1986c. *The family in ancient Rome*. Ithaca, NY: Cornell University Press.

Rawson, E. 1976. The Ciceronian aristocracy and its properties. In *Studies in Roman property*, ed. M. I. Finley, 85–102. Cambridge: Cambridge University Press.

Richlin, A. 1981a. Approaches to the sources on adultery at Rome. *Women's Studies* 8 (1–2): 225–50.

————. 1981b. The meaning of *irrumare* in Catullus and Martial. *CPh* 76:40–46.

————. 1983. *The garden of Priapus: Sexuality and aggression in Roman sexual humor*. New Haven: Yale University Press.

————. 1984. Invective against women in Roman satire. *Arethusa* 17 (Spring): 67–80.

Rickman, G. 1980a. *The corn supply of ancient Rome*. Oxford: Clarendon.

————. 1980b. The grain supply. In *The seaborne commerce of ancient Rome*, ed. J. H. D'Arms and E. C. Kopff, 261–75. MAAR 36. Rome: American Academy in Rome.

Robleda, O. 1976. *Il diritto degli schiavi nell'antica Roma*. Rome: Pontificia Università Gregoriana.

Rosaldo, R. 1986. From the door of his tent: The fieldworker and the inquisitor. In *Writing culture*, ed. J. Clifford and G. E. Marcus, 77–97. Berkeley: University of California Press.

Rostovtzeff, M. 1957. *The social and economic history of the Roman Empire*. 2 vols. Ed. P. M. Fraser. Oxford: Clarendon.

Rougé, J. 1966. *Recherches sur l'organisation du commerce maritime en Méditerranée sous l'empire romain*. Paris: SEVPEN.

Saller, R. P. 1982. *Personal patronage under the early empire*. Cambridge: Cambridge University Press.

Saller, R. P., and B. Shaw. 1984. Tombstones and family relations in the Principate: Civilians, soldiers and slaves. *JRS* 74:124–56.

Scarborough, J. 1969. *Roman medicine*. Ithaca, NY: Cornell University Press.

Schiller, A. A. [1935] 1971. *An American experience in Roman law*. Göttingen: Vandenhoeck v. Ruprecht.

Shackleton Bailey, D. R. 1976. *Two studies in Roman nomenclature*. American Classical Studies, no. 3. s.l.: American Philological Association.

————. 1988. *Onomasticon to Cicero's speeches*. Norman: University of Oklahoma Press.

Shatzman, I. 1975. *Senatorial wealth and Roman politics*. Collections Latomus 142. Brussels.

Smith-Rosenberg, C. 1986. Writing history: Language, class, and gender. In *Feminist studies/Critical studies*, ed. T. de Lauretis, 31–54. Theories of Contemporary Culture. Center for Twentieth Century Studies, University of Wisconsin–Milwaukee. Bloomington: Indiana University Press.

Solin, H. 1971. *Beiträge zur Kenntnis der griechischen Personennamen in*

Rom. Societas Scientiarum Fennica; Commentationes Humanorum Litterarum, 48. Helsinki.

———. 1982. *Die griechischen Personennamen in Rom: ein Namenbuch.* 3 vols. Berlin: De Gruyter.

Syme, R. [1939] 1979. *The Roman revolution.* Oxford: Oxford University Press.

———. 1958. *Tacitus.* 2 vols. Oxford: Clarendon.

Taylor, L. R. 1914. *Augustales, seviri augustales,* and *seviri:* A chronological study. *TAPhA* 45:231–53.

———. 1961. Freedmen and freeborn in the epitaphs of imperial Rome. *AJPh* 82:113–32.

Thomas, J. A. C. 1961. *Locatio* and *operae. BIDR* 64:231–47.

Thompson, L. A. 1989. *Romans and blacks.* Norman: University of Oklahoma Press.

Thylander, H. 1951–52. *Inscriptions du Porte d'Ostie.* 2 vols. Skrifter utg. av Svenska Institutet i Rom, 4.1–2. Lund: C. W. K. Gleerup.

———. 1952. *Etude sur l'épigraphie latine.* Skrifter utg. av Svenska Institutet i Rom, 5. Lund: C. W. K. Gleerup.

Tibiletti, G. 1953. *Principe e magistrati republicani.* Rome: A. Signorelli.

Todorov, T. 1985. *The conquest of America.* Trans. Richard Howard. New York: Harper Colophon.

Toynbee, J. M. C. 1971. *Death and burial in the Roman world.* Ithaca, NY: Cornell University Press.

Treggiari, S. 1969. *Roman freedmen during the late Republic.* Oxford: Clarendon.

———. 1973. Domestic staff at Rome in the Julio-Claudian period, 27 B.C. to A.D. 68. *Histoire sociale/Social History* 6 (12): 241–55.

———. 1975a. Family life among the staff of the Volusii. *TAPhA* 105: 393–401.

———. 1975b. Jobs in the household of Livia. *PBSR* 43:48–77.

———. 1976. Jobs for women. *AJAH* 1:76–104.

———. 1979a. Lower class women in the Roman economy. *Florilegium* 1:65–79.

———. 1979b. Questions on women domestics in the Roman West. In *Schiavitù, Manomissione e classi dipendenti del mondo antico,* 185–201. Pubblicazioni dell'Istituto di Storia Antica 13. Rome: L'Erma di Bretschneider.

———. 1980. Urban labour in Rome: *Mercennarii* and *tabernarii.* In *Nonslave labour in Graeco-Roman antiquity,* ed. P. Garnsey, 48–64. *PCPhS,* suppl. vol. 6. Cambridge.

———. 1981a. Concubinae. *PBSR* 49:59–81.

———. 1981b. Contubernales in *CIL* 6. *Phoenix* 35:42–69.

Van Gennep, A. 1960. *The rites of passage.* Trans. M. B. Vizedom and G. L. Caffee. Chicago: University of Chicago Press.

Veyne, P. 1961. Vie de Trimalchion. *Annales (ESC)* 16:213–47.

Waltzing, J. P. 1895–1900. *Etude historique sur les corporations professionnelles chez les romains.* 4 vols. Louvain: C. Peeters.

Watson, A. 1987. *Roman slave law.* Baltimore: Johns Hopkins University Press.

Weaver, P. R. C. 1964. *Vicarius* and *vicarianus* in the *familia Caesaris. JRS* 54:117–28.

———. 1972. *Familia Caesaris: A social study of the emperor's freedmen and slaves.* Cambridge: Cambridge University Press.

———. 1986. The status of children in mixed marriages. In *The family in ancient Rome*, ed. B. Rawson, 145–69. Ithaca, NY: Cornell University Press.

Westermann, W. L. 1955. *The slave systems of Greek and Roman antiquity.* Memoirs of the American Philosophical Society, vol. 40. Philadelphia.

White, K. D. 1970. *Roman farming.* Ithaca, NY: Cornell University Press.

Wilkinson, B. M. 1961. The names of children in Roman imperial epitaphs. A study of social conditions in the lower classes. diss. Bryn Mawr.

Willis, P. 1977. *Learning to labour.* New York: Columbia University Press.

INDEX